DATE DUE

~~NOV 20~~		
~~MY 29~~		
~~NOV 30~~		
~~FE 12~~		
NO 2 04		

DEMCO 38-296

NATURAL LEARNING RHYTHMS

How and When Children Learn

Josette & Sambhava Luvmour

Celestial Arts
BERKELEY, CALIFORNIA

Cover & text design by Fifth Street Design, Berkeley, California

FIRST CELESTIAL ARTS PRINTING 1993

Library of Congress Cataloging-in-Publication Data

Luvmour, Josette.
    Natural learning rhythms : how and when children learn / by
Josette and Sambhava Luvmour.
        p.   cm.
    Includes bibliographical references and index.
    ISBN 0-89087-699-1 : $12.95
    1. Child development. 2. Learning, Psychology of. 3. Early childhood
education — Parent participation.   I. Luvmour, Sambhava.
II. Title.
LB1117.L88   1993
370.15'23—dc20   93-33182
                                                        CIP

1 2 3 4 5 6 7 8 — 99 98 97 96 95 94 93

Many have come to teach the holiness of God,
but still there is not peace in the world.

Many have come to teach the holiness of man,
and still there is not peace in the world.

When many come to teach the holiness of children,
then there will peace in the world.

—Rabbi Schlomo Carlebach

To the warriors of consciousness who,
recognizing the sacredness of all life, have devoted
themselves to self-knowlege and service.

*T*able of Contents

Acknowledgments   *vii*
Authors' Note   *ix*
Introduction   *xi*

The Life Stages
The Life Stages   *3*
Body-Being   *17*
Emotional-Being   *37*
Will-Being   *61*
Reasoning-Being   *83*

Applications
Communication   *105*
Ritual Rites of Passage   *121*
Remedies   *143*
Authentic Education   *165*
Conflict Resolution   *201*
Society & Natural Learning Rhythms   *231*
On Divorce   *247*
The Evolution of Peace   *253*
Phases   *255*
Hesitancies   *256*
Life Stages   *257*
Rituals   *258*
Selected Bibliography   *259*
Bio Notes   *265*

Acknowledgments

This book would not have been possible without the help of the following people. We are deeply grateful for their support.

For courageous help at the beginning: Mayche and Richo Cech, Roger and Karouna Hodgson, Helen Parnell, Gabriel Ross, Nick Herzmark and Sidney Weisheimer. Also, the more than fifty people who contributed to supporting us while we wrote the first drafts of this book. Their faith has been truly inspiring.

For editorial help: Steve Beckwitt, Ron Miller, David and Ellen Albert, and Diana Reiss. Each of these people, Diana in particular, spent literally hundreds of hours scrutinizing every aspect of this book. If there is a flow and ease herein, credit belongs to these folks who gave from the heart as well as the mind. Additionally, Steve brought us on line in the world of personal computing, Ron has been a link to the holistic education network, David and Ellen provided social and philosphical insights and helped to create the structural integrity of this book.

To the children: It would take pages to list all the children that have been supportive of Natural Learning Rhythms. They have taken us into their hearts and we have taken them into ours. A partial list includes Nodja, Jeb, Sena, Roza, Abby, Jed, Jovida, Stephan, Kendra, Genevieve, Kale, W.B., Albie and Gray. Special thanks goes to our daughter Amber, risking emotional involvement when her friends thought it was "weird"; intense and intent during her five-day coming-of-age rite of passage; and most importantly, flashing her sparkling smile of encouragement at just those moments of confusion and despair. How fun and funny she and all our young friends have been.

For continued inspiration: Tom and Debby Weistar, who recognized the vision and have been unfailing in their attempts to bring it to fruition; Bill and Suze Copeland, genuine friends.

For publishing: David Hinds and Veronica Randall at Celestial Arts. Their good humor, availability and accountability has made this process both enjoyable and informative.

Last, we'd like to thank those who were there with us from the beginning, our parents Ernie, Marie, Irma, and Eugene.

Authors' Note

Because we are co-authoring this book, it is sometimes necessary to refer to one or the other of us in the third person. After some deliberation, we decided to refer to Josette by her full name, and Sambhava as Ba, the nickname given to him by the children.

Please feel free to write with any questions or comments:

Center for Educational Guidance
P.O. Box 445
North San Juan, CA 95960

*I*ntroduction

In the year 1799, on the eve of the nineteenth century, a stone slab bearing parallel inscriptions in Greek, an Egyptian popular script, and hieroglyphics was found near the mouth of the Nile river. This discovery made possible the deciphering of the pictographic writings of the ancient Egyptians and broke open a panorama on civilization's ancient past.

The quest for the key to human consciousness is as old as human history. From the Hindu's holy Vedas to the mystical Jewish Cabbalah; from the counsel houses of the Iroquois nation to the halls of the great Western universities; through education, psychology, anthropology, philosophy, and the sacred spirit—wise, caring people have sought to solve this mystery: *How do children grow and learn?*

Its answer will be the Rosetta stone of human cultural evolution. In discovering the inherent rhythms in human growth and learning, we shall gain the greatest knowledge of ourselves—both individually and as a species—by reaching deeply into our essence and drawing forth our most profound, most natural wisdom. It is then that we may create a culture and a society reflecting our full humanity.

The New Explorers

Today, as we approach the twenty-first century, parents and teachers have become the determined explorers continuing the quest for an understanding of human consciousness. In this search, we often grope our way along with few markers to guide our way. Are we disciplining our child in the right way? Have we given him a sense of love and belongingness? Will our child be able to take her place in society?

Nothing is scarier to us as parents than to expose our relationship to our children. We love them so much; we hope and pray we're "doing it right," and nothing, absolutely *nothing*, feels worse than the feeling that we are damaging a child.

Gayle, a shy but congenial thirty-four-year-old mother, had these very thoughts in mind when she spoke with a group of peers attending a workshop at the home of one of her neighbors. Doctors and homemakers, carpenters, clerks, and musicians, these men and women had come to grapple with family concerns.

Gayle lifted her hand, a sign that she was ready to speak. The other eighteen participants watched and waited. She began:

> Hi. I'm here with my husband Greg. We have three children; this is the second marriage for each of us. I had the older boy with my first husband, and Greg came with his daughter. The youngest is ours together.
>
> The two older children spend two-thirds of the time with us, and the rest with their other parents. We're confused about the best way to bring up all these children in the same household. There are just no role models on how to make it work.
>
> Lately, I see myself acting toward my children the same way my parents did with me, and that's the one thing I swore I never wanted to happen. We also see behavior in the older children that we don't like and wonder about the effects of the divorces on them.

As she spoke, Gayle's nervousness dropped away. By the nods of heads and quiet smiles of encouragement, it was clear that everyone shared many of her feelings. As the talk moved around the circle, more fears and concerns were voiced:

> How can I get out of the role of being a policeman?
>
> I hate it when I hit my children but I don't know what to do about it.
>
> How can I teach my child to honor the earth and all its people?
>
> How can we create a curriculum relevant to the 1990s and the individual needs of my child?

And more:

My child had a traumatic birth and first three years. Now he's acting out. Has his personality already been determined for the rest of his life?

I'm really getting to the point where I'm tired of battling with my teenager.

Drugs have invaded our neighborhood and home, and we don't know what to do about it.

I've been teaching for eight years, and if I don't find a new of relating to children, I'm going to quit.

Every one of these concerns is well founded. From the depth of our hearts we seek to nurture the child we love so dearly. From the height of our insight, we know that the evolution of life on the planet, and of the human species, depends on our ability to be with children so that they may live wisely and in harmony with their world.

It would be wonderful to live in a society that genuinely supported the family. Yet in the modern world, all too often, both parents must work to maintain a comfortable standard of living. Single parents, moreover, get minimal assistance in one of the most difficult tasks on earth: engaging their children and profession simultaneously. Family growth skills—ways to communicate clearly, resolve conflict, deal with divorce, or absorb a new child as a family member—are not part of any school curriculum. Professional counseling, if appropriate, is expensive and mostly unavailable to a large segment of society. And so we re-create the dysfunctional behavior patterns of our parents, grandparents, and previous generations. In an ironic twist, the family, and consequently most communities, has become an evolutionary backslide. Children around the globe pay the price.

The right relationship to children yields healthy, balanced grownups— grownups who can solve their own problems. We would do well to pay early attention to this fact of life. Presently, we're affected deeply by pollution, violence, substance abuse, and divorce, but those who are crucial to a solution, the children, are being destroyed as well.

This hurts.

Though all of us are aware that teaching has become an increasingly difficult profession, we frequently blame teachers for an educational system that simply does not work. Though curriculum requirements increase, then increase again, children seem to know less than ever. Classrooms are overcrowded and there is no time to pay attention to *social* learning, and there is little meaningful interaction between parents and teachers. The skills that are believed to help the United States compete in the international market are given special preference, yet even in those respects, our schools are failing.

Our ignorance about how to interact with children runs deep. All too often, children are seen as a burden. They must be rewarded and punished until they behave as we wish. We load our expectations of correct behavior, academic achievement, and intellectual communication on our children. Rather than disappoint us, they bend their backs to the task, and when they break or collapse, we read it as a failure.

As a society, we allocate a minuscule amount of resources to projects that investigate how children actually learn and grow. And when a financial crunch hits, the interests of children and families are the first to be sacrificed, as local, state, and federal budgets clearly show.

We need the time to consider who we really are as human beings. Despite the official veneration of Socrates in our learning institutions, "Know Thyself" has become a forgotten injunction. Both family and school have neglected to stimulate the child to *investigate herself*, to ask, "Who am I? What is 'family'? What is a 'parent'? What is a 'child'? What do I need, and what is the best way to provide it?"

Looking Forward

It is both heartwarming and empowering to see how many parents and teachers are now willing to look into their relationships with children. Something is wrong, and most of us can admit it. By tapping our inner store of natural wisdom, we can begin to reevaluate childhood and children, to access what we know to be authentic, and to reject the ignorance and myths that have been handed to us since our own childhood.

Children are like seedling oaks: Their entire potential is encapsulated in their being. With adequate sunlight and nutrition, they will grow into vigorous oak trees. On the other hand, when they are crowded or attacked, or when the soil is depleted, they must adapt to the imposition if they are to survive. Under such conditions, the seedlings will expend much of their energy snaking along the ground, looking for a patch of sun. Others will become spindly and weak. Still others grow well for a while, then suddenly become sick and die.

The trite aphorism that a developmental stage is merely "something the child passes through" denies the significance of the child's present moment. Such a belief isolates the parent from the child's message and can offer neither hope nor insight into solving current problems. This type of restrictive myth must go.

As we appreciate the diverse expressions of stage-specific wisdom, we begin to see the child, and his family, as truly unique. Our new insight buries the notion of a deterministic development in which the child is seen as trapped in a developmental cage and the parent is believed to have but a limited number of right or wrong responses. Rather, we seek to become free to respond to the individual child in the moment, fully confident that by doing so both we and the child grow in self-knowledge.

Every moment of a human being's life is of great significance. We are always growing and learning, and that which we learn in the present determines in large measure how we will behave in the future. A child growing up amid threats and violence will be armored; her behavior will be geared toward self-protection and her energy will be spent in defense, leaving little time to develop her natural wisdom and talent.

Yet there is a way out.

Until now almost all education—and we use this term to include parenting—has been designed to turn out "productive" children, rather than children who are developing according to their own natural rhythms and destiny. As John Gatto points out in his insightful book, *Dumbing Us Down: The Hidden Curriculum of Compulsory Schooling,* the intention of most schools is to produce good citizens, in other words, individuals who will fill jobs and support the societal status quo.

As far as authentic education is concerned, the question, "How can we turn out productive citizens?" is, as we used to say in Brooklyn, ass-backwards. This way of thinking prejudices the entire educational process, including parenting, teaching, and socializing. It turns education into a subtle, or not-so-subtle, form of brainwashing. And it creates a hierarchy of worth in which certain natural talents are valued over others. For instance, mathematics skills are taught with much greater urgency than interpersonal skills such as ways of honoring another student's opinion, or dissipating resentment, or methods for satisfying the needs of individuals in a group context. Can it be so surprising then that our society has produced sophisticated word-processor operators and a divorce rate of more than fifty percent?

We need fewer myths and a more committed search for authentic knowledge. The quality of an individual's education contributes mightily to his decision-making capabilities, including decisions about economics, war and peace, ecology, and family.

We have to find out just what is going on with the child. We need to ask:

> "How do humans grow and learn?"
>
> "How can we understand the meaning and purpose of the life process?"
>
> "How can we attune ourselves to the natural unfolding of human wisdom and intelligence?"
>
> "What is the proper role of parent and family?"

If these questions interest you, Natural Learning Rhythms will make your journey easier. While we cannot hope to provide the consummate answers, we do know—based on countless hours of fieldwork with children, working with hundreds of families, and deep study and contemplation—that a beginning can be made. We can empower ourselves, our families, and our children to live with the full measure of human wisdom, compassion, and intelligence.

We start with a simple observation about humans and nature, one that has described by wise people in every society: Over time, human beings, like all other living phenomena, progress through natural stages of development.

Throughout the ages much valuable work has sought to determine the nature of developmental stages, and during the last century, the United States and the Western countries have made invaluable contributions. Paradoxically, only a very small part of this important information is accessible to parents and teachers. And, except for the findings of a handful of compassionate educational philosophers, there's been very little meaningful work on the function and purpose of human development.

Jerome Kagan, chairperson of the Child Development department at Harvard University, has carefully researched a cross-cultural study of children, *The Nature of the Child*. It can be counted among the better works on education of this century. Regrettably, the book's erudite language limits its accessibility to many parents, and Kagan himself seems so bound by academic standards that despite his valuable findings he concludes that ". . . scientists have been unable to discover many profound principles that relate the actions of mothers, fathers, or siblings to psychological characteristics in the child."

Howard Gardner, a brilliant educational theorist whose *Frames of Mind: The Theory of Multiple Intelligences* reveals the diverse range of inherent human capabilites, is Kagan's colleague on the Harvard campus. Gardner names seven inherent types of human intelligence and asserts that each of us possess our own unique blend of these. The child and the society are best served, Gardner believes, when education matches the child's needs and talents, rather than imposing a standardized curriculum. His invaluable perspective could do much to humanize American educational systems, but again, an important text is barely comprehensible to even the above-average reader.

Many teachers have become angry about the inaccessibility of helpful information on education and developmental stages. The message seems to be that parents and teachers are somehow unworthy of this data, even though they are the ones who must develop curriculum, remedy dysfunction, and resolve conflict. Educators such as Gardner and Kagan must offer some concrete way we can use their findings.

Understanding Natural Learning Rhythms helps to bridge the gap between the hearth and the ivory tower, unlocking the "secrets" and exposing the wisdom inherent in the developmental process. We'll find out how to access that wisdom and assist the child bringing it to consciousness. We'll learn how adults grow by serving the child's development. And most importantly, we'll come to see our child for who she *is,* rather than who our society may believe she should be.

A Natural Response

In our fourteen years of parenting, teaching, and working with children and their families, we have seen that most people already have a meaningful knowledge of how children grow and learn. Indeed, when we describe the results of our research at Natural Learning Rhythms workshops, one of the most common observations of participants is, "I knew that already. I just never put it all together." Often they will recall incidents when, as parents or teachers, they were going to act in accordance with their children's natural rhythms, but their own childhood conditioning, or fear of disapproval, blocked their way.

In our many hours of fieldwork in human development, spending time with children and families in their everyday environments, we've observed children and collected much of the data that forms the basis of The Natural Learning Rhythms theory. We've also incorporated many examples we've seen of parents and teachers interacting with children in ways that nurture natural wisdom. During subsequent conversations about the interactions, educators often say that they know a particular technique works, but they don't know why. A mother who had problems getting her four-year-old to dress realized that her warm presence created an atmosphere in which the child willingly completed the task. A teacher told us how, by establishing a sense of community in his fourth grade classroom, the children's ability to absorb academic material increased dramatically. After a workshop, the reasons for success become apparent, and educators frequently devise new applications of their own techniques, and those of others as well.

Natural Learning Rhythms is not a "perfect-parenting" guide. Its goal is not to produce a "magical" or "radiant" or "intellectual" child. Such goal-oriented approaches prejudice our ability to see who the child is right now, in this moment. They inculcate guilt when their often impossible standards are not met, and they impose a system, rather than describe the learning process. Like the academic approaches that fail to provide specific, detailed applications of their insights, they have no day-to-day meaning for us.

Through Natural Learning Rhythms we can safely explore family wholeness, rediscovering what we already know about who we are and who our child is. When appropriate, we can identify the root of cause of family disharmony and create natural remedies to restore balance. Sometimes, in the process, we can even heal the wounds of our own inner child.

The Dance

When we drop our assumptions about who our child should be, we can begin to interact with her harmoniously, spontaneously, and responsibly: a process we have come to call "the dance." When we "dance," both the needs of the child and of ourselves are met in ways that bring forth a sense of cohesion and wisdom. For instance, an eleven-year-old's natural yeaning for inspirational models stimulates his parent to recontact inspiration in her own life. There is no discontinuity between the life of a parent and that of the child. There is no need to "be done" with the child so we can "do our own thing."

As an analogy, well-equipped dance studios have windows to let in the light and mirrors to reflect it so the dancers can see themselves. In much the same way, children serve their parents as both mirrors and windows. Much of their behavior mirrors their parent's present state of mind. Often, they reflect the parent's subconscious attitudes and desires: Unexpressed tension between parents, for example, may manifest in their children as sibling conflict, hyperactivity, or complacency. As Frances Wickes, and a number of other Jungian psychologists make clear, children play out the lives their parents wish they could live. Once deciphered, this mirroring allows important insight into who we are. When we "dance" with the child, we look directly into the mirror.

Children are also windows on the future, on what human society will be, on the fate of the earth we live on. As we watch them grow, we are witnessing human cultural evolution itself being played out before our eyes. After all, in these precarious times, it will be our children who will decide if we're able to regain our balance. The future of every species on the planet is sleeping down the hall. Dancing with the child brings home the inescapable truth that the future is determined by the way we engage the present.

xix

On our journey through the concepts of Natural Learning Rhythms we will encounter many dance steps. Most of them will be specific to a particular developmental stage and will show how meeting the needs of a child in each stage increases self-knowledge. With Natural Learning Rhythms as a family lifestyle expression, these dance steps come about naturally and continually.

More Myths

We've already discussed the common misconception that a developmental stage is merely something the child "passes through," and how such myths stifle our relationship with children. To give a sense of the scope and philosophy of Natural Learning Rhythms' effects, we mention several other myths here. These and others will be critiqued in detail later in the book.

♦ **Children say what they mean and mean what they say.**

Children play with *everything*, including words. Our society's perpetuation of this myth reflects our unending desire to glorify verbal/linguistic skills. In doing so we desecrate childhood by forcing the children to be little adults.

♦ **Nine-year-old girls mainly like to play with dolls and other girls, and nine-year-old boys mainly like to play with toys of violence and other boys.**

Children are unique. Each child expresses herself differently. Allowed access to their natural talents, nine-year-old children enjoy playing with many types of children, including those of the opposite sex. Everyone values genuine friendship. Gender bias is the basis for sexual discrimination, as well as the culturally disabling stereotypes of the logical, domineering male and the intuitive, mysterious female.

♦ **The child's personality is determined in the womb (or in the birth canal, the first month of life, the first six months, the first year, the first three years, or the first six years.)**

These theories address an important element of truth—that humans, sentient and vulnerable from the moment of conception, are deeply affected by the events of their lives. But it must be added that the multifaceted expressions of human adaptation indicate the possibility of attaining balance and harmony *throughout* life. More precisely, there are three major rebirths during the development of the child and several minor rebirths. The child's personality undergoes significant growth at each of these junctures. As we shall see, not only are new types of perception unfolding, but the very real possibility exists to rebalance early childhood traumas.

♦ **Being a dad or mom is harder when the child has a different biological father or mother.**

It is no more difficult to parent when the child is not biologically yours. Simply supply the natural needs of the child, and this creates trust and allows bonding. The genuine parent is the person who supplies the natural needs of the child; children love genuine parents. There are unique challenges in being a non-biological parent but they are no harder than in any other relationship with children. We'll address both divorce and parenting non-biological children in the last section of the book.

♦ **Behavior grows.**

In fact, behavior changes; it doesn't grow. And it changes in response to a variety of influences. Most importantly, behavior is under the guidance of the wisdom inherent to each of the developmental stages, which will be described in the following chapters. Stripped of the autonomy it appears to have in a clinical setting, behavior is a clear indicator of the child's psyche, having the same relationship to the child's overall health as a cough does to pneumonia, or a smile to contentment.

♦ **Rewards and punishments work.**

Rewards and punishments teach only how to avoid punishment. All behavior modification programs hurt children. They glorify behavior and neglect inner wisdom. They force the child to be who we want him to be, at the expense of allowing him to explore who he is. They create resentment and power struggles in the name of avoiding these selfsame struggles. Using bribery or an iron fist, they make discipline into a fearful word. Perhaps worst of all, they addict children to bribes and link power, violence, and fear.

♦ **Sibling rivalry is natural.**

When the family attunes itself to the natural rhythms of children, sibling rivalry exposes itself as an unneccesary if culturally accepted behavior that only makes sense in a competitive society that doesn't believe there's enough to go around. In many cases, we've seen sibling rivalry evaporate when an unhealthy family dynamic reaches balance.

♦ **Children know what's best for them and we should follow their lead.**

Children are wise and worthwhile in every moment of their existence, but there are developmental limits on that wisdom. Parents are here to guide, to cooperate with the natural unfolding of the child. Without naturally appropriate intervention and modeling, children become insecure, lose their inborn talent for exploration, and fail to access the depths of their inner wisdom.

Gathering Tools

There have been many approaches to child development. Many intelligent people share in the understanding that children grow and learn in a series of stages. Of the numerous developmental systems produced by the Western countries, at least five have originated in the United States during the twentieth century.

Is Natural Learning Rhythms different? Are those differences significant enough to justify your taking the time to understand them and, more importantly, to change your lifestyle to meet the developmental needs of your children?

Natural Learning Rhythms, extending the insights of Montessori, Steiner, and Pearce, makes this unequivocal statement: The qualities of a developmental stage are the outward expression of the wisdom that guides it. Stage-specific wisdom exists in each of us. It guides the unfolding of the child's life. The aim of parenting and education is to allow the child direct conscious experience of her stage-specific wisdom. The child's family is that group of people who supply her developmental needs and thus allow her connection to this inner wisdom.

All these differences add up to a new way of seeing the child. No longer can we claim to know how a child should turn out. Our aim is to allow the child direct experience of her stage-specific wisdom, not to impose our cultural prejudices on her. The issue is not whether the child will be a good Hindu, or a good American, or successful in business or painting, but whether she becomes strong and centered within herself. Once she does, the child is able to do whatever she needs to do to secure her liberty and fulfillment and thus take her place as an authentic member of her community.

Practicing Natural Learning Rhythms allows us to apply our developmental understanding with great skill. It's a sad truth that, despite the plethora of developmental approaches, only a few have been able to offer tools that families can use. Most of what has been written attempts to bring the child around to "good" or culturally acceptable behavior, rather than balance. Released from that constraint we become empowered with the ways and means to apply our knowledge and embrace our children with joy and enthusiasm.

The Life
Stages

1 ....

The Life Stages

Lepidoptera

Virtually everyone marvels at the nimble acrobatics of the butterfly, how it glides from one blossom to another sailing on the wind, how it somehow locates a mate in the midst of a vast forest. Though its flight patterns may be entrancing, however, they do not reveal the basic nature of the butterfly. Indeed, over the span of its lifetime the creature will reveal something more mysterious, something ancient and profound. Something not only about this particular butterfly, but about all butterflies—something about life itself.

Metamorphosis is a process beyond rational thought. Butterflies emerge from cocoons, cocoons are spun by caterpillars, caterpillars are larvae transformed, and larvae are the infant form of the species *Lepidoptera*.

From its conception, the entire life cycle of *Lepidoptera* is inherent in the larvae. All the potential of the insect, including the beautiful butterfly, is present and ready for its unfolding. This sequential development is *Lepidoptera's* natural rhythm.

To actualize this natural rhythm, each stage of its development—larvae, caterpillar, cocoon, and butterfly—must successfully meet the requirements for its growth. Given good food and a healthy, clean environment, its life stages progress and *Lepidoptera* reveals its startling mystery. The insect lives in a harmonious balance with its environment. This balance is the fruit of evolutionary struggle and has taken eons to develop.

In each of its developmental stages, *Lepidoptera* has different needs; the butterfly, for instance, drinks nectar while the caterpillar eats leaves. To feed the caterpillar nectar would be a violation of its natural rhythms, only thwarting its ability to grow. The butterfly itself would never develop. On a larger scale, the species would be unable to reproduce.

Each stage has its own ecological function, independent of the other life stages. For example, the caterpillar *in and of itself* plays a critical part in the forest's natural balance—whether it reaches the butterfly stage or not. It trims the trees and creates mulch in which seeds may grow. It also redistributes microorganisms. Furthermore, the caterpillar is prey for many species of birds and thus feeds the entire food chain. To treat it like a butterfly, even though butterflies may seem more beautiful, would be an affront to natural law.

Homo Sapiens

As with the butterfly, simply observing the behavior of a particular human being at a given point in her development will not allow us to see the true nature of the species *Homo Sapiens*. Human beings, too, are of a complex, mysterious, and ancient design.

Human beings also undergo natural life stages. The especially long period of human childhood, which evolved over millions of years, allows the unfolding of these stages, the natural rhythm of human development. This sequential unfolding, universally known as human development, *allows the manifestation of human consciousness*. Our extensive childhood is the time during which consciousness—physical, psychological, and spiritual—expands.

Each life stage is a new aspect of consciousness come to dominance. Within each stage, the child has the chance to play with this inherent wisdom, access its deep truths, and bring them to awareness. All life stages are necessary for consciousness to reach full maturity, full complexity. As with *Lepidoptera*, the successful completion of the life stages, the playing out of the measured cadences of our natural rhythms, allows the child to harmoniously integrate himself with our world.

Everything human is at stake here. In each stage, when *Homo Sapiens* finds the circumstances that induce growth, he is able to successfully harmonize with his environment. His evolution, and that of the species, is secured. When the opportunities are meager, everyone suffers. Were the opportunities unavailable, the species would die.

Society determines its future by the way it honors the life stages of its children in the present. We now know that children whose feelings are not honored will take advantage of and abuse both the environment and other human beings, as pioneering psychiatrist Alice Miller has so aptly expressed:

> Children who are lectured to, learn how to lecture; if they are admonished, they learn how to admonish; if scolded, they learn how to scold; if ridiculed, they learn how to ridicule; if humiliated, they learn how to humiliate, if their psyche is killed, they learn how to kill—the only question is who will be killed: oneself, others, or both.

Like society, the family also determines its future by the way it honors the life stages of its children in the present: A child not getting her needs met will disrupt the family. When a child's needs are satisfied, she feels joyful and confident, and parents waste far less time worrying. Unfortunately, good intentions and concern do not equal closeness or care. From the point of view of holistic development, the authentic family for a child is the aggregation of people who provide the growth opportunities *most in accord with her stage-specific needs*, her natural learning rhythms.

Stage-Specific Wisdom

Inherent in each life stage is a wellspring of wisdom, which allows that aspect of consciousness to be fully explored by the child. There are four different types, and we call them *stage-specific wisdoms*.

Stage-specific wisdom governs the unfolding of the life stage. Each wisdom has its natural rhythm of development. Each wisdom presents the child with the opportunity to make life-affirming evolutionary choices.

Each life stage also allows the child, and the species, to harmoniously integrate with its environment. The caterpillar fulfilled its purpose while a caterpillar; it did not have to wait to become a butterfly. Similarly, the child fulfills her purpose, both as an individual and a member of the species, by living in and deeply experiencing her current moment. There is no need for us to wait until she is a mature adult to validate or justify her existence.

As the caterpillar needed cut leaves and the butterfly needed nectar, so each different human life stage has unique requirements. The stage-specific wisdom selects nourishment according to its assessment of the child's developmental needs. It is disastrous for both individual and species to go against the dominant stage-specific wisdom and force feed the child an inappropriate food.

Profound and virtually inexhaustible, stage-specific wisdom allows the child to make contact and find meaning at the deepest level available in her particular environment. Stage-specific wisdom leads the child toward fulfillment of who she really is, now and in the future.

The job of the parent and educator is to provide the conditions that foster the most complete access to stage-specific wisdom. By honoring stage-specific wisdom we allow for the natural unfolding of the life stage. When the life stages develop according to their natural rhythms both individual and species grow and prosper. Our seedlings give rise to sturdy oaks, and everyone gets a chance to be a butterfly.

Great educators have long been aware of stage-specific wisdom. Maria Montessori wrote about "a vital force active within us . . . which guides [our] efforts." She called it *horme* and said that it ". . . belongs to life in general, to what may be called the divine urge, the source of all evolution." Then, Montessori unmistakably identified stage-specific wisdom: ". . . psychological maturation . . . changes its form at each level of development *because the horme changes its type."* She goes on to speak of "explosive changes" inwardly directed. These changes take place with the guidance of inner wisdom.

Rudolf Steiner, the founder of Waldorf Education, the esoteric discipline of anthroposophy and author of many books on education, pointed directly toward stage-specific wisdom with his brilliant interweaving of movement, language, and meaning in the young child. "Walking does not merely mean that the human being ceases to crawl and acquires an upright position. It means that the child attains to the equilibrium of its own organism with the cosmos. . . " And, "The relationship between physical equilibrium (action of the hands and arms) and psychical equilibrium forms the foundation which enables the child to come into contact with the outer world through the medium of language." In other words, there is a wisdom coordinating all these activities, and that wisdom springs forth from the meaning inherent in life and universe.

Joseph Chilton Pearce has been the most outspoken defender of the wisdom inherent in the developmental process. He sees existence itself as a biologically coordinated plan for the growth of intelligence. As

Pearce succinctly states "The biological plan is wrecked when the intent of nature is met not with appropriate content, but with the *intentions* of an anxiety-driven parent and society."

We can hear recognition of stage-specific wisdom in almost every attempt to perceive the whole child. Thomas Armstrong chronicles the many extraordinary expressions of children in his book, *Radiant Child*. Ken Wilber traces the thread of wisdom in children as it leads to recognition of wholeness in *The Atman Project*.

It's time to firmly establish stage-specific wisdom as fundamental in all interactions with children. *Natural Learning Rhythms* delves deeply into the nature of the four stage-specific wisdoms: their character; what conditions allow deepest contact with them; how they evolve; what their implications and applications are for communication, restoring balance, resolving conflict, creating curriculum, blending non-biological families, creating ritual and ceremony, and evoking the spirit of cooperation.

The Life Stages

Every child goes through four life stages. We call these life stages Body-Being, Emotional-Being, Will-Being, and Reasoning-Being.

The unabridged *Random House Dictionary* gives seven primary definitions for the word "being." Every one of them adds to the understanding of the life stage as defined in this book:

- ♦ **the fact of existing**
- ♦ **conscious mortal existence**
- ♦ **substance or nature**
- ♦ **something that exists as a living thing**
- ♦ **a human being**
- ♦ **God**
- ♦ **that which has actuality**

When writing the names of the life stages, we capitalize "being" to emphasize that each particular stage-specific wisdom governs all aspects of the corresponding life stage:

1. Body wisdom governs the Body-Being stage and is accessed through the body. Body wisdom uses sensation to receive information.

2. Emotional wisdom directs the Emotional-Being stage and receives information through feeling.

3. Will-Being is under the guidance of Will wisdom, which interacts with its environment through assertions and challenges.

4. Reasoning wisdom guides Reasoning-Being. Reasoning wisdom works via thinking.

Body-Being begins at conception and ends at approximately the age of eight. Emotional-Being lasts until about twelve, Will-Being until fifteen or sixteen, and Reasoning-Being until twenty-two. Ages are very approximate. Still, as we shall see, there are quite precise ways to determine the succession of the stages.

Using case histories we will explore these stages in the following chapters. We'll examine the transitions between stages, how to make direct contact with the child's stage-specific wisdom, and the particular aspects of each stage. On the way we'll shatter some bankrupt assumptions, do a few family dance steps, observe how love and trust develop between parent and child, and describe the child's perception of herself as she grows.

New Names for New Concepts

For many people, the Natural Learning Rhythms system resonates deeply with knowledge they've already sensed inside themselves; this both excites and perplexes them. Not surprisingly, a number of them want to know who we are, and how we developed Natural Learning Rhythms. We're often asked how we came to name the stages as we have. Why create new terms? Why ask people to grasp a new vocabulary?

Because the development of these terms coincided with the development of the whole system, which also coincided with our growth both as a couple and in individual self-awareness, these questions are best answered with a brief biographical narrative. We hope this narrative will allow easier access to the material and to us, to let you know who you're about to spend time with, to bring us closer as friends.

Fifteen years ago I (Ba) was living in Hawaii. I was running a small preschool, experimenting with many of the practices that would later become Natural Learning Rhythms. Josette became one of the teachers. We worked this way for the next five years, increasing our contact with children through home schooling. I took a double masters from California State University at Sonoma in psychology and early childhood education. Josette did intensives in Waldorf education and transpersonal psychology. Meditation remained, and remains our primary source of inspiration. We studied philosophy, anthropology, and religion extensively.

As time went by, people in our community began to come to us with family-related concerns. We noticed our relationships with children were becoming easier and easier. One day a parent remarked that we never seemed to use rewards and punishments with children, and asked us how we did it. We thought about it, and realized we never had. But we didn't know why.

Through careful study and fieldwork, we found inadequate the common belief that behavior defines the developmental stages. Such a theory simply did not do justice to the nature of the child. With a different eye, we returned to the literature on the same subject to see if anyone had looked deeper. Yes, there was a school of thought that envisaged the stages as an expression of something more fundamental than behavior. Nevertheless, there was something wrong, or rather incomplete about how these stages were defined.

Montessori named her *horme*, yet it comprised only a small part of her contribution. Her followers hardly spoke of it. We didn't know why. We'd confirmed her observations about absorbed, centered, balanced children tens of times. Steiner's esoteric approach was well articulated. His followers preached it and we'd corroborated his observations about the interconnectedness of all aspects of a child's growth. Yet, Steiner's esoteric terms depended upon interpretation. Specific discussions with leaders of Waldorf education showed that they had no cohesive, consistent understanding of what he meant. Assumptions abounded. And because of the lack of common understanding among the theorists and practitioners, Steiner's philosophy was not comprehensible to many parents.

So it went. Pearce's *Magical Child* caused a stir, but he had few practical applications, and he was seeing through the adult's, not the child's eyes. *Magical Child Matures* confirmed this evaluation. In educating children Pearce believes that "the final goal is the only criterion: development must be in line with our ultimate goal [which is spirituality]." But who is the child? And who best knows her destiny?

Ken Wilber certainly identified the spirit and wisdom inherent in human life; *The Atman Project* is perhaps the most erudite look at child development ever. Two problems: The study is difficult to decipher due to Wilber's use of esoteric and arcane terms; and more importantly, the child is seen as a "person becoming" rather than a presence. Childhood's value, to Wilber, is in the preparation for adulthood, not in and of itself. In *Radiant Child*, Thomas Armstrong tried to remedy the problem but could only provide us with an amorphous transpersonal spirit appearing in some children at some times. The spiritual leaders we contacted, including pastors, priests, rabbis, and yogis, attempted both individual statements and round-table discussions about child development, ending only with conclusions that reinforced the correctness of their particular religious practices.

We were dissatisfied, to say the least. We had put in a number of years of fieldwork, spending time with children in all arenas of their life—learning, playing, being in nature, vacationing, doing chores, as well as helping them clarify ideas about sexuality, career choices, and family. In the same way that Jane Goodall lived with chimpanzees, we lived with young humans, and in the course of it verified the existence of inherent wisdom in children. We had access to tantalizing studies whose results yielded important but partial information about the nature of this wisdom. And our experience of contacting this wisdom was easy; we never had to bribe or coerce children to enjoy disciplined, creative learning/playing together.

We moved to California. Children labeled "difficult" and "hyperactive" became a part of our life. We made contact with teenagers. We studied, debated, gently experimented. Our own family grew stronger. Children were attracted to us and parents came for advice. We sought training in family counseling. Families shared their intimate concerns with us. We wondered where these experiences would lead.

Eight years ago we began to see a light in the distance. Then, as if a dam had broken, all the pieces of our work and experience rushed to fit together. We realized that stage-specific wisdom is impersonal, playing through each of us, providing the opportunity to fully explore an ancient, venerable aspect of our *wholeness*. Each kind of stage-specific wisdom (body, emotional, will, or reasoning) has a set of optimum conditions that, when met, best serve the full development of the child's consciousness. These wisdoms are of the essence, as expression of wholeness. They contain the fullness of who we are at that moment of growth.

Our success with children was due to the fact that we were providing the conditions that made it possible for the stage-specific wisdoms to blossom. And then we saw it: When the inherent wisdoms read the world as safe, they deliver all the information the child needs to live a balanced healthy life—to fulfill his own destiny. Right away, we saw the applications: restoring balance through contacting the stage-specific wisdom, creating curriculum, devising developmentally appropriate rites of passage, engaging communication, and resolving conflict with developmental sensitivity.

We were awestruck. The implications of this understanding crossed boundaries from anthropology to general semantics, through all of psychology right into myth and ritual: To tell the truth, at this moment we backed off, frightened; it appeared that we had caught a tiger by the tail. There is no more tender issue for a family than how they act with their child, and it is a tremendous responsibility to try and change it.

Eventually, however, our commitment to life and the end of unnecessary suffering reasserted itself, and strongly. Children were our focus. Finally we had some insight into the fundamental questions about childhood. We could answer the behaviorists. The theories of those great educators such as Pearce, Montessori, and Steiner, who had known of inherent wisdom could be reconciled. In essence, they were all trying to say the same thing, each from his or her own angle: Who has the answers to the child's needs? The child. Our job is to allow her access to the inner wisdom inherent in her whole being.

Being. The fact of conscious existence. That which has actuality. Of the essence. We knew we had to find a way to speak of these wisdoms that encompased their entirety, that spoke to transpersonal as well as personal aspects of humanness, that allowed for behavior, psyche, and spirit.

Being. No other word would do. We appreciated the difficulty some people might have with the new terminology but we found no existing expression that could convey what we needed it to say. So, as many clever children do, we made up our own. Seven years and a hundred workshops later, we're able to say that it works, it's not terribly hard to understand, and most people like having a fairly objective method for referring to their children.

In this book, we've constructed each chapter so that it contains short, clear descriptions of each life stage and its specific wisdom, as well as case histories and examples of the way the child in each stage acts in nature. In this way we hope to catch the fullness, the life, and the precise elegance each stage-specific wisdom embodies. We also hope to

11

keep you interested. Dry, academic descriptions are boring and frequently fail to touch the reader. We want to touch you. We believe we have exciting insights that bring joy to parenting, balance to children, power to the family, and ultimately health and peace to our communities, society and the world.

The Character Traits

As the child develops, his body and psyche undergo radical changes, though unlike *Lepidoptera*, his basic physical form remains the same. Let's consider the body first: Both a seven-month-old and a twelve-year-old child have recognizable human hearts, even if the infant's organ is considerably smaller, beats faster, and requires a different type of nourishment. The two different hearts have the same form and structure. But in order to serve the more mature child, his heart is nourished by a more complex variety of foods than mother's milk, and it beats at a different rhythm.

The same principle of consistency holds with regard to the child's psyche: Human beings are born with certain character traits that develop throughout childhood, yet whose form and structure are easily recognizable in all humans.

Each child is born with her own unique blend of character traits. When these traits are in balance with one another, the child enjoys the most complete access to stage-specific wisdom. When they are out of balance, stage-specific wisdom works to restore it. Our bodies operate the same way. When we are well, we can use our body for a great wide diversity of tasks. When we are ill, most of our body's resources are mobilized to fight off the illness.

The character traits express themselves differently in each developmental stage. For example, autonomy, as expressed by the eleven-year-old in Emotional-Being, is closely tied to community; the fifteen-year-old in Will-Being expresses it as fierce individualism. By understanding the stage and the stage-specific wisdom that governs it, we can ascertain the nature and health of each character trait. We can then intervene to restore balance where necessary for the child's well being.

The Remedies chapter includes a full explanation of the character traits, along with detailed charts of how to work with them in the family or classroom. We mention the character traits here as a reminder that each child has a uniqueness and wonder all her own.

Hesitancies

We often imagine human development as a smooth spiral building steadily upon itself over time. But in fact, growth and learning more often follow a sort of irregular waving line, interrupted along the way by fits and starts. As with evolution, a genuine change from one life stage to another requires a lull, a coalescing of energy and information to make the quantum leap.

These lulls, or *hesitancies*, allow time to prepare for the new psychological and physiological changes. During a *hesitancy*, the dominant stage-specific wisdom slows down the child's reception of information and her expression of new behaviors.

During a hesitancy the child may become difficult, fussy, or demanding. He may test or manipulate. He may exhibit regressive behavior, wanting to be treated like a much younger child, and deliberately *unlearn* much of what he already knows. Hesitancies are often accompanied by nightmares, poor health and by the tell-tale refusal of favorite foods and activities by the child.

Hesitancies are part of the natural process. The child is collecting all available energy and, at the same time, alerting the parents that an important change is about to occur. The child's awareness is about to expand tremendously.

Hesitancies *need* to happen, for the overall development of the child. They crop up between the life stages and periodically within them, and should not be mistaken for malfunctioning.,

When a hesitancy is treated in a hostile way (like an illness, for example) and is blocked, the stage-specific wisdom must come to the child's rescue and "insist" that the hesitancy occur. If the scene turns into a battle, the child learns that change and conflict are inseparable. She learns that taking the time to check her support systems, a natural and wise response, is not condoned. Worse, she exhausts herself trying to both please her disapproving parents, and to honor her innate wisdom.

Although age, intensity, and expression vary, all children experience hesitancies: The six-and-a-half-year-old child might be unable to accept any criticism, or perhaps he'll revert to tantrums. He might prefer playing with very young children. The ten-and-a-half-year-old child may suddenly become afraid of the dark, have wild nightmares, or insist on reading books she gave to her little brother years ago.

On the other hand, children emerging from a hesitancy often display remarkable advances in consciousness or in particular skills. One three-year-old might emerge from a regression able to string together cogent sentences, another might be able to handle longer separations from her parents. A third might come out of a hesitancy able to move with agility over diverse terrain. The outcomes are as varied for sixteen-year-olds as they are for toddlers. One teenager might emerge from a hesitancy highly competent in elementary calculus, another at the clarinet or basketball, a third in solving quarrels among her classmates. Each child manifests his newly honed capacity uniquely. Many children show a blend of new abilities.

The Life Stage in Three Phases

Each developmental life stage passes through three phases, which we call *receptivity, trial and error,* and *competency.* While not as pronounced or obvious as the transitions from one stage to another, phase-shifts mark a significant growth in the child's learning and intelligence, and are often accompanied by a hesitancy.

The child in the *receptive* phase of each stage exhibits a great deal of vulnerability. He has just gone through the birth of the newest life stage, and so he must perceive the world in a brand-new way. This newness is both awesome and compelling, and the child needs all the support he can get. He is wide open and ready to learn, absorbing all the information he can.

The moment comes when the child is "full," his capacity for receiving information is saturated. He now turns to playing with the new information he has gathered, and so begins the *trial and error* phase. He will experiment with a new kind of behavior, for example, stringing words together into cohesive sentences in Body-Being, or making personal commitments in Reasoning-Being. And he'll do this in as many different settings as he can, as long as he needs to, until he feels that he understands its particular power and meaning.

All that the child has learned through receptivity and trial and error come to good use in the third, or *competency* phase. This is the full-blown expression of the life stage he is currently in, and he directly experiences himself as body, emotional, will, or reasoning wisdom. At the climax of this phase, at the height of *competency,* the child prepares to travel into the next life stage.

The Child in Nature

The natural world is a microcosm of wholeness. Seamless, timeless, ever-renewing, the natural world brings each individual to fullness within the context of mutual interdependence. We clearly gain great insight into our natural rhythms by observing the child's interaction with the natural world.

Human beings are natural creatures. We need to spend time in nature, in environments mostly untouched by humans, such as forests, seashores, and mountains. As a whole, the natural world supports each of its parts. As such, it accommodates the child in a way that allows balance and health. Here, we can find out the most about the nature of the child.

To gain this insight, we ran a nature class for four years. Each Friday we would take approximately ten children between the ages of six and twelve for all-day excursions into nature. Our mornings began with a hike. After a couple of hours we would stop and usually play cooperative games. After lunch there would be more games, storytelling, and acting, then the hike home.

Every activity, whether active or passive, taught us much about children in nature. Something about the great expanse and mystery of nature opens the children in a way that reveals their actual disposition. Time in nature tends to dissolve the child's defensiveness. The way she interacts with the natural environment and the people she's with provides great insights into her psychological and physical well-being.

In addition to the insights, describing the way each stage-specific wisdom interacts with the natural world elucidates their rhythmic progression. We can easily see the increasing ability to relate to the complexity of the environment. We can also see the differences between body, emotional, will, and reasoning wisdom by the way children of different ages relate to the natural world.

Each of the next four chapters describes a developmental stage. For both insight and elucidation, we have included a section in each on the way the child in that stage expresses himself in the natural world.

*B*ody-Being

"The world stretches outward from my body," knows the child in Body-Being. "I am its core."

Body-Being brings to consciousness of *body-as-environment*. From conception until the age of seven the child has one primary job: to develop a working knowledge of her own body and the earth, the planetary body. Securing herself on the planet provides the foundation for all her future growth.

Body-Being delights in life and living by providing the child with an unbending inclination to live and to explore. To establish herself on the planet the child must *sensorially* enter into life. To the young child, the world is an unending stream of sensations. It is immense; she's tiny. Yet she must undertake a full exploration of life unfettered by unnecessary fears. How can she do so without being overwhelmed?

Body-Being's wise solution is egoism. The child believes she is the center of the universe, and the world an extension of her body. She sees life as revolving around her, as emanating from her, as a play in which she has the leading role. She counts herself first, and if you ask her to make everything disappear, she'll cover her eyes: If she can't sense it, it isn't there.

The World Is an Extension of My Body

Both the refined physical sensitivity and intense egoism central to Body Being can be surprising, especially when these characteristics occur in combination with one another.

Jan, who teaches kindergarten at a suburban private school, told us of an incident she felt epitomized the caring nature of her little ones. During class one day, a boy fell and cut his arm. The rest of the children gathered around immediately, and "wouldn't leave until they knew the boy was going to be all right."

Out of curiosity about the way children perceive the world, we asked her to review the experience. Which behaviors was she seeing as caring?

"How did the other children know the boy was hurt?" we asked.

"They heard him scream," she remembered.

"And did all the children come?"

"Yes," she said, "everyone. They all stayed until he was taken care of."

"Did any children who do not ordinarily get along with this boy come?"

"Yes, several. In fact, this boy is not one of the more popular children in the class."

"Did it seem to you," we asked, "that those children who do not like this boy had a sudden change of heart because he hurt his arm? Do you think it was the boy they were concerned about, even though previously they avoided him, or something else?"

"He was hurt and so they cared for him," she answered, but without her prior conviction.

"Did the other children show any particular caring for the boy once it was clear that he would be all right? Did they check in with him during the day to ask how his arm was, or do special things for him, such as carry his books?"

"Not especially. Now that I think of it, when he got into a spat with a couple of kids at the end of the day, there was no mercy shown for his injury."

As the conversation continued all three of us could see that caring for the hurt child was not the foremost concern of most of the children. But neither was the children's attitude one of disdain. In the end, to our collective amazement, we realized their primary focus was the boy's arm, not the boy himself.

Again, we need to keep in mind that Body-Being's children see the world *as an extension of their body*. It was as if the children had hurt their own arm. If the boy's arm did not heal, how could they know that their own arm could survive a similar injury? During Body-Being, it is essential that this question be answered. Establishing the body on the planet is the most important task.

Body-Being keeps the senses sharp. Every smell, sight, touch, taste, and sound stands out cleanly and purely. So do the mood sensations emanating from the people around her. The child in Body-Being is alive, aware, and present.

As the child grows, she learns through these sensations. She watches those around her very closely, absorbing all she can. The principal behavior mode of the Body-Being child is imitation. She can only respond according to the sensory data available. As she senses, so she does. Yet, wisdom lies hidden in sensory-based imitation—her survival itself depends on it. Imitation ensures the child will be like those around her, and so accepted and cared for.

All Body-Being's great tasks are accomplished through evaluation of sensory input and imitation. In learning language, for example, there is first an infinite variety of sounds that the child hears and imitates. He experiences the sensation of the sound in his larynx; he notices the reactions in the people around him; he associates secondary sensations, such as smells or touch. Often, feeding provides an opportunity to play with these sounds. There the child feels safe and is often lovingly touched while mama repeats definite sounds over and over while he eats.

The child continues to play, to imitate, to explore the power of sound. Soon he says something and the feelings his mother emanates become extremely pleasurable. Jolted by the pleasurable sensation, Body-Being prompts the behavior over and over again. Yes, this sound is connected to her, to his mama, to the one who holds and feeds, to the one whose scent and heartbeat have always been present. How delectable for the child. The great game of connecting objects to words; the child will never tire of it during Body-Being's entire reign.

Just as pleasurable sensations send a signal to repeat a certain behavior, so unpleasant ones warn the child away from a particular behavior. Naturally, the child will follow pleasant sensations wherever they lead and avoid unpleasant ones whenever possible.

Body-Being's capacity for *feeling,* in the emotional sense, is rooted in pleasant and unpleasant sensations. Unpleasant ones engender feelings of "badness." To the child, an event can be bad, the person causing the unpleasantness can be bad, or the child can perceive herself as bad.

When unpleasurable sensations violate her egoism, these sensations make her angry. She especially dislikes any violation of the body or the family. If the unpleasantness is beyond her control it makes her unhappy. She loses her zest for life. Pleasant sensations, on the other hand, generate a feeling of gladness.

These four basic and simple feelings—bad, sad, mad, and glad—represent the limit for Body-Being's sensation-based emotions. More than adequate for survival, they constitute the feeling repertoire of the child. They support the child *in her body* without making excessive demands.

Reasoning also exists in only the most rudimentary form during Body-Being. The child can, for example, compare objects based on sensory experience. He may even perhaps accomplish some minor abstractions such as "sharing" and a sense of "tomorrow" through application of rules learned either palpably or by rote. But this is neither an understanding of morality or a genuine appreciation of time.

Body-Being's perspective of self and the world, of body-as-environment, produces a retributive sense of justice: an eye for an eye. To Body-Being's child, fairness means equal quantities: there is little consideration for special emotional needs or the notion that "everything will equal out over time."

The Foods

Having begun its influence at conception, Body-Being has the child fully prepared for birth. All physiological systems are ready to handle the tremendous expansion of life outside of the womb. The brain, the mediator of consciousness, has its full complement of cells. But almost none of the "hard wiring" of the brain's neural pathways have been set, for that would severely inhibit the child's ability to adapt to his environment.

The one exception is touch. Body-Being uses the sensation of touch to guide the child safely through the birthing process and the first years of life. The sensations against her skin tell her where she is in the birthing process. Through tactile sensation, she knows that her body *is* and that she exists.

The emotional dispositions of those people close to her, especially her mother, also register. All sensations become part of her awareness and her memory. During the dramatic transition from the womb to the outside world she's *wide* open, and her experiences become deeply embedded within her nervous system. They are imprinted.

Body-Being uses the child's birth—the most creative moment of its incumbency—to allow direct experience of innate natural wisdom unfolding. Truth and spirit in the body. *Wholeness.* When conditions support the natural wisdom the lesson is learned. Without the proper support, imprinting still occurs but the lesson becomes distorted; the child's relationship to creativity suffers and she loses some of her inherent power. Body-Being must then work at *restoring* balance, rather than *operating from* balance. And, though not impossible, modification of imprints is difficult.

Born. The child knows where he is and what to do by *how he is touched.* His sense of self, his awareness depends on the tactile milieu.

Loving touch translates as safety. Safety allows exploration, connection, the willingness to make contact. Loving touch: baby registers the message "all's right in the world" immediately. He thrives on it.

Loving touch provides the essential food in Body-Being's diet, though not by itself. The baby's psychological balance requires other kinds of nutrients as well: *security, warmth, and flexibility.* As with physical diet, each child requires a unique blend of emotion-nourishing foods. And Body-Being senses immediately whether these are present in a form the child can metabolize.

Security is physical and psychological safety. *Warmth* is not merely a temperature, but the sensation of intimacy and appropriateness. *Flexibility* means the ability to yield, to be pliable, to engage in give and take, and to be open to modification. Like loving touch, these foods directly nourish the body. Body-Being craves them. When they are not present Body-Being spends most of its energy directing the child to search for them.

Properly nourished, the child engages her natural learning tools, imitation and exploration, wholeheartedly. She trusts the information she has gleaned from inner sensation, and uses it to unlock the secrets of her environment. Nurtured by loving touch, security, warmth, and flexibility, she will spend the next seven years playing, alive in every moment, moved by her innate curiosity to gently challenge herself to find out just what to make of the vast world around her.

Security

Rose, a vivacious six-year-old girl, loves to climb. Every chance she gets she's up a tree, on a roof, or over a fence. One day I (Josette) was visiting her family when we heard cries from the nearby cedar. When I reached the tree, I saw Rose high on a branch, hugging the tree trunk.

"What's up, Rose?" I asked casually. "Something the matter?"

"I'm scared," she whimpered. "I climbed up here but I don't know how to get down. It's too high."

"Just stay there," I said and began to climb. When I reached a branch from which I could catch her if she fell, I stopped. "Hey Rose, are you still afraid?"

"Yes."

"Where in your body do you feel the fear?"

"Here," she said, pointing to her navel. "Right in my tummy."

"Can you take a deep breath into your tummy?"

Rose tried a few shallow breaths. I asked her if she felt better, but she said no. I asked her to try to breathe again. After five minutes she said that her tummy wasn't so tight anymore.

"Well, then climb down," I said. "I'm right here to catch you if you fall."

"It's too high. I'm scared again."

I asked Rose to breathe some more, then met her request to climb to a branch closer to her. Then she agreed to try to come down on her own, as long as I was right below her. When she reached the bottom she exulted in her experience. She looked up the cedar tree and said, "Wow, Mom, I climbed all the way up there and all the way down."

As we have said, the child in Body-Being decides which activity to explore based on sensory experience. The child either finds it pleasant and explores it, or unpleasant and turns away. Due to taste, for example, she may well choose white sugar over spinach, regardless of nutritional considerations. Similarly, if climbing higher is the positive sensation in exploring a tree, she may not take careful notice of the strength of the branches. Body-Being's child might also forget to look down.

Sensation-based decision-making raises the sometimes touchy issue of security. When an over-protective parent keeps the child "secure" from risky exploration, the parent conditions the child's experience. This conditioning limits Body-Being's exploration.

Many of us are aware, from our own experience, that providing security and intelligent guidance is the heart of the parenting process, and we let our good sense prevail. When the environment challenges the child, participate in such a way that the child has the full experience of her exploration without threatening her well-being. Be prepared, for instance, to suggest an alternate tree if the first one doesn't meet safety requirements. In the case of a child who eats too much sugar, provide other foods that allow the same sweet taste sensation.

Flexibility

Some time ago Andy, an attentive, earnest man who attended one of our workshops, was particularly affected by a discussion on the importance of flexibility. Generally, he explained, he had allowed his four-year-old son Sam to play with just one game or toy. Now he was returning home and had resolved to stop restricting his child's access to his belongings.

Two nights later Andy called us. That morning Sam had woken up in a good mood and they had played with his toys. But by mid-morning the toddler's mood changed for the worse. Andy had not limited access to the toys. When Sam wanted one, Andy got it down. Yet in a short time, Sam had gone through all of them and, thoroughly frustrated, had begun to cry. At that point Andy lost patience and the rest of the day was spent in disagreement.

In talking with Andy, we slowly we reviewed exactly what happened with the toys. We learned that as soon as Sam was finished with a toy, his dad put it back on the shelf. The child could have any toy, but only one at a time! In the end, though he hoped to be less restrictive with his son, the rigidity of Andy's neatness still deprived Sam of flexibility.

For Body-Being's child, flexibility leads directly to self-empowerment. By finding an environment willing to bend to her needs, the child can operate on body-as-environment with the most freedom and exploration. But this empowerment can only occur within a secure context. An unsafe environment contains no flexibility.

Excess

Just as deprivation of flexibility or security injures the child, so may excess. Developmental foods must be present in a balanced, healthy form.

> "My mother had swaddled me in scads of blankets," recalled Cristina, one of our clients. "I was so hot I couldn't breathe. She cooed and attended me, but never heard my message. Instead, I lay there writhing in frustration. It took me years to come to terms with that experience, and to understand its connection to my extreme aversion to being closed in by anything."

Cristina's mother erred to the side of too many woolen blankets—literally, a case of too much warmth. In a similar discovery, many educators of the Free School movement realized that too much flexibility does not serve the child: Aimless, she'll often follow the most pleasant sensation with no sense of its ultimate value for her. These free school educators, who had at first simply waited for the children to initiate activities realized that guidance, structure, and limitations are also vital to the child's well being.

Body Language

Body-Being's child plays and plays. Basing his game on imitation, he takes off into endless creative combinations.

Though he can roughly determine the relationships between words and objects, he cannot yet master their full meaning or power in the form of language. Therefore, he must have some exact means of communicating with his parents. His body provides that way.

What you see is what there is. Sensations register in the body of the child, and through careful observation you can see them. Her face, her shoulders, her muscular tension all reflect her sensation experience. For the child, this is not the time for acting. The aim is survival, no games or masks. Body-Being's language is body language. By learning to read it, we discover the value each experience has for our child. Over time, we come to know who she is and what she needs to have profound contact with her innate wisdom.

What You See Is What There Is

When the educator or parent learns to read the language of the body she begins to see through the child's eyes. She can both understand how the child prioritizes her values and provide remedies for difficult situations.

Julie's five-year-old son, Tris, would often play roughly with his new baby brother. The rough play bothered Julie, but even more alarming was the rigidity that would come over Tris's whole body whenever the play became intense. When she contacted us for counseling, she wondered whether Tris was jealous of the new baby, and if so what to do about it.

At the time, Julie was also in the process of separating from her husband. Mike had agreed to continue supporting the family since he felt that mothering was a full-time job.

25

When we arranged the counseling session, we enlisted the aid of our eleven-year-old daughter, Amber, who played with the children as soon as they arrived. In this way, a family environment—safe, secure, and flexible—was set up, rather than one resembling conventional therapy. This would allow Tris to relax, become comfortable, and more closely approximate his everyday behavior.

After hearing of the turmoil in their lives and their description of Tris's reaction to it, we weren't at all convinced that Tris was jealous of his brother. Instead, we believed that the main components of the boy's anxiety were the separation of his parents, a confining city apartment lifestyle, a crowded playground as the primary play territory, the parents' ignorance of the needs of Body-Being, lack of integrity by each parent in their interactions with each other and with Tris, Julie's physical illness (she suffered from lupus), and the arrival of the new baby. In some ways, it would have seemed logical to suggest remedies for each of these factors and end the conference. Certainly, there would have been some improvement, and Julie and Mike would have been satisfied. Yet we felt that if we could figure out the priorities in Tris's life, remedies could be applied with more speed, precision, and quality. Was the baby brother in fact the cause of Tris's difficulties? Leaving Mike and Julie behind, we went to spend some time with Tris and find out.

We found Amber and Tris playing in the barn. Hiding behind a bale of hay, we showered them with handfuls of cracked corn. We'd taken them by surprise, and they laughed and counterattacked with armfuls of straw. Soon everyone was jumping from bale to bale, throwing hay on each other, and laughing uproariously. After fifteen minutes of fun, we asked Tris if he would like to take a walk through the woods to find wild mushrooms. Amber said she had work to do, and so we went alone.

We walked and talked and became friendly. Eventually we came to a fallen tree with lots of mushrooms growing under it. On our bellies, we explored the mushrooms together, then sat on one of the branches to rest and take a drink.

Speaking easily, as one friend to another, we brought up all the various factors that had been identified as contributing to Tris's discomfort. Many were brought up more than once, as the conversation allowed. All the time we were observing Tris's body, especially his face, as often an expression will pass quickly across the face that reveals the child's true reaction. Through these observations we learned the relative importance of each factor for Tris.

We returned home and Amber showed up to play with Tris. We told Julie and Mike of our experience and our tentative conclusions. Tris was having the most difficulty with the lack of resolution in Julie and Mike's relationship, and in Julie's inability to play with him due to her sickness. When his baby brother came up, Tris was all smiles.

A second set of problems centered on Tris's sense of having "nowhere to go." Body-Being children rarely criticize their home, because home is all they know and is critical to security. When talking with Tris we switched back and forth from home to playground several times. The tension in Tris's face and shoulders proclaimed that both places threatened him.

Reflecting Tris's priorities, we prescribed a six-week remedy regime. The parents were to seek professional help to resolve their relationship within a month. For the duration of Julie's illness, she was to spend her strongest hours of each day "one on one" with Tris. We recommended that Julie, Tris, and the baby move. Tris needed a home/play environment free from the disabling memories of his parents' fights and his reputation as a playground bully.

He also needed more, not less, interaction with his brother. They were to sleep in the same bed, instead of Tris sleeping alone while baby slept with Julie. Julie was urged to include Tris in her time with the baby. He could help with the diapers and take care of the baby while Julie rested.

Within the next six weeks, there was dramatic improvement. During the last four, Tris's physical rigidity disappeared, and the brothers were getting along well. Plans had been made to move to the country. Tris was looking forward to the change and wondered if he could move close to Amber's house so he could play in the woods.

Hesitancies in Body-Being

Somewhere between two and three years of age a hesitancy occurs in Body-Being's development. The child may become obtuse, difficult, demanding, testing, manipulative, or fussy. He may want to be treated like an infant and/or turn his back on things he loved to do. This is not a test of wills designed to exasperate the parents, but treating it as such has led to the deceptive—and rather mystifying—notion of "the terrible twos." For the child, it's a time to check support systems, as we've said; it's also a time for energy to coalesce so that he can move onward.

Hesitancies occur in all children, though age, intensity, and expression vary. The next hesitancy in Body-Being often occurs around the age of six-and-a-half. This child might be unable to accept criticism, or revert to tantrums, or become easily upset by broken promises. She might prefer playing with very young children, wet her pants, or become extremely introverted.

The sudden growth in abilities that often follows a hesitancy also varies from child to child. One three-year-old might come out of the regression able to sing well, another might be able to handle more responsibility, while a third might be able to explore the dark. Each child is unique in his manifestation of his newly won capacities. In any case, hesitancies allow us to see that seemingly disfunctional behaviors are often part of the natural growth pattern.

A Hesitancy at Two-and-a-Half

Suddenly one day, John, age two and a half, would not let his mother change his diaper. Sometimes he would resist for days at a time. He refused all baths, wouldn't change clothes, wouldn't greet people, and disrupted preparation of meals. Previously, helping with the preparation of meals—washing vegetables or sitting on the kitchen counter stirring a bowl of batter—had been one of his great joys.

After a telephone consultation, Joan realized that John was probably in a hesitancy. She rearranged her schedule to accommodate John. No stigma was attached to his behavior. When hygiene demanded a change of clothes and a bath, she gently told him that he was to be washed. It was not John's decision, but Joan's. Joan did not argue, but firmly, with as little force as possible, accomplished the task.

No social expectations were placed on John. He could say hello or good-bye as he wished. Many times Joan refused invitations to other people's homes. If Gordon, the older brother, wanted to have visitors, Joan played with John in a separate room.

At the end of three weeks, John's verbal skills exploded. Complete sentences, even paragraphs, came forth effortlessly. All regressive symptoms disappeared. John's social affability returned twice over.

All the dominant qualities of a hesitancy are present in John's case: refusal of favorite events, regressive behavior, and intractability. John was giving a clear signal: "Slow down. I need time to assimilate the changes in my growth." He was regrouping his energies. Equally important, he was alerting us of the imminence of his great leap forward.

The Trial and Error and Competency Phases

The emergence from the hesitancy at two and a half signals the end of the receptive phase. Staying in the present, endlessly exploring, ever-sensitive to the right balance of loving touch, security, warmth, and flexibility, the child tries out behavior after behavior from her repertoire. Within a couple of years Body-Being knows which behaviors have the most potential for the highest consciousness of the child. It's then time for mastery.

Egoism runs rampant during competency. The child believes, "I am here, I belong, I can do anything." The exploration of her physical body culminates in investigation of the genitals. As always, investigation occurs within the realm of sensation.

The egoism does not stop with genital exploration. Some children see themselves as able to ward off danger, to negotiate the physical world no matter how difficult, to marry someone much older and have babies together, to handle responsibility beyond their capacity, to master difficult subjects and skills.

"I can do it!" believes the child. "The world is an extension of my body, and I am the center of the world. I can master my body and I can master the world."

Body-Being in Nature

Nature effortlessly communicates its lessons to Body-Being's child in the language that the child understands. Body wisdom responds to the nature's *wholeness*. The playful interaction between Body-Being's child and the natural world reveals each of their inherent qualities.

Wanting to know her better, we watch the child's body carefully, noting her tenseness, noting her ease. Over time we note the changes. Which interactions speak to the type of child she intrinsically is? Which reveal dysfunction? Which behaviors reflect the nature of Body-Being? How well does the child access loving touch, warmth, flexibility, and security in nature? How well does she explore? Does her style reflect her natural life-positive egoism or is she encumbered by self-consciousness?

In Friday Class, the nature class we taught for four years, "Hug A Tree" is a favorite activity. In a wooded area, the children pair off and one is blindfolded. The other child picks out a tree and, using a deliberately confusing route, leads the blindfolded child to that tree. The blindfolded one then explores the tree with all senses except sight. Using a different but equally confusing route, the blindfolded child is led back to the starting point. The blindfold removed, the child has to find the tree.

In our experience, children between five and eight almost always find the tree. Children between three and five years old do better than those twelve to fifteen years old. Grown-ups who treat the game seriously and explore the tree with good concentration do quite well, but those who just go through the motions do worst of all.

The five to eights, in the highest competency of Body-Being, are at their peak of sensation awareness. Even sightless, they make excellent sensation-maps of their world.

Yet on our Friday walks, we noticed that for some reason these same Body-Being children would mindlessly pull leaves off plants, try to put bugs in glass jars, and dangle lizards by the end of their tails. Why do children who can map the world so accurately through sensation sometimes treat that world so barbarously?

The answer is egoism. Their sensation experience refers only to themselves, not to the experience of the lizard. The lizard is there to be explored. Dangling the lizard is a tactile pleasure and yields the sensations of power and control. *Sensation* and *sensitivity*, we noted, are not the same thing.

Genuine sensitivity requires feeling. When a very young child just doesn't comprehend the message about "the feelings of the animals," many parents resort to threats as a way to stop their child from hurting the family pet. The child may well stop, to please the parent, to avoid the unpleasant sensation of his anger. But after age eight it is only the unbalanced child who attacks living things. That child, under the guidance of Emotional-Being *feels,* and her feelings bring a reverence for life.

How can we moderate this barbarism in Body-Being children when it appears? One intelligent teacher has created an activity in which the students pretend to be plants lining a path. Then a child passes through and the students, insensitively but without undue violence, push or pull at him. Without undue moralizing by anyone, sensation is linked to sensitivity.

Just as we have seen children come to understand nature, we have also seen nature revealing the innate qualities in an individual child. One Friday last year, our nature class of children ranging from six to twelve hiked down to the river. On arrival, the older children quickly organized a cooperative water game. But all the children younger than eight decided not to play. They stood by the riverbank and watched the rippling waves, or found pretty stones and set them on shore to dry.

As the sunshine grew more intense, we initiated cooperative swimming lessons. Again, the response from the older children was immediate, enthusiastic participation, while the younger ones refrained. Feeling no need to be social, they preferred to be by themselves and explore other parts of the river and beach. These young children experienced the lack of adult pressure as warmth, the chance to explore at their own rhythm as flexibility, and the approval of their teachers as security. At the same time, we teachers were able to observe and learn many things to help us grow more intimate with each of them.

On that particular afternoon we were able to watch Allan, ordinarily a very active child, sitting quietly in the sand sorting small colored rocks into groups by color, his attention riveted, his body relaxed.

Forty minutes later I (Ba) approached him. His eyes gleamed serenely. With a gesture Allan invited me to sit and view his work. He had taken each rock he found and placed it on a color continuum ranging from one end of the rainbow to the other. The overall effect was startling and beautiful. What meticulous precision had been expressed here! Though I couldn't tell where one color stopped and another started, seen as a whole all seven colors were instantly obvious. When I turned to complement the boy, he'd already turned to finding new rocks.

Though the beauty of his work deeply impressed me, in other ways Allan's calm, contemplative behavior was puzzling. Usually, this boy was a whirlwind of physical energy. I talked it over with Josette. We knew the child's father spent much of his free time either playing sports or watching sports programs on TV. Was Allan's frenetic behavior due to imitation, wanting to please his parent?

Our subsequent weeks' observation in Friday Class proved this to be likely. To deepen our investigation, we unobtrusively began to set up situations in which the child could explore nature on a small scale, with protection and quiet. Without fanfare, Allan's innate disposition toward color and handwork took hold. Told of our findings his parents fortunately supported the child by buying the materials and providing the quiet space that he needed. His intensity began to be focused on what he was doing instead of those around him. When those around him remarked upon his clearly evident transformation, Allan wondered what all the fuss was about. To him, his behavior was the most natural thing in the world.

Body Talk

Let's look at another example of an adult closely attuned to the child in Body-Being. At an advanced Natural Learning Rhythms workshop,

Maria, a resolute and confident mother of three, told us a story about observing her six-year-old neighbor Hannah while camping. Maria's attention was first drawn to Hannah in the forest with her playmates. At first glance the little girl appeared to be playing as she always did. But something seemed off, and Maria took the time to observe the child's body closely. Hannah's characteristic smile, which usually came and went naturally, instead remained frozen on her face—even, Maria noticed, while the child was running down a steep path. The sight jolted Maria. She'd always assumed that smile meant the girl was happy.

When the frozen expression persisted for several days, Maria politely asked about it. Turning on her abruptly, Hannah said, "I'm just being happy. Leave me alone."

Maria knew better. Waiting until the campfire that evening, she told a simple story about how she used to be afraid in the woods as a little girl. She told of how the fear affected her body; how she used to get so scared she "couldn't even to the bathroom."

The next morning, the little girl spoke of her own fear. She said she was angry because she didn't know *why* she was afraid. Maria asked gentle questions. Knowing the child was still in Body-Being, she didn't probe for emotional feelings, but stayed with concrete memories and questions about the way the fear felt in the girl's body. Together, they simply followed the history of child's bodily sensations. It was not long before it became clear to both of them that the fear had started when her parents divorced. "You still wish they were together, don't you?" Maria asked. Then the girl was able to cry.

By observing the child's body, Maria entered into the child's reality. She knew that Body-Being's children most precise communication is the body's reactions to the sensation they are experiencing. A frozen smile means a frozen heart, no matter what words the child speaks.

The Dance

We don't "bring up" our children, we *dance* with them. In dancing with them, we become free ourselves and our children are freed from the burdensome belief that we "did it for the child." Each time we meet the child's developmental needs we allow ourselves the chance to expand our self-knowledge. Each family member fulfilling her natural role allows harmonious integration with self, species, and society.

The family Dance enriches and is a graceful, intimate experience in which everyone wins. We'll discover as many dance steps as there are children and situations. Each parent's work is to recognize and practice the dance steps appropriate to her family.

Unbridled Love

At birth the child's senses are vibrantly alive. Touch is fully functioning. Honoring these conditions means having a birth that is safe, warm, quiet, and soft. It includes as few drugs as possible and a calm presence by those attending. And it takes place in an atmosphere of loving touch, with a mother and family ready to hold the infant.

Those of us who have had the privilege of being present at a child's birth know that nearly always love cascades through the room. Birth unmistakably reminds us of our commitment to life, and of the miracle of humanity and everything around us. We stand humbled, ready to protect the child's right to a good and decent existence. This moment of transcendence, revelation, and commitment is ours because we fulfill the natural birthing needs of the child.

Love of the child is crucial for both individual survival and continuity of the species. The birth event is often surrounded by so much love that, even when natural conditions are less than perfect, most of us experience this tremendous emotion anyway.

I (Ba) was born in King's Highway Hospital in Brooklyn in 1947. My mother was drugged and my father was isolated in the waiting room; he didn't touch me until two full days after birth. He already had two healthy boys . And so, he has recounted, while he looked forward to meeting me, he hadn't accounted for the great love he would feel as a result of the birth. As soon as he held me, he ended up trembling with joy and renewed commitment to his wife. We'd started to dance.

The Value of Observation

Many of us have been taught that the sustained time commitment that children require—and thrive on—is a burden. In our culture, spending large amounts of time with children is not accorded a high value, even when someone is getting paid for it. Frightening as it may be to acknowledge, deep down the belief is that *being with our children is not in our own best interest.*

It is quite true that children in Body-Being do require consistent integration with the elders in their world. Herein the dance takes shape, affording us the rare opportunity to study the unfolding of ourselves, both as an individual and a species.

Can we begin to understand our own individual evolution by watching our children? Did we form our habits, postures, and values in the same way that our children form theirs? Do the growth stages of the child mirror the rhythm of evolution for our species? For all living organisms? Can we understand the nature of adaptability by observing the human child?

Engaging these questions increases our compassion for all life. We see where we are similar to other humans and where we are different. We get a sense of just how long time has been struggling to produce something as marvelous as a human being. As observation attunes us to body wisdom, we begin to see it everywhere. Respect for the child as wise and worthwhile grows, for she expresses this ancient wisdom right before our eyes.

The Importance of Attachment and Separation

At some time every parent feels the pain inherent in the attachment/separation paradox. We wish to hold and protect our child; yet at the same time we realize that experience, independent of parental filters, furthers the child's growth. Each life stage contains such lessons.

The mother's attachment to her child begins at conception and increases in strength throughout gestation; yet, inevitably, the moment of detachment arrives. Birth separation calls for tremendous output of energy by both mother and child.

The attachment/separation lessons become more dramatic as the child grows: Where is the parent to find the vigor to enforce the natural separations? We are faced with a quandary. The more wholeheartedly we surrender to our work as parents, the more likely the separations are to occur. The healthy child grows to autonomy within his developmental capabilities. We welcome that autonomy, and we also wish it away. It takes time and energy to properly provide the conditions for autonomy, and we know it's right for the child, yet she may be clinging, and often we're not so ready to give up our role either.

During Natural Learning Rhythms workshops, participants devise new dance steps for each life stage. A woman named Elizabeth, in a particularly lucid moment, mentioned breast-feeding and weaning as attachment and separation dance steps in Body-Being. For herself, she explained, breast-feeding is a sensual, intimate experience. Soft, tender, and joyful, it positions the mother and child in loving, nurturing embrace. Attachment deepens. As the child grows, it begins to need new foods. The weaning separation must come as the child learns to feed herself and eat solid foods. Weaning, like birthing, is not an ultimate separation, but a restructuring that better reflects the needs and capabilities of mother and child. By letting go, they grow closer, not further apart. When the attachment to breast-feeding is surrendered a more fulfilling relationship ensues, and mother and child each experience this seemingly contradictory truth.

35

Loving Touch

Body-Being's children need *loving touch,* and our society is forgetting how to touch at all. The majority of work sites, high-tech products, and urban environments substitute symbolic communication for direct tactile contact. Artificial, inanimate objects comprise the great majority of tactile experiences.

Lacking natural stimulation, our tactile skills and senses atrophy. We tend to put our children in cribs, strollers, car seat carriers, baby walkers, or on chemically treated rugs or linoleum floors. We also let them play with bad-tasting, rigid plastic toys and chemically treated synthetic fabrics.

Parents of Body-Being's children need to practice loving touch to over come socially induced tactile disability. By touching lovingly, grown-ups also reawaken Body-Being within the child. We begin to get "in *touch*" with warmth and intimacy.

Body wisdom's loving touch empowers us all: parent, child, family, and community.

*E*motional-Being

During the reign of Emotional-Being, the child comes to know the world through *feelings*. From approximately age eight through twelve, the child learns to decipher his own feelings and those of others. By doing so, he comes to recognize his own interrelatedness with all life. Honesty, justice, and fairness—the beginnings of compassion itself—are the essence of Emotional-Being's wisdom.

❦

A short time ago a friend named Bill came to our home to visit, and we went for a swim in a nearby river. Drying off on the shore, he mentioned that he and his wife were worried about their oldest son.

> "Jeremy has been getting out of bed every morning, taking a shower, brushing his teeth with half a tube of toothpaste, and combing his hair!" When we smiled at the boy's behavior, Bill became annoyed.

> "I'm not joking," he insisted, "this is serious. Two weeks ago we had to drag him to the shower. I don't think he has once brushed his hair without being asked in his entire life. His clothes were always dirty and full of holes; now, he has my wife ironing his jeans!"

We felt delighted with Jeremy's behavior because it signaled the beginning of this eight-year-old's transition into Emotional-Being. The boy's parents, however, were sincerely concerned. Bill went on to say that he and his wife were seriously considering therapy for Jeremy. The boy, ordinarily gregarious, was now very shy. He was also showing renewed interest in his baby brother and for the first time was asking for the opportunity to care for him. Whereas before he would hit other children when threatened, Jeremy now became withdrawn and moody, or abruptly angry.

After the additional information Bill gave us, the gravity of the situation became apparent, and we stopped smiling. The problem was not with Jeremy, who was simply manifesting the labor pains of Emotional-Being's birth, but with his parents. They were about to commit their child to the pressure of formal therapy simply because he was expressing his natural self.

Emotional-Being is truly a kind of new birth. It stops the child's world. Understandably, Jeremy overreacted to compensate for his feelings of vulnerability, hence the preening and exaggerated emphasis on hygiene.

Jeremy's story is special but not unusual. Many Emotional-Being births have caused us to smile and to keep smiling. In one instance, our nine-year-old neighbor decided to join us for an outing to the movies. Instead of his usual tattered jeans and stained T-shirt, he showed up in a formal dress shirt and tie. In another instance, an eight-year-old girl suddenly became furious when her mother suggested that she change from her swimsuit to dry clothes on the beach. The mother was perplexed, for the girl had been changing in public her entire life. In yet another seemingly overnight transformation, a very physical eight-year-old responded to his younger brother's teasing by sitting in a corner and sulking, a reaction so unusual that his mother called a physician. Another young boy suddenly became terribly interested in being on time, and infuriated his parents by insisting they rush from one place to another.

For children, the transition from Body-Being to Emotional-Being, from the known to the unknown, nearly always has some fear associated with it. Only focused, grown-up caring can ease this fear. In the United States, many children go through this transition in public school with at least twenty-five other children they barely know. There, interpersonal relationships often become confused. It is extremely difficult for teachers, already taxed by inadequate resources, to provide the requisite focused caring.

As Jeremy's story shows, little details often indicate big changes in the child. Every behavior is an invaluable clue to the child's present moment. When Jeremy combs his hair he says, "There are other people out there and I care what they feel about me."

Jeremy's father had attended workshops with us, so we were able to remind him of what he had learned about Emotional-Being. As a parent he was about to be "midwife" to his son's *becoming*. His modeling would be of paramount importance. Caring, concern, honesty, justice, fairness, adaptability, and adventure were the required nutrients. He and his wife should consider now how they were going to supply these foods for Jeremy. It would be an ongoing experiment, but consideration of these nutrients during transition would help them connect more deeply with Jeremy. Their family could then enter this new stage in the best of health.

The transition from Body-Being to Emotional-Being lasts about eighteen months. During the final stages of Body-Being, alerted that its ascension is soon to arrive, Emotional-Being heightens the child's receptivity to feelings. Though still constrained to basic feelings—mad, sad, bad, or glad—the child now feels these emotions more keenly and deeply.

Emotional-Being assesses the child's life, both his inner and outer worlds, and recognizes a challenge: an egoistic child who perceives himself the center of the universe. How can Emotional-Being open him to perceive himself in relation to others? What will stimulate this growth? What will open the child to inherent emotional wisdom?

The Hinge between Body- and Emotional-Being

Emotional-Being responds by making the child fully aware of death, the fact that he will one day die. With this awareness, the child's perception of himself as filling the universe is swiftly reduced to one of being a very small part of it, with a very definite end. The realization shatters his egoistic illusions; his body, he realizes, is not the center of the universe, but only the center of his own perception. There is a big universe out there, separate from his body, of unfathomable dimensions. Adrift and vulnerable, he turns to others, most frequently his family, to try to cope with the immensity of his new understanding.

Existence, wholeness, includes death and life and all living creatures. The child is here, on this planet, living with these people, for a limited time only. Awareness of death not only connects the child to wholeness, it connects her to her survival by connecting her to her community. From the depth of her being she yearns to connect, to feel caring and be cared for, to be present and to understand.

The discovery of mortality destroys the cloistered existence of Body-Being. It leaves the child *wide* open, reborn. Something new has been revealed, a truth she could not have imagined: Creation includes destruction. Anything new depends upon the transmutation of the old.

During Emotional-Being's birthing moment the child imprints the connection between creation and destruction. At the precise moment she believed most strongly in her body, she has just become aware of her own death. Once exposed to the destructive aspect of creativity, the relationship of death to life, it will take all of Emotional-Being's reign for the child to emotionally accept it.

Children both receive and react to the awareness of their personal death in very different ways. The critical variables are the child's inherent character (her predispositions), her education during Body-Being, and her everyday environment.

When the child feels his mortality without filters it brings his interpersonal relationships into sharp focus and leaves him open to the great lessons Emotional-Being has yet to teach. But Emotional-Being is oh-so-careful. If parents and community do not support an unfiltered appreciation of death, or the child's consciousness is not ready to deal with it, Emotional-Being masks the information. It might use dreams, hold back the intensity of the feeling, or delay the awareness. It might try to rally support by stimulating fears in the child, including nightmares, unwillingness to be alone, and dread of the dark. Through these messages the child's awareness of her death is meted out in doses that she can digest and her environment can support.

Death and the Onset of Deep Feeling

In her extremely important book, *On Children and Death,* Elisabeth Kübler-Ross describes the progressive development of the child's perception of death and dying.

Very young children have no fear of death, writes Kübler-Ross. By the age of three or four, however, their view changes, and ". . . in addition to the fear of separation comes a fear of mutilation. This is when they begin to see death in the environment." At four or five years, children begin to speak about death as if it were a "temporary happening."

Finally, by the age of eight or nine, ". . . children, like grown-ups, recognize the permanence."

In our work with families over the past twelve years, we have asked scores of children about death. Their answers confirm Kübler-Ross's observations.

Children in the Body-Being stage relate to death only through sensation. When exposed to death their concern is limited to separation anxiety, and fear of body mutilation. But listen carefully to the newly born Emotional-Being child. In some way, often shyly and hesitantly, she will reach out and ask about her own death. Nine-year-old Caroline, for example, insisted on querying several different religious leaders. In her letters to them she would briefly introduce herself and then, in capital letters, ask, "WHERE DO I GO WHEN I DIE?"

Noemi, another nine-year-old, had a dream of flying and woke up exhilarated. When her mother inquired about her unusually buoyant mood, Noemi answered, "I've been given my answer about death."

Ten-year-old Brent was a regular member of our Friday Class. One wintery morning he came to class clearly despondent and sulked for much of the day. At first we thought his sadness stemmed from his father's recent desertion of the family, but no matter how many times we broached the subject Brent always dismissed the event as unimportant. Gently throughout the day we kept the issue alive. Finally, by mid-afternoon Brent's frustrations spilled over and he began to talk.

"It's not him," Brent said through painful, angry tears, "it's me. Last night I wished him dead. I wished he was *dead!* Now what? Does that mean I've got to die now? Do I have to see him when I die? Why can't I go somewhere where he'll never be?"

Most of the class heard Brent's outburst. We decided to circle up. Each child shared her beliefs about death. Younger Body-Being children spoke mostly of heaven. Emotional-Being's children accepted heaven as a possibility but also wanted to know whether "good and bad count" when a person dies. A lively discussion ensued. The younger Body-Being children asked to be excused.

Feelings ran hot among those that remained. In a rudimentary fashion, these Emotional-Being children debated spirituality, philosophy, and authenticity of scripture. Each child spoke fervently; each was deeply offended if his remarks met ridicule. Brent, still upset, brought it all to an end when, in a quiet, trembling voice he said, "Just try wishing someone was dead from deep in your heart and then see how you feel."

Contrary to popular belief Brent's honest expression of his suffering brought the class closer together. The children felt connected as they heard their own heartfelt concerns mirrored by their peers.

Over the years we've studied how to bring up the subject of death with children. We've found them quite willing so speak about death once they realize we are acting as their friends. We do not judge their perceptions. We accept what they say, which usually leads to their questions about our perceptions of death. When we respond, we do so truthfully. To us, what happens after death is a mystery we do not fear. Lack of fear allows us to experience life as alive, creative, vibrant. Most of the children we've encountered accept this simple explanation, for it allows them to explore their own feelings more deeply.

Discussing death is healthy for children, when it is done mindfully and in accordance with the child's developmental needs. The child must have the chance to explore her own feelings about death and its relationship to life. Otherwise, Emotional-Being has no opportunity to expose its deep wisdom.

Stephen's Story

Many adults still remember this traumatic discovery of their personal mortality, though not all of them can say how it has affected their later lives.

Stephen, a father of three, teaches a nature class at an alternative elementary school. Introduced to Natural Learning Rhythms at a workshop, he's been practicing for about three years. He told us this story of his own discovery of death:

> When I was nine my parents decided to go on vacation and leave me at home with my twelve- and fifteen-year-old brothers. A woman from the neighborhood came to fix dinner each night. After we ate, she cleaned the dishes and left.
>
> That weekend, both brothers went out and left me at home by myself, contrary to my parent's wishes. Around ten o'clock that night I went to bed. I felt intensely lonely, even though our garden apartment was attached to houses on either side, and if I'd raised

my voice, I would have woken fifty neighbors. As I lay in the dark I felt very small and alone in a very large world. I was very uncomfortable and so I tried to sleep. I remember when I closed my eyes, a huge array of stars appeared. Everywhere, there were stars and more stars. They seemed to go on forever.

I got scared and opened my eyes. But the feeling of immensity was everywhere. Something was really disturbing me. I tried not to think about it, but the more I resisted the more frightened I became. Finally, a terrifying awareness burst open inside me and I started to sob: I was going to die someday. My life would one day end.

A year earlier, I had gone through the death of a close grandmother, but no other experience had caused emotions of the magnitude of what I was now feeling. I called my oldest brother at his girlfriend's house and asked him to please come home. He was preoccupied, however, and told me to go back to sleep and not to worry. Now I had nowhere to turn. Unable to cope with my feelings, I occupied myself by recalling all the facts I could about my favorite baseball team: the star pitchers and their earned-run averages, the best hitters and their batting scores. In this way I passed the hours and finally fell asleep.

For several months after that stressful weekend passed, the fact of my imminent death would come to mind as soon as I lay down in bed. I developed insomnia. My parents became alarmed, but I could not explain to them the terror I felt. Instead, I would think about baseball statistics as a way to pass the sleepless hours.

This fear persisted on and off for ten years. I learned how to recognize the initial stages and, using baseball imagery, to divert my mind from it. At eighteen, a near-death experience in an auto accident radically changed my understanding of death. I realized that a part of me would continue to exist after my body died. In a sudden realization, I saw that the fear that plagued my efforts at sleep was the fear of death. And that my emotional development had been frozen years earlier, when I was left alone at nine years old.

At this point, my burden of fear dissolved. I could literally feel my heart opening. Feelings long repressed, such as a longing for justice for all, came rushing into my awareness. I knew at once that this repression had occurred at nine when I was overwhelmed by

43

the fear of death. Now, my close brush with death freed me from the fear, and I gained new insights on my own life history. In my adolescence, I professed an intense concern for oppressed people; now I saw that my identification with these people had more to do with my anger at my own feelings of oppression than with genine concern for the well-being of others. I saw my rebellion against parents and the 'establishment' in this same light. Now my sense of the world changed. I felt connected to all life. I felt the suffering of the oppressed and the oppressor and cared for them equally. In nature I reveled. I felt both lovable and capable of love.

Many people are emotionally disabled by the brutal handling of death awareness at Emotional-Being's birth. While the current trend seems to be leaning toward more open acknowledgment of death in relation to terminal illness, our society's steadfast taboos still prevent discussing death when the family is healthy. When members of a family—even a happy, close one—are unable to openly examine how death may impact their lives, then, very likely, they may find it difficult to deal compassionately with a favorite aunt who has cancer, or not to be somewhat callous in the face of war crimes. They may also be unable to connect with their Emotional-Being child who has begun to ask critical questions about death and transcendence.

Community and Vulnerability

Emotional-Being is born. The child's consciousness: profound vulnerability, hunger for relationships, no experience with the feelings upon which these relationships are built. Aware of the mystery of death, knowing no solution. Open, seeking: "Who knows something about this mystery?"

Emotional-Being puts the child in direct *feeling* relationship to her family, her community, and her society. She feels the feelings of the significant people in her life. They become her models. Are they honest, just, caring, and adaptable? Are they hypocritical, dictatorial, vengeful, or rigid? She feels her own emotions and creates a *feeling-representation* of who they are. From it, she forms a personal concept of goodness, fairness, and justice.

Emotional-Being reads hypocrisy, cheating, severity, and authoritarianism as *unsafe*. The child's feeling-representations are shaken, and Emotional-Being's energy is spent on self-protection, constantly guarding her against the hurt she feels in the presence of such models. Then Emotional-Being can only bequeath survival wisdom, which guides the child to use feelings defensively to secure himself against an unsafe world. The child's perception of I-and-Other degrades into Me-against-Them. Human connections become riddled with strain, cunning, and cleverness as trust atrophies, cooperation degenerates into competition, cliques form, and the differences between the sexes turn into a war.

Emotional-Being is loath to turn the child away from her family and community, but in the face of extremely hypocritical models it will do even that. Negative models may also generate the compensatory feelings of fantasy, hero worship, and fanatical loyalty in the child. Such reponses somehow balance the dire suffering, yet, as we shall see, they create even greater problems down the line.

Healthy Food, Good Models, Deep Wisdom

Emotional-Being, like each of the life stages, depends on certain foods to stimulate the ancient wisdom at its command. Taking the path most conducive to survival, which almost always means maintaining connection with immediate family and community, Emotional-Being directs the child to the most nutritious foods available. To honesty. Justice. Adventure. Caring. Fairness. Adaptability. To the people who live in accordance to these attributes. To good or "right" models.

These healthy adult models do not need to be "perfect." If the child never sees an adult make a mistake and aknowledge it, how can the child *learn how to learn* from her own mistakes? Models who pretend to be perfectly just or fair strike the child as pretentious.

In the presence of right models and healthy foods blended to satisfy the needs of the individual child, Emotional-Being's gift, its deep emotional wisdom, springs forth. Ultimately, that child is able to feel *transcendence,* an extraordinary connection to the mystery that moves her beyond daily worries to a sense of wholeness, to a feeling that justice and fairness permeate the universe.

The child's impulse toward transcendence surfaces naturally in reaction to awareness of mortality. From around the age of nine-and-a-half to ten-and-a-half, Emotional-Being moves the child to investigate every context in which she feels spiritual inspiration. She scrutinizes her world for transcendent possibilities.

For many children, religion often seems to hold that potential. The presence of religious officials at marriages and funerals, the community support, the promise that herein lies information about life after death, the hymns and the myths, the grandeur of religious buildings, and the costumes and accoutrements all combine to create a powerful attractor for the child's natural need to feel transcendence. These aspects inspire the child. He opens to the teaching. If the teaching truly leads to just a few moments of transcendent feeling, the child will be rid of much of his fear of death. He'll connect to wholeness, to cycles, balance, and harmony. If the religious teaching does not bring the direct experience of transcendence, then the bitter feelings resulting from uncovered hypocrisy, disappointment, and shattered faith prevail.

Religion is but one means for the child to pursue transcendence. There are others as well, for Emotional-Being makes the feeling readily available to him. The simplest recipe involves only five modest ingredients:

- ♦ **the child**
- ♦ **the right foods**
- ♦ **the family/community**
- ♦ **nature**
- ♦ **an appropriate myth**

The myth, a tale that involves entering the unknown and facing death in order to fulfill one's purpose in life, plays a critical role in opening the child to her inherent emotional wisdom. Myths tell of the creation of the world and human society, of the need for faith and courage, and of the destruction of fear. Mystery evoking, mystery confirming, myths remind the child of the existence of life in death. Myths inspire. Myths can be brought to children as part of ritual rites of passage, storytelling, or in drama classes.

Honesty and Justice

Learning to trust the emotional wisdom of children takes patience and courage. Here's the story of one teacher who persevered and reaped the rewards.

John teaches at a Waldorf School, where teachers stay with the same classroom of children from the first through the eighth grade. For the last two years, John's rapport with his class had been deteriorating. When he approached us with his difficulty, his class was entering the fourth grade, and so most of the children were in the Emotional-Being stage of development.

John could clearly point out how he lost contact with his class: He could no longer transmit the material and had become impatient with any transgression of classroom protocol. He had turned into a disciplinarian. Some of the children cowered before his stance and performed the tasks he demanded, but they did so without creativity. Others openly rebelled.

A sensitive man who cares deeply for children, John cringed when he understood the nature of the classroom dynamic and his part in it. He'd heard that we advocate a way of being with children that supersedes the policeman's role, and he came for advice.

After a carefully listening to John about his attitude and practices in the classroom, we suggested some simple changes. First and foremost, we asked John to *invite the class* into the solution process. Whenever John noticed signs of classroom rapport deteriorating, he could offer the class his perceptions, and most importantly, his feelings, including those of inadequacy and helplessness when faced with this problem. He would then ask the children for solutions. In short, we asked John to be honest, and through honesty to appeal to the emotional wisdom of the children, instead of being rigidly defensive.

Honesty to Emotional-Being children means being truthful about your feelings that relate to the issue at hand. Of great importance, it also means expressing those feelings in a way that includes the children by honoring their developmental wisdom. It would be only partially honest for John to say, "I feel angry because you talked in class, so you have to stay after school." In this case John names his anger, but uses it as a punishment. He places blame on the children, which makes them feel guilty and resentful, and in doing so misses an opportunity to contact emotional wisdom.

An honest statement from John would sound something like this: "I feel angry. All this talking is going on and I feel the need for us to concentrate on math. You're talking and we're not getting our work done. What should we do? How can we work it out? What are your feelings about this?"

True to the nature of Emotional-Being, the children ate up John's honesty like pizza at a party. They were able to articulate their contributions to the problem. Fair, workable solutions poured forth. Of great surprise to John, the children did not take advantage of his honesty, but used it as an opportunity to create a class more in line with everyone's needs.

We've seen such transformations occur again and again. Every day we witness the daring justice of Emotional-Being's children: Two ten-year-old girls giving up the opportunity to ride a horse in favor of a friend who, they said, was "having a hard time at home and needed to be with the horse"; the children in our nature class willing to take time off from play to work out conflicts within the group; half a dozen eleven-year-olds working for hours on a mailing to end clear-cutting of a forest based on their own feelings of connection to the Earth.

The child's sense of justice is yet another window through which we can view her developmental sequence Emotional-Being's *affective* justice, because it reflects the feelings of the moment, improves on Body-Being's *retributive* justice. At the same time, Emotional-Being's sense of justice cannot take into account past history or the future, the more complete vision Reasoning-Being's *rational* justice will embody.

Clearly then, parents are not the principle source of moral law for the child. That honor belongs to the inherent wisdom in each of us as expressed through Emotional-Being. We serve that wisdom by meeting the child's need for justice.

Adventure and Adaptability

While the following case history links adventure and adaptability—two key nutrients of Emotional-Being—in everyday life, they often turn up separately. Adaptability may be modeled in various contexts: in the give and take of the family, in finding new solutions to academic problems, or in relaxing standards that impose upon the child. Adventure also appears in many forms: bike riding, attending a concert or sports event, or visiting different cultures, even in the same city. Both adventure and adaptability strengthen the child in Emotional-Being.

Marsha's daughter Cindy had continual feelings of non-specific anxiety. She clung excessively to her mother and had recurring worries about scary stories she'd heard long ago.

Marsha considered Cindy's Emotional-Being diet and decided her daughter needed more adventure. She planned a camp-out, during which they would awaken at one in the morning and climb a nearby mountain peak to watch the sunrise. Cindy agreed to the plan, but had some doubts as to her mother's ability to lead the expedition.

Several weeks later, on the way to the campsite, Marsha lost the trail. Cindy was upset, and they spent half an hour discussing her fears. Without losing patience, Marsha carefully showed Cindy how they could adapt to the difficulty. One way was to embark on new strategies for finding the trail. The second was to amend their original plan and approach the peak from another direction. There was no need to abandon the project because of a momentary setback. They soon found the trail, chose a place to camp, and went to sleep.

At one o'clock in the morning Marsha woke up her daughter. Though somewhat frightened by the darkness, Cindy was intrigued by the adventure, and they started off. Half an hour later, they lost the trail, and again Cindy became upset. Again, Marsha outlined adaptation strategies.

Only the success of the previous afternoon gave Cindy the courage to continue in the dark of the night. At the crack of dawn they reached the mountain top and witnessed a glorious sunrise. Five hours later, Cindy, reveling, was still reluctant to come down.

Your Model Is Your Teaching

Making an "emotion-" or "feeling-model" of significant elders in the child's life is part of the natural learning rhythm of Emotional-Being. This does not mean that the parent is supposed to be a perfect model. Simply understanding the needs of the child and being sensitive to the family creates a healthy model. Since right modeling is crucial to Emotional-Being development, we'd like to offer some insights into some models that work, as well as some that don't. For many caring grown-ups, trying to live up to a modeling ideal is a strong temptation. In real life, however, these overly strident attempts often lead to discomfort and confusion. Consider this case history:

Joseph and Jeri love their two children very much. They attended a Natural Learning Rhythms workshop where the concept of modeling struck them as especially important. When they returned home, Joseph and Jeri decided to become the "perfect" models. From that time on, nearly every activity with their children was evaluated before they engaged in it.

Over the previous two years, they had been debating the merits of natural foods versus standard supermarket fare; sometimes these debates turned into mild arguments. The arguments were eliminated, as were their ongoing discussions about the morality of paying taxes for nuclear weapons. Joseph also stopped complaining about his phone company job. Jeri stopped being physically demonstrative toward Joseph because she feared its effect on their eleven-year-old daughter.

This extreme discipline did not however produce a paradise. Indeed, the quality of their family relationships deteriorated daily. Within three months, everyone was fighting and no one knew why.

The truth was that up until that time, Joseph and Jeri had been satisfactory models. When they became aware of the importance of healthy models, however, they had become self-conscious. This heightened self-consciousness resulted in family friction. Inevitably, something had to give.

At tea one afternoon, another couple with whom they'd taken the workshop gently pointed out the unnatural and unnecessary striving in their attempts at correct modeling. This valuable insight helped to dissolve the tension. Joseph and Jeri returned to their natural style of parenting. They *knew* that they were okay as long as they supplied the basic foods. Now they also had the comprehension to back up their actions.

These days, the family laughs about those three months of "perfection." They also wonder if the lack of trust among the people of the world is due, in part, to insecure parents overcompensating by subjecting their children to "morally perfect" models.

Parental modeling based on cooperation and consistency not only supports Emotional-Being's development, it also strengthens the family as a whole.

Peter, Barbara, and their family are leaders in a struggle to end river pollution. Their two daughters, seventeen and fourteen, and an eleven-year-old son, are home schooled. Whenever possible all five work together on their river conservation project. With tasks that do not need all five people, they are careful to rotate partners.

Sometime back, activist colleagues recommended that each family member specialize in a different aspect of the anti-pollution campaign, to increase the efficiency of the whole. When the family tried this new strategy, however, they found that competition developed for the tasks that were the most attractive or that best matched their personal whims, slowing down the job and mucking up the works.

For Barbara, Peter, and their children, unity through cooperation continues to be the top priority. This approach keeps all family members happy and harmonious and this in turn attracts others to their cause. The children are centered and skilled, and they interact competently with people of all ages and types. The consistent modeling of cooperation has allowed a sharing of family values beyond Peter and Barbara's highest expectations.

It would be pleasant if children were able to absorb the lessons of right modeling and screen out less positive influences. Unfortunately, both positive and negative models affect children in the same way: One's model is one's teaching, even if that modeling is hypocritical. In the case of Sean, we have witnessed its results.

Sean's parents divorced when he was four years old. Because the father rejected his son along with the boy's mother, Mary, from that time on Sean lived exclusively with her. Three years later Mary met a new man, Gene, and eventually they married.

Around the time of the wedding, Sean was exhibiting random outbursts of extreme violence and frequently expressed cynicism toward his mother and other females. Intellectually precocious, he often used his high grades as a way of showing off. No one could get close to him.

Gene entered the family circle aware of Sean's problems. He liked Sean and was committed to Mary. In a short time, Sean responded to Gene's concern and to the stable family environment. He and Gene became good friends and enjoyed many activities together; they even talked about Sean's feelings for his genetic father.

Thus, Sean's models were mostly intact as he came into Emotional-Being. During the next two years his spells of violence disappeared. He began to help other children in school. His relationship with his mother and other women mellowed.

As time went on, Mary became pregnant. Sean was excited and looked forward to playing with the new baby. His "dad," as he proudly called Gene, really wanted the baby. Sean was happy for him and for his mother. But as the birth approached, Sean felt subtle changes in Gene. All of Gene's attention seemed to focus on the coming baby. Though Sean's rising despair was obvious to nearly everyone, Gene never saw it. Gene pretended that his feelings toward Sean were unchanged. Sean knew better. His mother tried to reassure him. Sean didn't believe her and resented her for "bullshitting" him. When the baby was born, Gene, like many other parents in his situation, felt a stronger attachment to his new child than to the one who was not his genetic offspring.

Sean's world fell apart and his violent behavior returned. Cutting sarcasm was unmercifully hurled at his mother. He hated his new sister and openly said so. The family, already under stress from the baby's birth, was in constant upheaval. And Gene, unwilling to admit the changes in his own feelings, now attacked Sean. Months of bitter exchanges between Mary, Sean, and Gene followed.

At the beginning of the new marriage, Sean had been able to risk attachment to a new dad because of the vulnerabilities that accompany the early years of Emotional-Being's dominance. In accepting Gene as a "dad," Sean was able to overcome much of the negative experience with his genetic father. Had Gene not cared for Sean, or had he joined the family outside the window of Emotional-Being's emergence, it is unlikely that this bonding would have occurred.

To Sean, Gene's model was pure hypocrisy. The boy's old desertion wound, of which Gene was aware, was ripped open. All Sean's new healthy feelings about dad, mother, family, and society were instantly poisoned. Tragically, two years later, Sean came to the conclusion that he was merely a convenient person for Gene to "suck dry to satisfy his own sentimental needs."

This part of the story ends with no winner. Two years later Gene and Mary divorced. After a custody battle for the baby, Gene ended up with minimal visitation. Sean, his mother, and his sister started a new home alone. We'll return to Sean's history in our discussion of Will-Being.

Hesitancy in Emotional-Being

During the two-year span from about eight-and-a-half to ten-and-a-half, the child's consciousness expands by leaps and bounds. It will encompass her own death, her emotional connection to self, family, and community, and the possibility of transcendence.

Such prodigious expansion cannot go on forever; the receptive phase is now over. The time has now come to contract, to *hesitate,* to stop and organize all this new information. Before the child turns to the trial and error phase when she will experiment with the different feeling-patterns she has absorbed, a breath must be taken, support and security checked out, residual fears expressed—and hopefully worked through.

During this hesitancy the child is often extremely sensitive to criticism. Uncertainty, especially about feeling accepted, becomes unbearable and he may very likely react with bossiness or timidity. Other reactive behaviors include withdrawal, turning inward, and enduring loneliness, depression, or physical sickness.

During the hesitancy Emotional-Being's child wonders: How friendly is it out there? Where is it safest? What energy must be put toward my protection? Where was direct experience of inspiration? Who uses words that refer directly to feelings?

This evaluation usually lasts two to six weeks. When it's over, the hesitancy ends and the trial and error phase begins.

Drama and Reading During Trial-and-Error

53

The child will spend the next two years engaging those people and activities that best address Emotional-Being's concerns. Through play, she refines her *feeling-representations,* or emotional impressions of others, until they are in accord with her feelings about herself and her world.

Two new skills greatly enhance the child's ability to play: proficient reading comprehension and drama. Through drama he gets to safely explore the wide range of feelings that don't enter his life on a day to day basis. Each experiment adds to his repertoire of feelings, thus enabling him to extend his connection to family and community. Combining drama and myth allows the child to act out scenarios of death and transcendence.

Emotional-Being's wisdom infuses the child's reading comprehension with a capacity to feel the meaning in the literature. Innuendoes become apparent, and her understanding of character and plot expand dramatically. Adventure, mystery, science fiction, and inspirational biographies thrill the child. Through reading, she vicariously travels to new worlds, trying on the characters to determine their meaning to her. She's usually definite in her likes and dislikes, thereby telling her parents what type of child she is and which avenues of inspiration she's most comfortable with. For some children, music and the visual arts play a similar role to reading.

Mixing quiet interior explorations, such as reading, with public displays, such as acting or socializing, yields countless combinations of feeling experiences. The Emotional-Being consciousness records every one that the child attempts. Those experiences that allow him with the most complete relationship to wholeness, those embodying justice, honesty, and fairness, will be the ones chosen by the child for the competency phase. This last phase will also bring the child to an honest appreciation of mortality and transcendence. Now patiently able to resolve difficulties, to listen to the feelings of all involved, to delay gratification somewhat, the child practices again and again those sets of emotional behaviors that make him feel good about himself, his community, and his world.

Emotional-Being in Nature

What a marvelous interaction there is between nature and children in Emotional-Being. Stunned by the beauty and majesty of nature, these children feel enthrallment and wonder. Life and death, symbiotic relationship, and the merit of awe and glory resound throughout nature. Emotional-Being hears and responds.

For the past nine years we've been homesteading ten acres of land in the Sierra foothills. One day last summer, while several children were visiting us, I (Josette) came upon a king snake eating a gopher snake in our garden. Excited, I called to the children. Incredibly, the main battle was being fought underground. Only the bottom halves of the snakes were outside the hole. Sometimes these halves would lash about violently, other times they were quiescent. The Emotional-Being children watched transfixed for about an hour, then continually checked back to note the progress of the battle, which ended four hours later.

Friday Class has been an excellent laboratory for observing Emotional-Being children in nature. During our hikes we notice time and again that the children's main focus has been the relationships *between* various aspects of the natural world rather than its individual entities.

From time to time we ask a discreet question or two to verify our observations. A child sees a redtail hawk. When we inquire, he tells us he is considering the hawk's relationship with its family and its prey. Later we find coyote scat on a rock, and the children want to know how the other forest animals react when they come across it. We sit on a decomposing log observing the many life forms feeding off the decay, and the children immediately turn the conversation toward cooperation among diverse life forms.

One eventful day stands out in our memory because of the classic example of the interaction between Emotional-Being children and nature. That weekend, we had decided to have a camp-out in the state park with our Friday Class. All the attending children were in the Emotional-Being stage. It was May, and a late spring rain left the air clean and cool with soft cirrus clouds in the evening sky.

After setting up camp, the group began to explore. Suddenly, a girl shrieked with delight. Everyone rushed over. She'd discovered a tree carpeted with thousands of cocoons in varying stages of development. We watched one of the wooly cocoons tremble, and from within, before our eyes, a butterfly emerged. Magnetized, every child stood by the tree for the two hours until sunset watching the cocoons.

The rain and the long dusk made for a particularly spectacular sunset that evening. We ate a light meal around the campfire. Dusk turned to darkness and the moon had not yet appeared. Ba asked the children to lie on their backs and stare into the starry night. Quietness enveloped us. The sky expanded without end. Occasionally a child would sigh as a deeper state of relaxed peace came over her. Inspiration. Gratitude.

After about an hour Josette sat up, prepared to put out the fire. The group had had a long, exciting, and strenuous day and we were certain the children would pass into an easy, gentle sleep. We were wrong. Something had happened. Six of the eight children sat up with her. Captivated by the fire, they began to talk.

Great wisdom was expressed by the children that night. With clarity and undogmatic insight, they spoke of the necessity of change. Using wolves as an analogy, they considered ways in which a community both supports and inhibits change. One child remarked on the way wolves cooperate with one another during the hunt, and how the females unselfishly protect their pups. Another child countered, reminding the group that the pack's hierarchy is so rigid that any deviance can be met with an attack by the leader. Next, beginning with the observation that "rabbits are cute," they went on to explore the relationship between rabbit and fox. They felt a deep understanding of the role of both, spontaneously realizing that the interplay of predator and prey allowed balance and harmony in the whole of nature.

The conversation turned to the immensity of the sky. One child wanted to visit other planets. He wondered if it were possible to do so after death when he "wouldn't have a body anymore". A discussion about death followed and lasted well into the night.

Curious at first as to what happens after death, attention soon moved on to fears about death. Then a child remembered the cocoon tree, and a lively debate ensued: Do we simply transmute when we die, like the cocoon into the butterfly, or do we end like the butterfly itself, metamorphosing no more?

During such activities as our camp-out, we as teachers are able to observe and feel, learning much about the children and their relationships with family and community. This process occurs effortlessly and has been replicated by many parents and teachers familiar with Natural Learning Rhythms. Sometimes we can empower the children to connect in more wholesome ways, especially if their issues only concern one another. More often we turn to the parents, diplomatically share our observations about their child, and hope they can provide the proper diet.

❦

A last important observation on Emotional-Being children in nature: Even in the face of the breathtaking phenomena of the natural world, Emotional-Being children, when they feel safe, repeatedly choose to explore one another as their favorite activity. This is really not so puzzling, if we remember that, in their natural world, the I-and-Other relationship is fundamental.

To Honestly Dance

Emotional-Being's children bring the fierce beauty of fairness and justice into our lives. They require us to be honest, to be fair, and to be caring. Their struggle to understand their own mortality brings up the most fundamental questions of life and death, of religion and spirituality, of survival and the meaning of human evolution.

The special wisdom expressed by Emotional-Being children make clear the consequences of our acts. In very real terms, we can either meet the entreaties of emotional wisdom, or opt for extinction. We can model justice, or risk that the child will not feel the value of the social group in our survival as a species. We can provide the child with a forum expansive enough for her ocean of feelings, or impair her appreciation of her interconnectedness with life. We can create opportunities for inspiration, or inadvertently teach that the body is supreme, so that the child loses all feeling for the future, all veneration for the struggle of her ancestors.

The Value of Right Modeling

As parents, acceptance of our role as models causes us to face who we really are. Do we have unresolved tensions from the death of a loved one? How do these tensions manifest in relationships with our children? Honoring the child's first deep concerns about death and spirituality requires us to investigate our own personal attitudes about death and spirituality.

Authentic modeling is a result of the parent's genuine inquiry into his own heart of hearts, and from courageous engagement of whatever answers he finds within himself. His modeling teaches the child how to relate to these two most important aspects of being a human.

57

Children in the Emotional-Being stage engage in more complex social interactions than very young children do. Parents are faced with a new sophistication in their children and their children's friends. How will they respond? Will the parents favor their own child over another? Will they be honest about their reactions and interactions? What will they model?

As parents, I (Ba) and Josette sometimes face predicaments in which our daughter Amber's feelings have been hurt during episodes with friends where feelings are concerned; she feels wronged and wants us to intervene on her side. It is very tempting to give in to our darling, loving daughter. Working together as a couple, we must remind ourselves to maintain fairness and find the best solution for everyone involved.

At first Amber found our stance confusing; she felt that we, her parents, should unconditionally represent her. After several more experiences we all recognized the great benefits of impartiality. Now that Amber feels certain that a just solution will be sought, she feels empowered and unhindered by self-consciousness and manipulation. She's not trying to prove her point and win our approval, but rather is trying to bring resolution. By not favoring our own child over another, we've learned a tough but enlightening lesson in attachment and separation. When we let go of our protective tendencies, we entered a much more responsive relationship with her. Personal integrity and commitment to fairness, equality, and justice evoke *family wisdom.*

Emotional-Being and World Peace

An important part of who we are as human beings is our social identity. Our best defense has been our social structures; without society there would be no *Homo Sapiens.* Therefore, as we dance with the Emotional-Being child, we gain knowledge about our species as well as individual self-knowledge.

Given the important role of culture in our species' evolution, healthy social adaptability is a crucial ability. Emotional-Being children insist that we keep current, and adapting ourselves in every context is the most important evolutionary lesson for any species. Emotional-Being thrives on adaptation, and parents provide the food. Parents learn the meaning of adaptation, where to find adaptation and how to make it palatable to their children.

To say that the healthy development of justice and honesty in Emotional-Being's children is the foundation for world peace is no simplistic exaggeration. For children of this age, each interaction between people, no matter how seemingly trivial, is significant. The sum total of these interpersonal relations, when projected onto the grown-up behaviors of the citizens of a nation-state, provides the underlying tone of world politics.

Little hurts poorly handled turn into big resentments. When children find no expression for hurt feelings, emotional wounds become raw and infected. With repeated emotional trauma, children are disempowered. They lose trust in themselves and others, and create buffers against the pain. These buffers may take the form of false pride, bullying, exhibitionism, or obsessive identification with a team, a gang, or an institution.

The act of helping children resolve resentments and disputes teaches adults how to do the same with each other. Paying attention to the small details in our child's life reminds us that all events are simply a collection of small details. We learn to be present, to be mindful.

Ecological sanity, achieving a harmonious balance between ourselves and the environment we live in, is an essential ingredient for world peace. During Emotional-Being the child becomes conscious of the interconnectedness of all living things, and she develops her deepest feeling-based knowlege about ecology.

Ultimately, such feelings determine our grown-up relationships with other people and with nature. By honoring them, our own inner sense of ecological sanity can begin to guide our choices. It is through Emotional-Being's wisdom that we learn to relate to each other and to every other aspect of our environment in a balanced way.

*W*ill-Being

If the journey through childhood were a river flowing to the sea, Will-Being would be the whitewater rapids.

With the onset of Will-Being, the urge to individuate and pursue freedom races through the child's consciousness. As she burns off the dross of childhood, she will need to explore herself as a discrete entity, identified solely with her own needs. She will mature physically, and become able to procreate and to establish herself as a responsible individual. She will clearly say, "I stand alone."

At the same time, though, she has never actually stood on her own before. The upshot: an undertow of insecurity. That friction—the urge toward freedom against the undertow of insecurity—provides the compelling energy fusing in the core of Will-Being's wisdom. That energy is the raw energy of life. No creature can exist without will.

Earliest Signs

In the height of Emotional-Being competency, puberty changes begin and the child starts to realize that he is responsible for his actions. People feel his emotional maturity and are drawn to share more intimately with him.

What a difficult moment! The child *must* develop her individuality or she will flit from one emotional drama to the next, never fully developing her natural talents, nor finding the personal boundaries so important for her own welfare. It's no easy job: Will wisdom has very little to do with the sense of community, justice, and fairness so endearing in the Emotional-Being child—and parents mourn its disappearance.

As a result, Will-Being's arrival, unlike most births, often occurs within an atmosphere of fear and mistrust. Few recognize why Will-Being's fierce energy is needed, or how key its role is in the child's evolution, as well as the evolution of the species. They do not see that Will-Being provides the strength for the solidification of the child's uniqueness. Frequently, parents and teachers dread the challenge implicit in the child's individuation. Will-Being generally emerges suddenly and willfully, and parents feel they are losing much of the control they had over the child.

Instead of attempting to muffle this vital expression, Will-Being's arrival should be honored powerfully and dramatically. A formal prescribed observance—ritual rites of passage—work best. A ritual signals safety; it gives permission for Will-Being to unveil its own wisdom. Old "kid-like" attitudes can be understood and set to rest; the child's new individuality can be recognized, appreciated, and accepted. In the presence of elders who have wrestled Will-Being's rapids and emerged whole and joyful along with him, the child feels his own courage. For everyone it can be a tender moment, full of honor and respect. In chapter seven, we detail such coming-of-age rituals.

Birth of Will-Being

As the child's body grows bigger, his mind can absorb more information. Society lays claim to this new power through higher expectations. Will-Being's spirit urges the child: "They want you to do more. You can choose what to do. Assert yourself. Is this challenging? Does it help you gain your individuation, your freedom?"

The secondary sexual characteristics appear: pubic hair, breasts, and testicles develop. Will-Being prompts: "You will become an adult. You'll probably have a child some day. What kind of world will it be? What are your ideals?"

The insecurity of never having stood alone before surfaces. Will-Being implores: "Find your peers. Define yourself in relationship to them—they share in your present struggle. Experiment with various identities. Find the people who won't ridicule you or make you feel insecure."

Insecurity, heightened sex drive, increased personal power, knowledge of an uncertain future, and intense social needs confuse the child. Will-Being counsels: "Find your own personal space. Learn to defend it.

Insist on doing some things alone. Express yourself as different, unique—even at the expense of consistency."

Though we've described Will-Being's stimulus in words, the child is more likely to experience urges, "callings," dramatic feelings, pressures, stresses, and forces. At times he'll feel compelled, at other times believe he is in control of himself and the situation. In every case he'll be moving toward a greater sense of individuation and freedom.

Will-Being: A Natural History

Jessica and Margot, two lively twelve-year-olds who regularly attended our Nature class, were showing all the signs of their entrance into Will-Being: a defense of individuality, a shedding of "kid" behaviors, discomfort with other children in Emotional-Being, careful assessment of potential allies, reluctant but inevitable challenges to authority, reluctant but inevitable confession of ideals, the desire for separation, and intolerance of imperfection.

The change in Margot and Jessica became most apparent one Friday in class while we were practicing "Indian listening" at the river. The activity required silent concentration as we cupped our hands around our ears to hear variations of wind and bird calls. Just as the class became quiet and attentive, Christy, a nine-year-old known for her habitual complaining, loudly declared that she was bored, and that the activity was "dumb and a waste of time."

Over time, the class had evolved several strategies for balancing Christy's complaints, and most of the children were not unduly upset. Sometimes Jessica or Margot would take on the responsibility of helping her. This time, however, something else happened. Margot proclaimed that Christy was "her own person who should not be denied."

Everyone was stunned by Margot's choice of words, including Margot herself. The sense of change in atmosphere was palpable. Margot seemed embarrassed at the attention the whole class focused upon her. But Jessica stood at the edge of the water, and as Josette immediately noticed, a "look of recognition" entered Jessica's eyes.

The following week, for the first time, Jessica refused to participate in "Hugger Tag," formerly one of her favorite games. She told us, "I just don't want to and don't try to talk me into it because I'm not going to play." The rest of the class began to play, but soon Margot too dropped out. She sat on the other side of the field from Jessica and did not talk with her. When Josette approached Margot to ask why she wasn't playing, Margot spontaneously threw both arms straight out with palms facing Josette. It was the clearest "Stop!" signal we've ever seen. Josette turned back to the game without a word. For the rest of the day Margot and Jessica had nothing to do with one another, and they resumed their interactions with the group.

Other subtle shifts occurred in the next few weeks. Jessica and Margot preferred to play with either the six- to eight-year-old children, or the elevens and twelves. If partnered with an undesirable nine- or ten-year-old, they would politely rearrange partners. When met with resistance, they would be curt and challenging. In addition, if they did not like an activity they simply would not participate. Still, when we asked, their parents told us that the two girls were not spending any more time together than usual.

Then, about two months into this three-month sequence, they began to vocalize their opinions about everything that happened in class. Sometimes they would reinforce each other's position; more often they would speak for themselves: "That game's only for little kids," or "I should be allowed to choose my own partner," or "Christy's a brat," or "There should be more older kids in class." Most opinions were complaints voiced while engaging in an activity which made dialogue impossible.

The following week Ba suggested the class hike to a mountain lake. On the way Jessica said, "Hiking is boring. You can't even really talk to anyone while you do it." Ba heard her, stopped the class, and called for a circle.

Jessica refused to join. Ba asked her to repeat her remark. She refused. Josette asked if she liked Friday Class. "Not as much as I used to," Jessica answered, "but it's OK."

"Why won't you circle up so we can talk about it?"

It was not Jessica who answered but Margot. *"Circling's dumb sometimes."*

"What's dumb about it?" Josette asked. At this moment we were on a steep slope. All the children had gathered around, with considerable difficulty, to hear the conversation. Yet we could not pass up this opportunity for engagement.

Margot replied heatedly. "I mean it's good for kids to share and to make circles, but this endless listening to kids who I don't like is a drag. I mean I care about them but I don't really care about what they have to say about my life. I mean it's my life, you know what I mean? I'll decide what to listen to, even if it's in a circle."

Jessica said nothing, but this time the girls locked eyes and giggled. Then they went off arm in arm. Once again we talked to their families who said the girls still were not spending a great deal of time together.

Class met again on a breathlessly hot summer day. We decided to go on a short hike to a lake. One of the ten-year-old boys, who was having a rough day, argued, pushed, shouted, ran ahead, lagged behind, and disrupted two games. Finally, the class circled up to address the problem. Jessica and Margot joined the circle. They told the boy in terse, almost cutting terms, to get his "act together." They placed responsibility squarely on his shoulders and were unwilling to listen to any mitigating circumstances that might, in part, account for his behavior.

Eventually, the class proceeded to the lake. In the water, the boy continued to be a nuisance. Jessica and Margot began to defend whomever the boy bothered. The boy yelled at them. With resigned exasperation, Jessica and Margot insulted the boy, called the other children to them, and instructed them to exclude the boy.

I (Josette) pulled Jessica and Margot aside. I was a little angry and spoke forcefully.

"What's going on? This doesn't feel right."

Jessica and Margot responded to my anger with defiance. "He's acting like a jerk," Jessica said, "and it's not good for anyone if you baby him along. And it's no fun either."

"You're just letting him get away with his stuff and everybody suffers," Margot added. "Nobody likes him."

"We have ways of working it out," I answered. "Ways that were all right just a couple of weeks ago."

"So what? This class isn't fun anymore. We're really not interested in working things out and listening to everyone's boring ideas. We want more excitement. More challenges." While Margot was saying this, Jessica was nodding her head excitedly.

"But what about the hikes and games? Aren't they challenging?"

65

"They were," Jessica burst in. "But not with these kids anymore. We want older kids. I mean the younger ones are OK because they are cute."

"How about the kids your own age?"

"Some OK, some not OK. Mostly not OK. Worst are the others, though."

"Have the kids changed? Have the games changed? What has really changed?" My anger was gone. My questions were supportive and respectful.

Jessica answered, "We have, I guess." A hint of fear came into her voice. "But why? And what does it mean?"

"What do you think it means?"

"All I know," Margot said, "is that I don't want anyone to tell me what to do. I want to make up my own mind."

I continued to gently inquire. "Not even me? Not even your parents? Your older brothers? Each other?"

"I'll listen," she said, "but I'll make up my own mind. And not with these dorky kids, either."

"Are you saying you don't want to come to class anymore?"

Jessica and Margot looked at each other. They liked me and Ba and they enjoyed Friday class. Several significant seconds of silence followed.

Jessica proceeded cautiously. "It's not that we don't like you or don't think Friday class is a great way to be with friends, it's just that. . ." Jessica faltered but Margot finished strongly.

"It's just that we need something more," stated Margot. "And we don't want to be held back."

"I agree," I said. The girls smiled with relief. "And I can give you some clues as to what is going on. I can explain some things about the way all children grow and learn. I think if you listen closely and understand, it will really help. It's going to take a few minutes, so before I start I need to know that you are willing to listen with good attention and without interrupting. I don't want to lecture, so don't take it that way. It's just that to understand the whole you've got to give me some time to explain the parts. OK?"

I was not surprised when Margot and Jessica enthusiastically agreed to listen. When children experience change they like to know why. They like it when they feel you are talking about them and their experience.

"All forms of life grow in definite stages. Do you remember the cocoon tree? The cocoon is one stage of the four stages of life for the insect family Lepidoptera. The other stages are the larvae, caterpillar, and butterfly. In each stage the insect eats completely different foods. The caterpillar eats leaves, the butterfly eats flower nectar. Humans also go through life stages. And each stage has different needs and different forms of expression. Are you following me? Have I lost you?"

"Not me," Margot said.

"Me either," from Jessica.

"OK, so what I see happening is that you are switching from one stage to the next."

"But where were we, and what are we getting into?" Margot asked.

"First, I want you to know that almost every society has recognized the existence of human life stages. The stage you are entering is one of the most well known. I call it "Will-Being." A child in Will-Being needs to be an individual, to express herself as she sees herself, without anyone defining who she is but her. Along with that comes the need for personal space so that she has a territory to work out her self-expression.

"There's a reason for your change in attitude. Have you noticed that you have very little patience for the kids in class who are just a couple of years younger than you?"

"Yeah," Jessica said. "They're really getting to be kind of a pain in the neck."

"That's because they are acting in ways that most remind you of parts of yourself that you want to leave behind," I explained. "Your move to be an individual means you've got to burn off those childish behaviors that no longer work for you. You're growing up and there's a time in which old stuff is dropped. You are in that transition."

"OK, I get it. But that doesn't change the way I feel about those kids or some of the other stuff in class," Margot charged. "What you're saying doesn't make me want to do anything different than I've done it."

"I'm not trying to convince you to act . . ." I started. But Jessica interrupted me.

"She's not telling us we're good or bad," she said. "She's telling us what's happening so we don't have to feel bad about our changes."

"And," I said with great relief, "I'm sort of hoping that now that you have some idea of the process so you'll be more comfortable and kind in the way you play it out."

"I see other parts of my life that make more sense now, Josette," Jessica said. "Some of the stuff with my parents and the different ways I'm looking at all my friends. But I don't understand why I care so much about what people my own age think about me if I'm supposed to be into my individuality."

"Have you ever felt such intensity about being an individual, yourself, before?" I asked.

"No, not like this," Jessica responded.

"Neither have your peers. You're in this together, trying it on for the first time. Do you ever get scared when you feel the strength of your changes?"

Jessica thought for a few moments before answering. "Yes, but I don't let myself think about that too often. If it comes up, I try to push it away."

"OK, fair enough. The same thing's happening to most of your friends, though each of you does it in your own way. So you're drawn to each other for support. And you know you're in it together through clothing, slang expressions, and taste in music. As a grown-up friend who cares about you, I want you to know that all that is healthy. I support you in those changes."

"But I don't see us staying in this class anymore, do you?" Margot asked.

"No, I guess not. I just want to thank you for sticking it out with me, both in class and in this conversation."

Jessica and Margot grasped the psychology with ease. There were no hard feelings, not even with the boy who had been a nuisance. From that moment on Jessica and Margot became closer and closer. For the last year they have been virtually inseparable.

Sensitive Respect

How Will-Being thrives on sensitive respect! When the child's assertions are honored as explorations of individuality, when the same latitude is shown to her experimentation with identities as to the infant when she learned to walk, when the community supports freedom, will wisdom shines, revealing the value and meaning of each identity. With a minimum of self-consciousness and an absence of guilt the child accepts the process of her own becoming. She learns to discriminate which identities allow her deepest access to wisdom. She begins to shape her individuality. Full freedom exploration energy pours forth.

Here's how we practiced sensitive respect with Margot and Jessica. Many grown-ups would have tried to modify Margot and Jessica's behavior according to their own values. A belief in "class unity" might have been enjoined to inhibit Margot's defense of Christy, or to force the girls to circle up. "No put-downs," a concept now in vogue, might have been used to control the girl's insults of the troublesome boy. Both reactions would have evoked popular approval; neither would have allowed the girl's consciousness to access inner wisdom and in due time find the most healthy behavior.

To act with sensitive respect is to interact with the child free from ridicule or derision. It means to honor the individuation process by respecting the ever-changing personalities even though they are short-lived. Humiliation of any sort, but especially in public, destroys sensitive respect. Violation of personal space is equally destructive. Rather than confront Margot's defense of Christy and add to her embarrassment, Ba suggested the safe space of the group circle. I (Josette) accepted Margot's refusal to join Hugger Tag without question or refute. We inquired into their personal lives without the focus of undue attention. When the girls started to complain we did not label them as "complainers," but instead examined the meaning of those complaints. We didn't take any of their behaviors personally. We proceeded slowly, waiting for them to declare their intentions. As their understanding grew, we offered a deeper perspective, including access to their own psychology. Finally, we supported Jessica and Margot's decision to leave the class.

Balanced Diet, Deep Wisdom

In addition to sensitive respect, Will-Being's favored diet also includes contact with peers, private space, challenges in the realm of success, lots of action, and the opportunity to express and act upon *ideals*. A Will-Being banquet provides an active challenge that involves ideals and peers.

Offering the child a balanced diet of these nutrients grants conscious access to deep will wisdom. Family trust grows. The child's assertion serves the aim of individuation, not rebellion. His insecurity reminds him to get on with the work of finding healthy identities, instead of being cheapened into a receptacle for guilt and blame. Free exploration evolves as a family activity.

More deep wisdom. Connection to peers allows Will-Being children of varying backgrounds to appreciate one another. They learn to tolerate the people of their own generation, the ones with whom they'll share the planet for the rest of their lives. Appreciating ideals keeps the Utopian vision alive. This quest for a perfect society fuels cultural evolution.

A Reaction to Rubbish

The delicate balance between assertiveness and insecurity makes Will-Being's reign quite fragile. Harmful foods have immediate and dire consequences, and Will-Being reacts quickly and decisively when they are ingested.

When exposed to ridicule Will-Being recoils. The child's experience: poisoned. Not safe. Individuals not welcome. Pull back.

When exposed to threat of failure Will-Being contracts. The child's experience: contaminated. On guard. Insecurity is a weakness. Be self-conscious.

When limits are imposed Will-Being retreats. The child's experience: imprisoned. Violated. Freedom unattainable. Be defensive.

All Will-Being can do in the face of ridicule, threat, and imposition is attempt to protect the child, who is then left with a limited repertoire of cunning behaviors. Sometimes conform. Sometimes rebel. Sometimes conform and rebel. Defend through sarcasm and cynicism. Be passive.

Be aggressive. Be passive-aggressive. Get out. Deceive. Show off. Hide all experiments. Listen to their lectures. Break their windows. Do well so they'll leave you alone. Do poorly so they'll leave you alone. Do whatever they want so they'll leave you alone. The bottom line: Don't solidify an "I," or they might find out where you are.

Choice and Challenge

Freedom to choose—an exquisite achievement of the evolutionary process—fuels the child's individuation. Freedom of choice also serves the species: It leads to more niches explored more creatively. Will-Being stimulates the desire to be free, to choose the life the child believes best, to fulfill her destiny, to be *whole.*

Again and again Will-Being directs the child to choose, well knowing that her choices will be naive and often short-lived. It insists she assert her right to choose. It further insists that she asserts her individuality, asserts her insecurity, and asserts her right to defend either. Often, the child asserts for assertion's sake, unconcerned about the "facts" at hand, aware only of her need to try on a personality, to build her understanding of identity.

Assertion breeds challenge, and challenge provides the opportunity for the child to define herself in relation to her world—to discover limits and boundaries. Whether the object is family, community, nature, school, or peers, Will-Being provokes the child to use assertive challenges to mark where she begins and where she ends.

Through these assertions Will-Being ascertains the details of the child's world. What kind of support does she have when facing the critical issues of freedom, responsibility, and individuation? Is she met with sensitive respect or ridicule? Can she co-create her boundaries or are they imposed upon her? Does she have ample opportunity and support to probe her ideals? Is she presented with challenges in the realm of success or must she endure constant fear of failure?

Two Reactions to Assertion

At a recent workshop Andrew, a wry, unassuming man who minced no words, complained about his thirteen-year-old. "It seems like my kid is getting dumber as she gets older. A year ago she was helpful around the house, she wrote letters to save the baby seals, and really cared about her younger sister. Nowadays she listens to obnoxious music *constantly,* and dyes her hair a new color every month. She's threatening to put a ring through her nose. Worst of all, whenever I try to help her with anything, she tells me I'm wrong. Then she shuts her bedroom door and won't come out." All those in the room listening to Andrew laughed and nodded their heads.

It's a very common reaction for parents to resist Will-Being's assertions, and often the child then rejects the parents. Many times this mutual rejection marks the end of childhood, which is terribly sad, because Will-Being actually marks the *beginning* of the second half of childhood. The more painful the rejection by the parents, the more "destructive" the child's assertion becomes. We are all familiar with this sequence in our own lives and in society. Put another way, the less sensitive the parent's respect, the more violent the child's rebellion. Assertion does not always mean green hair or a pierced nose. Assertion does not have to be a rejection of family and family values. In some healthy families, in fact, assertion has a transformative rather than a rejecting character.

The Traynors are a content, closely bonded family. They share prayer, music, and religious philosophy. Recently Roger, the father, approached us about his son, fourteen-year-old Troy.

Troy had arrived at a new interpretation of the New Testament and insisted that the entire family agree with him. The family discussed the matter, but both parents, while acknowledging Troy's insights, did not fully agree with his interpretation. In the past, the whole family would have simply let the matter go. But this time Troy was not satisfied. He felt personally offended that a resolution was not reached.

The evening he came to see us, we talked to Roger of Troy's need for assertion. As seems to happen so often with Natural Learning Rhythms, Roger immediately understood and spontaneously devised a healthy family-centered response. He suggested to Troy that they enter into a deep investigation of the New Testament with full commitment toward one interpretation or the other. That might mean more study, meditation, seeking out New Testament experts, and examining their own lives in minute detail. Troy agreed immediately, glad for the challenge.

In the end, the Traynors actually came to an interpretation neither of them had suspected. The experience not only changed the way they understood their religion, it changed the way they approached interpretation. A greater tolerance for all family members and for all religions grew out of the process.

Troy's determined assertion had triggered a valuable family transformation.

Challenge in the Realm of Success

With sensitive respect, we should try to create challenges that allow the child in Will-Being a high likelihood of success. Challenges that lie beyond the child's capabilities undermine her new, fragile sense of self. Challenges successfully met bring out feelings of individual confidence and responsibility.

In the Emotional-Being chapter, we told the story of Sean, a boy who had lost his father, then gained a stepdad, only to lose him as well. The destructive behavior Sean took up after each episode of abandonment, including physical violence toward his mother and sister, made his future look bleak

73

But several years later, as Sean entered Will-Being, an unusual remedy broke his most destructive patterns Making use of our professional contacts, we helped him enroll in a creative writing class at the local university. The course challenged Sean's greatest strength, his precocious mind Sean's subsequent and anticipated success in this class reduced the tension in all parts of his life. He is beginning to be kinder to his sister and to lean less heavily on his mother

Willow, a thirteen-year-old girl, was homeschooled for the first twelve years of her life. Last September she decided she wanted to go to school in order "to find out if I can do what the other kids can do " She had set up her own challenge

As her family assessed her request, Willow's motivation became clearer. Grades were not important She'd always found cliques distasteful and didn't want to be around large groups of children who had been through school together. She liked learning at her own pace but wanted to be in an academic setting with other children. In a shy way, she desired intimate experience with a cross section of her peers

The family profiled their collective needs. Together, they chose a small alternative school with a strong academic program. Willow was given sensitive support. Her parents would not intercede with her teacher unless she asked them to or they discussed it with her first. Her grades were her own. If she didn't meet the requirements of the school, home study still remained an acceptable option.

The year came off splendidly. Willow chose her challenges and had her successes. As she grows into Will-Being, the ideals she expresses and the challenges she creates become more complex and encompass larger ranges of experience. She feels safe and enjoys the new challenges.

Ideals and Peers

When a child accepts the fact that he will become a responsible adult, he often develops a profound desire for the world to be "perfect." Children in Will-Being thrive on ideals and are impatient with imperfection. They will accept responsibility in society—but only on their own terms.

The projection of ideals underscores the importance of peers. For the teen, to be oneself for the first time is frightening; to desire the big world to be perfect seems crazy as well.

Many parents, weathered by life's compromises, cannot support the child's idealistic projections. They feel hurt by the child's movement away from their values toward those they believe are naive, anti-social, or self-defeating. Then, only peers can share and understand the child's experience.

Exploring ideals with peers allows children in Will-Being to define their own world-view regarding school, community, and society. This defining occurs while the child still lives in his parent's home where, hopefully, he has the benefit of sensitive, respectful guidance. Without such support, the individuation process crumbles before the ridicule and derision of others.

When I (Ba) was fourteen, and firmly in Will-Being, the Civil Rights movement came to prominence. I agreed with the principles of the struggle: Society needed to be free from discrimination.

Each Sunday morning during those years, members of my upwardly mobile suburban community came to our family home for brunch and political discussion. When the conversation turned to integration one day, to my surprise and chagrin I found that many of these second-generation immigrants accepted racist stereotypes and opposed any remedial civil rights legislation.

Though I had usually been a quiet listener, I shocked myself and my neighbors that day by forcefully asserting the case for civil rights. When met with opposition based upon what I believed was narrow dogmatism, I exploded, embarrassing everyone. Frustrated, I vowed that such injustice would not persist in the world when I grew up.

My parents scorned my position. Instead of letting me experience my ideals in action, they labeled me idealistic and immature. Their disdain bred rebellion, and I made an inner resolution to leave home as soon as I could.

Natural Learning Rhythms made it much easier to respect the Will-Being children in my life and therefore to avoid imposing that kind of chauvinism on them. When our fourteen-year-old daughter and her friends decided to defend animal rights, for instance, they were encouraged to investigate it thoroughly. Rides were arranged to demonstrations. Serious conversations took place among family and community members as to the value of the movement. Ridicule was banned. The children learned that peer relationships could center around important issues, that all opinions count, and that ideals are valid and worthy of exploration.

75

The Trial and Error and Competency Phases

Will-Being's reign lasts only about four years, and its phases succeed one another rapidly. Fueled by will power and with the help of peers, the child in Will-Being's trial and error phase boldly dons and discards personalities as part of her exploration of her ever-changing "I."

By the time she has reached the competency phase, the child solidifies an "I." If she's been unduly constrained she'll use her strength to fight against her bonds. If she's been left without guidance, her strength will be dissipated in random, uncreative explorations. But if she's been treated with sensitive respect and has been allowed to fully participate in the formation of limits, she'll use her strength to contact her individual freedom and personal power. She will have an "I" that she believes can stand alone.

Will-Being in Nature

In nature, freedom lives—unconfined, ever renewing, ever beckoning. Supremely challenging, nature calls to the Will-Being child, "Explore my diversity, assert yourself against my challenges, savor freedom in the realms of my vastness." The child responds by seeking thrilling, barrier-breaking adventures.

Of course, each child has his own unique definition of "thrilling" and "barrier breaking." One child may find difficult rock climbing the challenge they need, for another it may be conventional downhill skiing, and for a third it may be an overnight canoe trip with no dangerous episodes. Almost every natural environment contains a wide range of possibilities.

In every way, nature offers Will-Being's child sensitive respect. In the outdoors, the child finds circumstances that challenge her at her own level; she need not fear humiliation. As the child changes she can find a different natural environment that meets her new needs.

Twenty-eight-year-old Sven, a Yosemite Park youth guide, attended the Natural Learning Rhythms workshop. To our observation that nature offers sensitive respect to the child in Will-Being, Sven added an important refinement. He told several stories of inner-city Los Angeles teens who visited Yosemite's high country for the first time. On their backpacking expeditions, many of these teens found their own special places. At the evening campfires, the campers wouldn't divulge the location of their place, only that it was special and they didn't want it discovered. In each person's mind he had a place that belonged only to him. Sven suggested that this was an example of nature offering sensitive respect, for it allowed each teen to identify his own personal space.

Spending time in nature aids those Will-Being children seeking to remedy individual imbalance. Because so many of our children do become emotionally scarred in their first twelve years, this remedial quality is exceptionally important. Last August we escorted fourteen Will-Being children on a three-day whitewater rafting trip. The river guides who led the expedition had taken the Natural Learning Rhythms workshop and were familiar with the developmental needs of the children.

Jacqui's experience stands out as an example of the power of nature to restore balance to the child of Will-Being. She was a last-minute addition to the journey, having heard of it through a friend of a friend, and she had only two casual acquaintances among the other children. Yet she decided she had to go.

Jacqui had attended a small, exclusive private school her entire life. Her mother ran a day care center and Jacqui had spent many of her free hours attending to the small children. When we met her, she was preparing to enter the public high school the following month. A bright girl with all the gifts needed to succeed, Jacqui expressed no particular apprehension about going to school. She did, however, shy away from peers.

Our plans called for each child to take a turn guiding the raft down the river. Jacqui's turn was to come on the second day. On the first night she had the responsibility of organizing the preparation of the hot food. She did so efficiently but managed to offend her two co-workers by being overly bossy. A pattern was becoming clear: Jacqui behaved in either a diffident or overbearing way.

Guiding a raft successfully through the rapids depends upon unambiguous communication among all raft members and a keen appreciation of the subtleties of the river. Jacqui's turn to guide began early in the morning. She and I (Josette) sat in the same raft. Soon we approached a rapids. Jacqui's directions reflected remarkable skill at evaluating the river, but her delivery instructions left much to be desired. She shouted at her crewmates and didn't wait for their reply. She criticized them when they didn't respond immediately and in the exact way she'd demanded. Jacqui gave the distinct message that if we shot the rapids successfully it was due to her expertise, but that if we failed if was most certainly our fault.

We didn't capsize, though we came close. Once we made it out of the white water, we hit a calm stretch and began to bail water out of the flooded craft. The other children grumbled loudly within her hearing. Jacqui seemed tense, exhilarated, and a bit exhausted. I caught her eye, intending to offer some advice about communicating with the other children. But her look told me she was intent on this challenge and wanted to succeed.

Soon, another rapids appeared. This time Jacqui took control of the whole situation. All she changed was the way she delivered her directions. Even as we entered the fast-moving water the children sensed the change in her. A vibrant thrill of anticipation passed through all of us. The rapids turned out to be very steep with two large boulders jutting up in difficult places, but we knew we'd make it if we worked together as one. As soon as we reached the calm water "high fives" were passed all around. This time Jacqui was right in the middle of our spontaneous celebration.

That night she was a helper in building a sweat lodge. She cooperated with everyone and never imposed. She was one of several children sharing intimacies long into the night.

The next day we were lazily floating around a river bend when we came upon a dozen vultures feeding on the carcass of a dead deer. Jacqui burst into tears. We beached for lunch and I took her aside. Without any prompting she told me of the death of her friend the year before. For the first time she truly grieved. The other children heard her sobbing. Pretty soon a fifteen-person conversation started about death and feelings, and each child spoke of his own needs and frustrations, not only Jacqui's. But she listened, shared, and learned. By the end of the trip, she had a good idea of what friendship meant and how she could develop the peer support she desired.

Wild Dancing

Put on the fast music and turn up the juice, for it's time to dance with Will-Being. The child asserts a personality and we try to dance with her; the child changes and we trip over our own feet. We then learn patience, humility, and attention to beat. Most importantly, we're reminded of the right to change, the freedom to choose direction, and the exuberance of being ourselves.

Join the dance. Let the fire of Will-Being burn off your outmoded attitudes and behavior as it burns off those of your child. Hear the child's ideals and fuel your own. As you dance, feel yourself stretch. Enjoy the freedom to challenge your world as the child challenges hers. Let this fiery energy invigorate your life. It's a dance of rejuvenation for the parents and a dance of maturation for the child.

Exploring Sexuality

The cleansing fire of Will-Being's wisdom can work for the whole family.

Caroline, a very attractive girl of fourteen, came home from school one day muttering to herself. When her father asked her what was up, she withdrew. When her mother inquired, Caroline said that "school is dumb and they treat the kids like jerks." Further questioning revealed that Caroline and her classmates had been lectured to about sex education, and that she had found the talk trite and misleading. She already knew all the biological information; she wanted to know about the "real thing."

"Doesn't anyone think I can handle myself?" Caroline asked.

The question went straight to her mother's heart. She recalled having the same feelings at fourteen. They were a close family, and so with Caroline's permission, her dad was brought back into the conversation. In a remarkably open gesture, Caroline's parents invited her to ask any questions she liked. They would answer as completely and honestly as possible. Caroline asked about morals and ethics, and about relationship practices in other societies. She voiced apprehension as to her ability to love and give of herself.

Every question Caroline asked caused her parents to reexamine their own attitudes and practices concerning sex, romance, and love. In this straightforward, often-difficult, and vulnerable atmosphere, all family members gained one another's respect. Caroline now feels her parents have compassion for her struggle. They can talk about anything together. Her parents have new appreciation for her maturity—her ability to question intelligently and be receptive to new ideas. Her parents also gained a new perspective on each other, because their reexamination of sex, romance, and love revealed habits they'd unconsciously accepted and opportunities they'd overlooked.

79

Separation and Attachment

To be the target of challenges can be stimulating; being rejected is uncomfortable and threatening. Yet rejection by the Will-Being child offers the parent new insight into the value of separation and attachment.

Assertive rejection by Will-Being's child strikes deeply inside the parent. Difficult questions arise:

"What is the real character of our bond?"

"What part of our relationship will endure?"

"Why is my child so intent on individuating, on leaving me behind?"

These questions arise from the pain of separation, occurring so unmistakably during this life stage. Yet when we accept this pain, we have the opportunity to ponder the questions. We have the opportunity for insight into our feelings, our expectations, and our way of relating to others.

Remember Yourself

The child asserts, claiming her individuality. When the parent accepts the child's new independence, a subtle process begins. A quiet voice murmurs, "Start preparing for your next life stage. Remember yourself. Have you satisfied your own individuation?"

Will-Being lets us know that our destiny is toward ever-greater individuation. She reminds us that we must continuously acknowledge our own freedom. As we grow, life suggests ever-increasing chances for freedom, and each chance depends on our maturity as individuals. Will-Being continually mirrors our relationship to freedom.

A Response to Substance Abuse

Many parents do not understand why substance abuse is so widespread among children in Will-Being. The following case history reveals much about the motivation of abusers; it offers some practical responses for parents and teachers as well.

Jack's parents divorced when he was three years old. His father remarried two years later. From that time until he was thirteen, Jack lived with his father's new family in a suburban town. Violence in the home between the parents and between Jack and his siblings was not uncommon. Boredom at school, little contact with nature, and strict rules for behavior added to the tension.

Jack started using cocaine when he was eleven years old, in the fifth grade. He managed to hide his drug use for a year, but one day his father was doing the laundry and came across a small cellophane packet of cocaine in Jack's pants pocket. His parents punished him severely. They made him promise not to do it again. Guiltily at first, then with growing defiance, he began to use a lot of crack cocaine. Two or three friends joined him. He started to deal. Heavy metal music captivated them. At thirteen, Jack was arrested. His father and step-family members felt personally betrayed, and suggested he try to live with his mother.

Jack's mother liked drugs, including alcohol, marijuana, cocaine, and nicotine. During the four months they lived together, Jack was often truant. He started to argue with his mother, and stole small amounts of cash from her. One day he stole a car, got caught, and was suspended from school.

At this point the court decided a foster home would best serve Jack. He had become acquainted with a wealthy bachelor, Arthur, a friend of his cousin. Arthur was willing to take him in "if he reformed." Arthur had pull in the community and persuaded the judge to suspend criminal charges. The judge subsequently ordered Jack to attend school at the local detention center and warned that if he did not improve under Arthur's tutelage, he would be sent to jail.

Arthur hired us to help. We believed that Jack would be more comfortable at this time of his life with a male counselor. I (Ba) took the case alone because of the obvious issues of masculine self-worth and identity.

Together, Jack and I explored his past. He came to see how he used drugs to avoid his pain, especially the pain of his mother's rejection. I never once criticized Jack for turning to drugs. But Jack insisted that more was at stake. He liked certain substances because, in his words, he experienced "lightness, joy, and freedom, if only for a second." Jack had contempt for those who denigrated drugs without having had this experience. He could see that in the beginning, with crack and cocaine, he was trying to overpower his feelings. But in the last year he had turned to LSD and marijuana, which, he contended, had induced his "positive" experiences.

Subjected by law to random urine tests, Jack stayed away from drugs. His feelings of boredom, resentment, and anger resurfaced. Jack felt grateful toward Arthur, who provided him with care, affection, and physical comfort, but he was chafing against the rules. Also, Arthur drank and gambled, and Jack bristled at his hypocrisy.

I complemented Jack on his discipline in staying away from illegal substances. The more we talked, the more interest Jack showed in psychology, especially his own. Jack believed that one of the most interesting aspects of his marijuana experiences were the insights he gained into himself.

Jack spoke; I provided a "reality check" by offering honest, straightforward feedback. Soon, Jack began to see his unique importance. He saw that his attitude toward life determined his drug use and that he'd "have to get it together" to make an intelligent choice in relating to these powerful substances.

All the time there was intense pressure on him to use illegal substances. Other children on his school bus smoked pot every morning. Arthur's rules were claustrophobic. His mother turned her back on him once again. All his developmental deficiencies were still unremedied.

81

I searched for Jack's passions and ideals. Finally I saw one: rock music. After much cajoling of Jack and Arthur, guitar lessons began. Jack never missed a lesson and learned to read music in three weeks.

Jack's musical talents have brought him into closer contact with his peers. Some of Jack's moodiness has lifted, and both parole officers and school teachers sense the change. They're worried however that rock music will bring substances into his life and that he won't be able to resist.

I'm worried too. I'm also worried that Arthur will carry out his threat to have "good old fashioned discipline"— corporal punishment—be the rule in the house. Arthur hates Jack's mother and is insisting she give him custody of her son. He also believes I'm too permissive with Jack, though he can't ignore the obvious improvement. Jack's walking a tightrope suspended between his own unresolved dysfunctional tendencies and an insensitive guardian and community—a tough place to be.

Jack's compulsive drug experimentation was an attempt to rebalance the pain of his childhood. As he grew more fully into Will-Being he desperately grasped for some way to experience his dreams and ideals. Throughout his childhood he perceived the environment as very hostile, so Jack's choice of substances has ranged from crack to LSD—from an addictive, supposedly pain-relieving drug that amplifies power sensations to a non-addictive substance with the reputation of inducing visions of perfection and beauty.

Moralistic anti-drug campaigns have no deep meaning to the child in Will-Being. Their occasional effectiveness is due strictly to the threat of sanctions. Yet threats and punishments often mean psychological starvation for the Will-Being child. They deny her the chance to explore ideals, peers, and individuality. If that threat is momentarily suspended the child may eagerly embrace drugs, just as the starving person rushes to food. The "forbidden fruit" becomes the object of intense desire.

Clearly, the healthiest and least expensive way to deal with the substance abuse issue is to provide the child in Will-Being with opportunities to meet her natural needs in ways that do not depend on such substances. This chapter has spoken of ways to do that in nature and with challenges in the realms of success and adventure. The chapters on Ritual Rites of Passage, Remedies, and Authentic Education contain successful methods for allowing this child access to these great foods in a balanced way.

Reasoning-Being

Reasoning is the most far-reaching aspect of inner wisdom. During Reasoning-Being the child gains a deep knowlege of past and future—of quarks and nanoseconds, of the universe and its billions of galaxies. Through her expanded awareness of time and space, the child comprehends her own individual growth, and the development of her family, her community, and the species.

Using the power of definition, the ability to explain the nature and essential qualities of an event, Reasoning-Being creates *meaning*. The child becomes aware of *why* she does what she does. The why, the meaning, can also include the concept of *wholeness*—whether of the molecular world, the astral world, the community, or the family. The child in Reasoning-Being comes to understand the *systems* that comprise the whole, and the relationship of each system to the others.

All Night with Isaac

Last October, a neighbor of ours named Judy sat with us during a community picnic. Though it was a day of rest and festivities, her red eyes and slumping shoulders hinted at exhaustion. In a tired voice she asked for our advice concerning her son Isaac, age sixteen.

Two years into high school, Isaac was beginning to question his parent's lifestyle, the one that he'd grown up with all his life. At the dinner table three nights before, Isaac wondered aloud if using the outhouse rather than the flush toilet, or reading by solar electric light instead of a utility-powered one actually made him a "better" person. When his father justified these choices by citing environmental concerns, Isaac interrupted. He said he'd heard his father's explanations before and understood them, but his own priority was to maximize learning, not to minimize environmental degradation.

An all-night discussion followed. Isaac never said his father was wrong, only that he wasn't sure he should follow the same path. Judy perceived her son as "agonized." At one point the father became angry, and Isaac cut him off. Only Judy's intervention prevented a major argument.

The following day she and Issac talked alone. He was wide awake and enthusiastically picked up the conversation. Isaac explained that this year, at the public high school, his schoolmates were from radically different backgrounds than his own and they were not bad or stupid. A number of them were quite nice and very intelligent. Furthermore, he saw that his neighborhood friends had the same desires and illusions as his newer friends. How could anyone claim that one lifestyle is "better" than another? It might be better for the parents, but he said, ". . . a person's got to find out for himself who he really is."

The academic and social challenges of Isaac's first years at high school satisfied his needs for the remainder of his time in the Will-Being stage. With peer support and no threat of isolation, he was able to try on new behaviors at his own pace. This year, however, Will-Being's assertions could not cover the expanding scope of Isaac's experience. With his burning questions, he returned to his primary support, his family, hoping to find some answers.

When Judy later suggested that she and Isaac find his father and reopen their dialogue, Isaac was eager to do so. Isaac's father was not. His statement had been made the previous evening, he said, and Isaac could now "make his own choices." Within seconds, four distinct expressions—hurt, dejection, resignation, and determination—succeeded one another on Issac's face. Judy saw them; his father did not.

Alone, Judy and Isaac continued to talk into the night. This time they also analyzed his father's reaction. At two o'clock in the morning, Isaac summed up his position: "Dad's just so sure that he is right. But I have to find out for myself. Didn't you? Didn't he? Shouldn't you help me? Shouldn't he?"

Judy agreed. Depleted, she opted for sleep. Before he let her go, Isaac extracted the promise that Judy would devise a way to help him find answers for himself. Seated on our picnic blanket the next day, Judy's question for us was, "How can my husband and I help Issac find out who he is? How can we hold our own values aside, and still maintain integrity with Isaac?"

When Judy had finished speaking we were quite excited. We described the qualities of the newly developing Reasoning-Being. She asked that we be specific.

"Judy," I (Josette) said, "think over all you told us. What was Isaac after? What was his aim in this huge expenditure of his energy?"

"He said several times that he's got to find out who he is," Judy answered. "In fact it was uncanny how he kept bringing the conversation back to asking questions and debating opinions, rather than endlessly arguing. It was tiring, but there was something really . . . *attractive* about it. He actually listened and tried to acknowledge me in the conversation. At the same time, we had to talk about what was bothering him or he got mad." Judy smiled. "No changing the subject or all hell broke loose."

"Are you saying Isaac couldn't control his emotions?"

"Oh no," Judy answered quickly. "I never saw him have so much control while discussing controversial topics. It was only when we digressed, or when his father got angry, that there was trouble." Judy paused. "Actually he even handled his father better."

"Was there any difference in what was considered a controversial topic?" Ba asked. "I mean, was there a new dimension to his considerations? More understanding of the interrelationship of the variables, that sort of thing?"

Judy thought for a while. "Well, " she said, "now that I think about it, yes. It was as if he was considering three things at once: himself, the world at large, and the particular topic. He continually questioned why, when, and how he came to a particular conclusion. He couldn't accept anything at face value, but he wasn't willing to deny it out of hand either. He wanted to look at it and wanted us to do it with him He wasn't saying we weren't right. He was asking how we knew, and why it was necessarily right for him "

"Are those fair questions?"

Judy sighed. "Fair enough, but a pain in the neck. I really don't want to go back and reconsider all these issues. Once is enough There are other things to do." Then Judy stopped, thinking about her own words. "But you know, it's fun, too. I mean, it's really nice to be part of Isaac's growth. And I know when I get some sleep I'll see I learned something new by dealing with him. It's always that way with my children. It's just harder some times than others."

What is Reasonable?

First, let us clear up some insidious misunderstandings of Reasoning-Being's wisdom that permeate our society.

Reasoning-Being is not merely intellectualism or symbol manipulation, nor data retention and retrieval. To reduce Reasoning-Being to these mechanistic faculties is like reducing a human being to a computer. It denigrates the natural process and ignores nature's most precious gift: intelligence connected to the *whole,* and the relative place of all events within the whole.

Genuine reason is built upon a balanced foundation of body wisdom, emotional wisdom, and will wisdom. Any act that violates the wisdom of these prior developmental stages is not *reasonable.* Weaponry, which destroys the body wisdom of security, is not reasonable. Violence toward children, which kills the emotional wisdom of interconnected-ness, is not reasonable. Dictatorship, which crushes the will wisdom of respect for individuality, is not reasonable. Every un*reason*able act jeopardizes the child and the species.

Gestation

The child's behavior during Will-Being both prepares her for Reasoning-Being's awakening and activates that awakening inside her. Urging her to break away from her childhood, Will-Being's wisdom stimulates the child's sense of responsiblity. By prodding the child to try on many personalities quickly, it heightens her ability to compare, experiment, systematize, and generalize. Using insecurity as a touchstone, it insists the child directly experience confusion and doubt.

Responsibility. Comparison. Systematization. Doubt. When these factors are present in the proper proportions, the child develops a crucial skill, the ability to *question.* By Will-Being's competency phase, the child has settled on a couple of personal identities. Simultaneously, her growing awareness of self has increased her ability to doubt and question.

At some point the doubt becomes overwhelming. The child realizes that even his firmest assertive declarations cannot fill the immensity of infinity. His passing identities cannot answer the questions that begin to burn in his mind and heart: "Who Am I? How do I know who I am? What is life? Why is life? How does this universe work? What is my relationship to it?"

Reasoning-Being's time has come.

A Hesitant Birth

Reasoning-Being has arrived. The previous ways of constructing reality must be wiped clean. Emotional-Being brought awareness of personal death; Will-Being, awareness of procreation and maturity. Reasoning-Being's way has already been indicated: doubt, and a quantum leap in perception of time.

Reasoning-Being begins as the hesitancy that ended the Will-Being stage, and this space will allow the child and family to prepare for the enormous changes it will bring. The irrefutable knowledge has hit: The various identities the child so staunchly defended cannot account for the world she now perceives. Born of doubt and confusion, the hesitancy creates doubt and confusion for everyone connected to the child. The sudden starts and changes of Will-Being stop. The parents do not know the answers to the child's questions. The direction of the child's life is thrown open to question, undermining whatever efforts the family has made for her future.

For the child, romantic identities adopted in Will-Being die. As Reasoning-Being dawns, students drop courses of study, political persuasions are reconsidered, and family relationships are scrutinized. Sometimes depression sets in, especially if the previous life stages were poorly handled. Some children can't bear the intense changes, refuse the opportunity to question, and instead turn to the military, pregnancy, suicide, or blind allegiance to a career.

The hesitancy's purpose is to draw everyone's complete attention and support to attend to Reasoning-Being's sacred birth. It's a dramatic moment. Reasoning-Being is the last stage of childhood. It holds the power to understand and heal the previous stages. By the end of Reasoning-Being the child will stand completely on her own, a potent player in the evolution of her species and planet. She'll also be able to conceive *wholeness*.

As the hesitancy ends the child confronts her ignorance. She accepts the need to find out all she can about herself and her world. She investigates and compares systems. Her personal history becomes very important as she realizes that who she was in the past partly determines who she is now, and that who she is partly determines who she'll be in the future.

Doubt no longer terrifies the child as it did during Will-Being. Instead it provides the impetus to question, pushing the child to investigate, compare, and experiment. For example, the child might look in the mirror and say, "Where did I come from?" In Will-Being, she might have uttered a remark that matched her particular identity of the week. Now, in Reasoning-Being, it may spur her to investigate the issue through evolutionary biology.

She then seeks access to coherent systems. Systems which have a past and a future, which lead back to the child's awareness of self, which connect her innermost processes with the world around her. A physiology student might look at a diagram of the lungs and realize that these organs have the same structure as a tree. The child also looks for big systems. Systems that connect grains of sand and distant galaxies, such as the chemist's periodic table of elements. Systems, such as evolutionary theory, which connect faraway histories with faraway futures. Systems that tend toward interdependence and holism, such as the theory of relativity, or chaos theory.

Unhealthy Transitions

The child's access to the deep wisdom of each life stage depends upon his experience in previous stages. Isaac's entrance into Reasoning-Being reveals a mostly healthy development process. Many children, however, have had significantly less healthy evolutions. Though the transitions they've gone through might appear quite different than Isaac's, the essential process and ingredients are much the same.

Lloyd, a personal friend, entered Will-Being with a poor Body-Being and Emotional-Being education. Not surprisingly, assertion manifested as rebellion. Idealism succumbed to cynicism and sarcasm. Lloyd sabotaged all parental limits and social norms. Reckless in regard to bodily safety, he graduated high school mostly on the strength of the school's desire to be done with him.

As Reasoning-Being dawned, Lloyd, insecure and despondent, left home. He traveled throughout the United States. Lloyd was in search of himself and knew it, and he was often scared. Eventually, his attitude toward his parents mellowed, but still he would not return home. His answers were to be found elsewhere. After a year he decided he needed guidance and entered the university.

Looking back, we can see that Reasoning-Being's arrival forced Lloyd to reevaluate his life. Initially rebellious, as Reasoning-Being solidified, his feelings toward his family changed. The rebelliousness softened. His "damn you all!" attitude transformed into a "search for something better." Reasoning-Being said "leave" and Lloyd heard and left. He still had the courage to explore.

Many young people do not have the requisite sensitivity to hear and implement Reasoning-Being's messages. Helen's Emotional-Being development was particularly bad. Her father drank every night and behaved abusively. Both parents demanded that she practice an empty, strictly formal relationship to Catholicism. Suburban life bored her. Her mother also drank, but not as much as her father. Helen suspected her mother of having other sexual partners, though she did not admit this to herself until later in life. By the time she was twelve her parents openly hated one another.

For as long as she could recall, Helen always wanted to be out of the house. In Emotional-Being, romantic fantasies were her outlet. By Will-Being, boys became the focus, and through them she hoped to fulfill her emotional dreams. At seventeen Reasoning-Being considerations dawned within her. Who was Helen? What avenues were open to her to find herself? Given her childhood upbringing and unmet developmental needs, she saw only a single investigative option. She became promiscuous.

Reasoning-Being's directives motivated Helen, but deep Reasoning-Being wisdom did not reach consciousness. Too many emotional needs had been neglected. Sex became a dream-like escape for her, and she craved the thrill of the adventure. She never asked herself who she was in relationship to what she was doing; it was all too stimulating. By eighteen she was pregnant, and more pregnancies followed.

We have met may children whose entry into Reasoning-Being was so poorly handled that they lost all interest in learning itself. Many women found themselves panicky about finding a husband and not freely investigating intimacy. Many men "chose" institutional job security instead of experimenting with their natural talents.

Sadly, as is too often the case, Helen spent years relating to sex and men only within this immature emotional context. Clear reasoning is vital to healthy relationships. Later in the chapter we shall explore this link more thoroughly.

Receptivity

Taking in data and exploring systems is the principle work of Reasoning-Being's receptivity phase. At the same time, Reasoning-Being prompts the child to analyze, investigate, compare, and experiment.

It also imparts a most important skill: attunement to the rhythms of a given system. For instance, if the child explores classical violin, she recognizes the need to understand theory and history, the integration of her instrument with others in the orchestra, her relationship with her teacher and the other musicians, the demands on her body, and the desire for mastery. She no longer merely projects a desired identity, for example, that of a "great musician." Instead, she carefully analyzes the requirements of the classical violin system and develops the appropriate program to reach her goal. She'll have to consider financial support, career opportunities, social implications, information from the other stage-specific wisdoms, and the relative importance of other interests.

A big task is at hand. Yet she can easily attune herself, for neither past nor future are intimidating. She'll define history, understand it as a system, and thus give it significance. She'll project a future, understand how it relates to her present, and thus give it meaning. She'll remember that she does not have full knowledge of who she is. She is investigating. Therefore the meaning she assigns to past and future will not be perfect, but her best approximation of the way things are. She's then free to treat the entire experience as an experiment.

The child will then have a quick, simple way to store, retrieve, and compare the data of the violin system. She'll do the same for personal history, and often compare the two. How did her childhood experiences affect her desire and ability to be a classical violinist? She'll apply the same approach to the future. How many years of practice are necessary before an income can be realized? What types of financial support are available along the way? As each issue arises she'll be able to work with it both thoroughly and efficiently. She'll reason.

Indeed, reasoning wisdom is so thorough and efficient that even a multi-faceted life-determining decision does not occupy all the energy of the child in Reasoning-Being. Other issues of importance, such as long-term social relationships, spiritual pursuits, political affiliations, and raising children, can easily be considered as well. There's also plenty of time for hobbies and socializing. Each issue is considered in much the same way as the example above, the decision to pursue the violin. Each time she'll receive the data; check with body wisdom, emotional wisdom, and will wisdom; compare, define, formulate a system, and give it meaning; then investigate and experiment. As she becomes proficient in this process, Reasoning-Being's receptive phase draws to a close.

The Foods: Nourishing Reasoning-Being

The key foods necessary for full and balanced development of Reasoning-Being are mature recognition and co-exploration. To offer mature recognition the elder acknowledges the importance and validity of the child's investigation. To participate in co-exploration the elder supports the child to come to a deeper understanding of the nature of his search or the data being studied.

The child under the guidance of Reasoning-Being is asking the most serious questions a human can ask. He wants *meaning*. When elders honor his search, when they support his inquiry by pointing him to the necessary data or by helping him define his task, they are welcomed and loved.

Most profoundly, Reasoning-Being transforms doubt into healthy skepticism. The child who utilizes healthy skepticism remembers that she is investigating who she is, not "investing" in a set of beliefs. She is inquiring into the nature of reality, not insisting on her opinion. She is experimenting with events *as if* they were real, less concerned with success and failure than insights and understandings.

Ultimately, she is playing with her newly found reasoning "toys." Elders often have trouble offering mature recognition to a child who is playing at reasoning; they find the child's interest in so wide a variety of subjects "unrealistic." Some remember their own late teens as a frivolous time; others were already seriously at work at job and family. Others have trouble with co-exploration. For example, some professors, having invested long years of work in a specific field of knowledge, may demand students meet certain arbitrary standards before they will be worthy of the lessons the professors have to teach.

As Will-Being's doubt transforms into Reasoning-Being's healthy skepticism, a new supply of potent energy is made available to the child. He gains more power and confidence. Everything is available for his inquiry! He has the time and the perceptual abilities. He can examine himself and the world. He is like a god; empowered, nearly fearless, able to do as he chooses, ready to commit to his chosen cause.

Commitment and Falling in Love: Trial and Error

Slowly but surely, Reasoning-Being's healthy skepticism turns into commitment. Personal commitment means to give oneself in trust; to consign oneself to the preservation of a position, issue, or relationship; and to intend duration. This capacity for commitment is unique to reasoning wisdom. Yet, at the same time, it is utterly dependent on the wisdoms of the prior life stages.

If Reasoning-Being and the other stages have developed in a healthy way, genuine commitment arises effortlessly. Reasoning-Being connects with Body-Being and the child gains the deep direct knowledge that he belongs on this planet, that his body and the Earth body are physically interdependent, and that he is safe, supported, and secure. Reasoning-Being links to Emotional-Being and the child feels connection with all life, at home in the human community, and conscious of death, transcendence, justice, and honesty. It hears Will-Being and the child knows freedom is his birthright, and he can take responsibility and become himself. Reasoning wisdom itself provides the child the ability to understand long-term engagement.

Commitment takes many forms. The act of falling in love is one of the most commonly known. Falling in love implies that two people feel profoundly interconnected, that they will honor one another's individuality and freedom, that they will be together in the future, and that they will work to ensure one another's safety. Such is the *reasoning* perspective on falling in love. Relationships not based on these principles often end in unhappiness and separation, for the developmental wisdoms were not taken into account.

The emergence of commitment marks the beginning of the trial and error phase. This is a very gradual process. Short-term commitments come first. Through trial and error the child can explore her differing capacities for different kinds of commitment. She can become a keen reasoner.

Specializations soon evolve. The child may fall in love, or she may accept the rigors of becoming adept in a given discipline. As the information from committed engagement registers, Reasoning-Being prods the child to deeper questions. If she's fallen in love, it will remind her to inquire into the nature of love. Can the experience be realized with more than one person? What are the implications of the existence of love for society? How has her love experience changed her perception and performance in her other commitments?

Reasoning-Being's aim in creating these deeper questions is to keep the child humble. Infinite mystery. Emptiness of projected beliefs. These qualities draw forth Reasoning-Being's most profound wisdom. Only the mind standing in awe of the richness of the universe and of the human capabilities is able to genuinely *inquire*.

93

Inquiry— A Trust Builder

Two tools foster mature recognition particularly well: inquiry and co-exploration. Through inquiry we pose a question; through co-exploration we probe and act upon it. Neither tool requires superiority of youth or elder. Both allow the opportunity for each person to work according to her own abilities in the gathering and evaluation of data.

You may remember times during your own Reasoning-Being development when someone asked questions that reflected a genuine interest in who you were and what you were doing. Perhaps it was a teacher who inquired into your single-minded obsession with a physics project, or an uncle willing to recount your family history, or an elder cousin who looked at your drawings and visited art museums with you. In their individual ways, each of these people was using the tool of *inquiry*.

When we inquire, we honor the person to whom we are speaking. Staying focused on the specific subject she has introduced, we gently but persistently keep asking questions until we are sure *we know what she means*. This may sound simple and obvious, but in fact, we often do not fully understand the meaning behind the statement. During inquiry, the child in Reasoning-Being has the non-threatening opportunity to look more deeply into her motivations for engaging her particular interest.

Reasoning-Being's child faces an important decision-making moment when he graduates high school. Should he take a job, go to college, learn a trade, or travel? What kind of college should he attend, and where? How will this decision impact family, friends, and his future?

Two summers ago, Dawn, an eighteen-year-old cousin of mine (Josette's), visited us for a weekend. She was facing these kinds of decisions and asked for help in sorting out her options. After dinner Dawn began to talk about college. After listening for a few minutes, I interrupted her.

> "I'm not really sure I understand what you mean by 'college.' What does being at a college really mean to you?" I asked.

> At first Dawn obviously thought my question superficial. But she had no ready answer. "I'm not really sure," she said. "Better job. New people. Fun social life."

> "What do you mean by a better job? Is there some particular field you want to pursue for which a college education is necessary? Or is it that a college diploma means more opportunity and a higher starting salary?"

> "Well, I love the communications field. Radio, TV, theater, and film are what I'd really love to study. I did a lot of that in high school. But the university I'd like to go to has a stiff math requirement. I'd have to go to summer school and then do really well to get in."

> "It's interesting," I said, "that you didn't mention your desire to study communications until I asked. All you talked about was a better job. How come? How strong is this desire?"

> "It really is my dream but I'm a little afraid of what it means," Dawn admitted. "I'm not sure if I can handle the big university scene or the academics. I don't really know if I'd like to be a public person, though it sure seems like it would be a great life."

> "What about the big university scene scares you?"

Dawn started to speak, then stopped and struggled for words. I waited patiently. Finally, stumbling over each word, Dawn said, "Being all alone with all those new people. I don't know if I'll match up. I don't know if I'll fall into their way of doing things and not get to find my own thing. I mean, that's sort of what happened in high school. I guess I'm the kind of person who is easily swayed by other people. Am I just going to get sucked into this wave? Or if I don't, is everybody going to think I'm weird?"

I connected Dawn's two concerns about college. "Is your interest in communications yours or the result of being swayed by your friends?"

This was clearly a question Dawn had never asked herself. Startled, she sat and pondered it. She could not avoid responding, since the question was in her own words and related to events she had defined as important. Her answer was surprising.

> My father has a lot to do with it. I've really been close to Dad since Mom died, and my working in communications would really make him happy. It's not like he pushed me into it. But I can tell he'd love it and I know I want to do it partly for him. But I really like it too. I'm glad we both like it. And I like the other people I've met in communications, but their influence has come more in social life than academics.

Simple, non-prejudiced inquiry had opened examination of Dawn's relationship with her father, her social life, her choice of profession, and peer interaction. Through inquiry she can understand the value she attaches to each event in her life, using her own words and definitions. She can now prioritize and act.

The three of us reached this degree of insight through inquiring into "the big university scene." Dawn had opened up several other approaches, such as her remark about the life of a "public person," that would have yielded similar results, had they been pursued.

We (Josette and Ba) followed every line of inquiry. By the end of the weekend Dawn had reevaluated her relationships with peers, father, needs in college, beliefs about communications, and her memories about her mother. All three of us were amazed at her new definitions and priorities. Every certainty she had espoused at the beginning of the weekend had been altered. Inquiry stimulated Reasoning-Being wisdom and the whole world looked different.

Dawn's choice was her own. We did not impose our values. We used her words. We asked and asked and asked. If more data were necessary, we would have aided in gathering it. Any interpretation of that data

95

would have been arrived at through inquiry, the subtle, powerful trust-building tool.

Recapitulation

The child in Reasoning-Being feeds on the opportunity to recall past events, consider them, and then weave them into a meaningful whole that broadens and supports her current perceptions. She seeks to recapitulate her own personal history and, usually, the history of her field of interest.

Jennifer, a client of ours who came to us while in Reasoning-Being, was bounced around for most of her childhood. Her mother abandoned her when she was five. She moved from one aunt to another until she graduated from high school. Jennifer was mostly unhappy and felt unloved. Upon graduating from high school we encouraged her to follow the trade of her dreams, fashion design. We'd been suggesting this throughout high school, but bogged down by curriculum requirements, she believed it unrealistic. Now, doubting the value of high school and buoyed by her new ability to look at the world, she agreed to investigate.

As she read about fashion design, Jennifer became depressed. She saw herself as lonely and grasping, and she wondered why. We helped her look at her childhood. She agreed to find and talk to all her primary caregivers.

She returned a month later amazed, confused, and more determined than ever to be a success. In fact, Jennifer saw herself as powerful and intelligent to have survived the difficulties in each of the homes of her childhood. She realized that the alcoholism, poverty, and feelings of being overburdened by another kid that each of her aunt's had experienced "were not my fault."

Jennifer's investigation of fashion design became more intense. She wanted to know not only what schools were available, but the history of each one, and more specifically, what she called their "tradition." The school she chose was expensive and out of state.

Jennifer went to school and she worked. Defying the label of "lazy" she was given throughout childhood, Jennifer achieved beyond all expectations. Nowadays, when asked why she put out so much effort, Jennifer answers, "I saw in a flash that almost everyone wanted me to be just like them. That's why they put me down. Well, I'm never going to let that happen. I feel sorry for them, but they are not going to pull me down with them."

The End of Childhood

Reasoning competency creates a healthy ego in an open-ended universe. The ability to move from specialization back to greater generalizations. The ability to hold microcosm and macrocosm in the same thought. Ultimately, the sure and certain knowledge that even Reasoning-Being is not the most precise mode of wisdom available to humans.

Reasoning-Being's instantaneous understandings seem almost mystical at times, for they include the expanded relationship to time. But reasoning wisdom does not describe the limits of human knowledge: Its knowledge is based on duality, the comparing of two discrete events in the universe. There still exists the observer *apart* from that which he observes. While reasoning wisdom is able to divide time into infinitesimally small divisions, afterwards there remains segments of that division.

The child in touch with Reasoning-Being competency recognizes these limitations. She will inquire more deeply. Is there a way of wisdom that uses body wisdom, emotional wisdom, will wisdom, and reasoning wisdom and yet lies beyond them? Reasoning-Being knows the answer is yes, and *intuition* is its name.

Intuition is the direct expression of inner wisdom. Non-habitual, non-prejudicial, beginningless and endless, as well as spontaneous, intuition cannot be conned or seduced. Neither subject nor object, it cannot be "taught."

And so both Reasoning-Being and childhood end at approximately twenty-three years of age, just when humans are in prime physiological condition to have children. As we saw in the dance section of the *Body-Being* chapter, one of the great gifts of the newborn to the parents is an experience of transcendent love. Yes, developmental rhythm, a manifestation of the sacred, is at work again. The birth of the child is an exquisite announcement of the existence of intuition.

Nature Redefined

Reasoning-Being's child re-creates the definition of nature itself. Her expanded time awareness—added to her feelings of doubt, confusion,

97

and humility—leads to a knowledge of nature on a grander scale than any previously conceived or imagined.

Excited and a bit overwhelmed the child asks: Does nature have meaning? Is evolution a random process, or is all life imbued with design and purpose? How can human beings find out? Why do natural phenomena exist? And the child doesn't forget himself: "Who am I?" he asks, "in this vastness and incredibly balanced complexity? What's my role, my function, my purpose?" It is nature itself that stimulates the interweaving of such considerations in Reasoning-Being children.

Our friend and neighbor Nick is one of these children. At nineteen, he knows more about the Sierra Nevada mountains than most Sierra Club experts, and he occasionally assisted us with our nature class.

One Friday, Nick led the class on a walk to a stand of old-growth pines in the foothills. Several parents joined us. As we walked Nick identified many of the plants along the path. One ten-year-old boy asked about a manzanita bush. Nick told us its name, and described its yearly cycle and the fragrant flowers it produces in spring. The boy smiled, nodded his head, and turned away. Nick continued to talk anyway. He told us of this plant's relationship to the local predators, which led to a full-fledged dissertation on human encroachment on the life of the forest and the future of the spotted owl. By this time only grown-ups were listening. They politely informed Nick that we had to move on to keep up with the children. Nick, enraptured in typical Reasoning-Being fashion with the wonder of botanical systems, had hardly noticed their absence.

Not all people of this age group voice their observations and deductions. Several years ago when we were visiting relatives in Hawaii, we came across eighteen-year-old Leo, sitting by the ocean shore. He'd been staring out to the sea for about twenty minutes and we wondered why. We sat down and inquired. He'd spotted an ocean current about a quarter mile out. He was wondering where it went and if early Polynesian navigators had used it to make their way across the waters. He explained that he knew little about the ocean and felt humbled by its vastness. Within two weeks, he had joined an ocean canoe club and had begun to study navigation.

Nature enjoins Reasoning-Being's child in co-exploration by meeting questions with answers that lead to deeper questions. Reasearch in astrophysics showed Irene, a college sophmore, that the same elements that comprise the stars are found in our bones. Fascinated, she immediately found herself asking her teachers and peers if they believed her findings shed light on the origin of life on earth.

In a uniquely Reasoning-Being way another student, Leam, wanted to know about his brain in its "primal state." He spent the better part of two weeks in a sensory isolation chamber. He came away wondering about the connection between the "mind" and the "brain" and began intensive research in physiology, psychology, and philosophy.

A third student, Amelia, watched a sea snail struggle, then die when it was washed upon the shore above the waterline. At that moment, she told us later, she felt a deep understanding of Buddha's first noble truth: "All life contains suffering."

Open-ended: such is the character of Reasoning-Being's inquiry, and the way of nature itself. To the reasoning mind, the issues of origin, of purpose, of creation, and of death are open territories to be investigated. Dogma will not suffice. With all the knowledge and power of the great wisdoms of childhood now manifest, how can we answer the questions that burn in our collective human heart?

99

Dancing with Reasoning-Being

Sit down, open your mind, and get ready to dance with Reasoning-Being. This is the dance of examining all data without prejudice in the service of meaning and definition, of the power of knowing of the *whole*.

Dancing with the child while she learns her reasoning skills—comparison, experimentation, investigation, discernment, and recapitulation—enhances our ability to use these skills. Dancing parents often immediately apprehend the value and significance of intimacy and commitment, of the need for humility in order to reason, of the multilayered sagacity inherent in nature, and of the paradigmatic power of expanded time perspective .

Dance of the Species

The whole of humanity rejoices in the Reasoning-Being dance. We welcome home the child who kept herself separate during the stage of Will-Being. We reunite as individuals, as family, as tribe, and as community, recognizing one another and our common need to investigate life and universe.

As parents, we have to surrender our attachment to being the primary intimate companions of the child, which is difficult for us yet necessary. For the species itself, a moment of fruition has arrived, for the child accepts the responsibility of evolutionary continuity. She creates a bond to her lover and to the larger whole, enhancing the life of everyone.

Reasoning-Being's expanded sense of time reminds the parent of the fragile web of nature and human relationships, so critical to human survival and happiness. And that the past has led to the present and the present affects the future. Something clicks. We realize that we are creating the future by the way we act in the present.

With Reasoning-Being: Stepping Beyond

During young adulthood, many of us did not have a full opportunity to access Reasoning-Being wisdom due to insensitivity to our own developmental needs. Stimulated by our children's needs, and working under the auspices of mature recognition and co-exploration, we now have the chance to heal this deficit.

We've seen this happen with two couples who are our neighbors. Serge and Mary, parents of three including nineteen-year-old Nick, never had the time to fully investigate how clear-cutting impacted the Sierra mountains. They had no formal background in any academic discipline and admitted to feeling uncomfortable about their lack of knowledge, but they worked against clear-cutting anyway.

Jesse and Robyn had the same experience during the debate about damming the Yuba River. They had little factual knowledge, but they did have a strong desire to keep the river pristine. They have two children, including Stephanie, who is twenty.

The two couples are old friends. At least twice a month they have dinner together, sharing information about their respective causes and about their children. For two years Serge and Mary's son Nick has been studying the Sierra clear-cutting issue. Jesse and Robyn's daughter Stephanie has been involved with the Yuba for more than three years.

One night, at dinner, Mary began telling her friends about the Sierra. She told of the length and breadth of the range, of the composition of the soil under old-growth trees as compared to soil composition in replanted forests, and of the need for biological diversity to sustain various plant and animal species. When she faltered, Serge had the missing information. When Mary finished Jesse and Robyn thanked her for the information, then proceeded to give a detailed description of the environmental data relating to the river fight.

When they finished, both couples sat in silence for some time. Then all four started talking and laughing at once. All the information about their respective endeavors had been garnered from their children. As they thought about it, they realized that their information had been steadily increasing for quite some time. The couple's visits had become more information-oriented, though they had failed to notice it. At this dinner, however, the truth was unmistakable. By staying in close touch with their children's interests they had substantially increased their expertise and power in the world.

Now, a year later, their knowledge is formidable. Both sets of parents know more about nature than at any time of their lives. Their political views are more clearly defined and they feel more comfortable expressing them. Their understanding of the scientific method and scientific research tools rivals that of many a professor. They know how biological and geological events are dated. They can deeply consider the succession of life forms.

In short, by participating in the child's expanded time perceptions the parents expanded their own. Rather than seeing the world in a way that had solidified twenty years earlier, the parents have the privilege of meeting the moment influenced by the questioning mind of Reasoning-Being.

In another instance, a mother healed an old emotional wound by honoring the emergence of Reasoning-Being in her child. Gloria, forty-five, had divorced Dan's father, Dale, when Dan was three. A bitter, extended custody battle followed. Once on their own, Gloria had sidestepped most of Dan's questions about his father. The issue had come up again when Dan was thirteen, and Gloria told him a bit more, but not the whole story. She believed that he was too young to understand the sexual issues that came between the couple, and the impact of Dale's use of cocaine. Now, at eighteen, Dan was asking again. This time Gloria knew she must make full disclosure.

In reviewing the divorce event with Dan, Gloria went through an illuminating transformation of her feelings. Her son's questions went to the heart of the issue. Why had his dad turned to cocaine? Were the problems of lying and sexual incompatibility attributable to the cocaine, or were there pre-existing issues? What was Gloria's contribution to the relationship's demise? Had Gloria examined her own childhood to see if any of her conditionings had been blocking Dale's happiness?

By the end of their encounter Gloria felt a new compassion for Dale She felt lighter in spirit than she had in years. She'd even identified blocks in her own sexuality that she now wished to correct And she dropped her cold neutrality about Dan and Dale interacting. She invited her son to investigate whatever part of his own life he believed to be important and vowed to offer support whenever possible. Through this thoughtful co-exploration, Gloria resolved her old issues, therefore freeing herself and allowing Dan to deepen his Reasoning-Being inquiries. Such an experience leaves the child open to the next developmental gap: the contacting of his own intuition.

Applications

Communication

Take a minute, close your eyes, and think back to your most satisfying experience communicating with another person or a group. How did each person treat the others? Did only one dominate the interaction, or did a sense of communion prevail?

The word "communication" (as well as the terms "community" and "communion") derives from the Latin *communis,* meaning "common," or "belonging equally to more than one, or many." In this book, communication means "the deriving of mutual understanding between two or more people." Each person comes with the intent of *both* giving and receiving.

Unfortunately, today's culture often disregards the *common* aspect of communication, and the term is frequently misused to signify a simple transmission of information. Watching television, for example, is not communication. Standing in front of a classroom and lecturing to students is not communication. In both of these cases, information travels one way only—one person imparts, others absorb; one person empties, others fill up. Neither party has entered into a *common* arena in which both are mutually enriched. Indeed, the college lecturer or televised entertainer may receive money, recognition, or a sense of accomplishment for her work, but seldom will she have the chance to receive the responses or thoughts of the individuals who make up her audience.

Real communication establishes a bond of trust. Both parties have come to listen and to speak, to take in and to offer—to reach an understanding that eclipses their preconceptions. To do so, each has taken into account the other's position—his opinions, moods, and capabilities. Neither party aims for agreement or even compatibility so much as for synergy, the extraordinary moment when the whole of their common under-standing becomes greater than their individual ideas.

The same basic considerations so crucial in communication between adults also apply to communication between adults and children.

♦ First, work to extablish a context agreeable to all parties and appropriate for the type of communication you antici-pate. (It would be foolish, for instance, for a group of peo-ple to try to debate philosophy on a crowded subway, and wise for a parent to let the answering machine take the phone calls during an important talk with a child.)

♦ Next, take care that the act of communicating serves the common understanding. Choose words and subjects that invite others to offer their perspectives.

Successful communication with children depends upon how well we honor their developmental needs and capabilities, and their uniqueness. It depends upon how genuine the parent is in his intent to create a new real-ity with his child. Is the parent listening to learn, speaking to support? This is the only way that the simple miracle of communication can flourish.

Listening with Undivided Attention

Eliot, a well-paid computer engineer, was struggling with personal issues connected to his job. He strongly objected to the way his company used his programs to design weapons, and he also wanted to spend more time with his family than his work schedule allowed. Linda, his wife, sympa-thized with him, but had concerns about their financial security. Though they'd had several discussions, no resolution had been reached.

One evening Eliot came home especially angry and confused. He really wanted out of his workplace, he said, but he felt trapped by the need to earn a good living. Linda sat down with him to talk. For the first time they tried to come up with realistic financial alternatives. Then the phone rang.

It was Linda's mother calling. The two women spoke for about five min-utes. When Linda got back to Eliot his impatience had returned. Just as the couple found the lost thread of their conversation, their fourteen-year-old daughter Marti came bounding in, asking permission to visit a friend. By the time they finished negotiating with Marti, Linda had to go check on the dinner roast. Ultimately their conversation was pushed far back into the night. Eliot and Linda did finally talk, but they were both tired and far from their best.

Interruptions are the bane of communication. They divide attention, and undermine the delicate intimacy required to speak of our needs and come up with possible solutions. Like many of us, Eliot and Linda often find they have to make superhuman efforts to keep their focus. Their communication and, ultimately, the quality of their life suffers.

Indeed, even with the best intentions it is difficult to maintain undivided attention. Will partial attention do? No. It didn't work for Eliot and Linda, nor has partial attention worked for any other couple we know. To be resolved successfully, Eliot's concerns required care and consideration. Linda had to be present, and able to listen and suggest. She couldn't communicate in the face of the interruptions.

Divided attention ruins communication with our children too. You may remember an instance from your own childhood when a grown-up's attention was diverted just when you really needed it. Perhaps you were telling your parents about your new part in the play, or confiding in a friend about your father's death, or listening to some great truth from the lips of your older sister—just when the interruption came. Do you remember your feelings?

We can offer undivided attention to our children in the same way we offer it to each other: Physically, make eye contact often, especially while listening. Whenever possible, literally "line up your heart" with the child's heart; this will put you at their approximate height. It will help allay the child's sensations and feelings of intimidation at being little in a very big world. Gauge the distance between you carefully—close enough to allow the child to feel intimate support, and far enough to allow her autonomy.

Undivided attention benefits any kind of communication, yet it is one of the most difficult things to achieve in our complex society. There is so much to explore, so many ideas and technologies to assimilate. Electronic intrusions, such as television, radio, telephones, videos and digital billboards draw our attention constantly. Personal concerns can distract us too: A sick parent or an important social event may take us far away from our children. Single parents, often solely responsible for earning an income and educating the children, have additional pressures. All these pieces together mean that providing undivided attention can be an awesome task.

Yet, we can do it. We can treat our interactions with our children as if they are, for that moment, the most important event on earth. Consider it from this angle: If you were to have the President to tea and the phone rang, would you answer it? Would you spend more than a minute making a phone date for later? Would you keep the TV on while you were conversing?

We can extend the same courtesies to our children. To us, they are more important than the President, though we may sometimes forget it. We can make the physical environment conducive to communication:

- ♦ Eliminate the electronic intruders (telephone, television, and radio) while communicating.
- ♦ If the child interrupts while you are busy, make a date for later rather than giving ineffectual half attention.
- ♦ If the child complains that he won't be able to remember his message by that time, jot down a few key words and remind them to him later.

In short, we adults can do all the things for our child that we'd do for one another—and for the President. This is how we begin to live up to the original dictates of communication: *belonging to all.*

In our home, we post the Chinese character for the verb "to listen" on the bulletin board. It is included on the next page. All the elements of undivided attention are present: ears, eyes, heart, you. We use it to empower every family member to both demand and extend undivided attention. If one of us has let our attention become distracted, any other family member can simply point to character to help make her point. Because we all use it, all of us respect it.

Being Empty: Listening without Prejudice

Everyone in Stan's family is a baseball fan. They watch the televised games and root for the San Francisco Giants. While Hank, Stan's father, has never overtly put pressure on Stan to play the game, he enthusiastically supported Stan in Little League, and greatly and openly admires the major league players.

You

Eyes

Undivided
Attention

Ear

Heart

At age eleven, Stan wanted to quit playing organized baseball. He had never been proficient at the game and wanted to pursue new interests. Because he'd always had a good relationship with his father, he came to tell Hank of his decision. I (Josette) was visiting Stan's mother and observed their interaction through the window.

Hank was mowing the lawn when Stan approached him. When Stan said he wanted to talk, Hank flipped the machine to idle, but didn't turn it off. Because of the noise, he missed Stan's rather shy opening comment about quitting.

"What's that?" Hank yelled over the sound of the motor.

"I don't want to play Little League anymore."

"What? What's that? Why not?" Hank's face reflected confusion. He turned off the mower. "This sounds serious, son. What's up?"

"I just don't want to play. I'm not that good, it's not really fun, and I want to do other things."

"Have you really thought this one through? After all, you've always really liked baseball."

"I still do. I probably always will. I just don't want to play on the team anymore."

"Has something happened with the coach? You know, I could go and talk to him if you like."

"No dad, it's not the coach. He's a nice guy. It's me."

"Have you spoken to your mom about this? Shouldn't she be in on a big decision like this?"

"No, I haven't. I came to you first. I figured if it was OK with you that it would be OK with Mom."

Hank put his arm around his son's shoulder "Well, maybe what we ought to do is talk it over with your mother. In the meantime, you can sleep on it and maybe change your mind."

As the conversation drew on, Stan became increasingly dejected He decided to make one last attempt to communicate

"I'm not going to change my mind," he said with some force "I want to quit so I have time to do other things."

"What other things?" Hank's question had an edge to it.

"A bunch of other things. I want to try to play the guitar and learn how to sing and use the computer and press . "

"Wait a minute there, son, wait a minute That's a lot of things. Now, do you know anything about the guitar or singing? And are you going to learn all those things in the little amount of time you'll have from quitting baseball?"

"No, I guess not. Look, maybe you're right. Let's talk it over with Mom and see what she has to say about it."

"OK, son, if that's the way you want it, that's what we'll do."

Stan never found the support he needed. He lost trust in his father. Stan did not have the opportunity to explore his feelings in the safety of his family His primary model, his dad, never heard him

The simplest rule for listening without prejudice is: *Be Empty.*

Don't be in a hurry to fix, improve, criticize, mend, smooth over, or teach. Listen, try to ascertain the child's (or grown-up's!) motivations, and respond to her *inner wisdom*

Listening without prejudice energizes a powerful communications circuit between parent and child. The child knows she's been heard and feels safe to risk expressing her perceptions and desires. This information, in turn, helps refine the parent's ability to see the child's motivations, to understand the "why" of the child's behavior more quickly and easily— and to reflect the child's moment. For the child who securely trusts her parent, mirroring stimulates *inner wisdom.* She understands the effect of her behavior; whether it be forgetting to feed a pet, or acting cute to gain approval, or lying about where she's spending time to avoid a discussion of ethics.

The truth is that each of us attempts to listen without prejudice many times each day. Placing ourselves in the presence of art, music, or a movie, we try to hear the inherent message. Or we may attend a scholarly lecture, or listen to a friend work his way through some thorny problem. For that moment, we drop our biases. Adopting this same attitude with children encourages closeness and harmony in the family.

Children are wise and worthwhile; their expression reveals incisive knowledge about themselves, their parents, their community, and, as we have seen, the very process of evolution. Listening to them without prejudice, being empty, allows us to partake of this knowledge—to connect with our children at their most dynamic.

Paraphrasing is an enormously effective technique in communicating: It helps keep a listener present as well as empty and open. Paraphrasing means telling the speaker what she just said, in your own words. It is a simple and powerful tool, yet many people resist using it. Their reasons vary, but often include the following:

"It sounds idiotic to repeat what I just heard"

"I feel like I'm insulting the other person."

"I listen and I don't have to prove it."

"I assume you're listening or you wouldn't be sitting here with me."

While there is some truth in all these comments, none of them detract from the bottom line: paraphrasing *works*, and it works especially well with children.

In everyday life, most of us already use paraphrasing, in both mundane and dramatic situations:

111

♦ A Body-Being child will approach us, crying, and tell us she's fallen and bruised a knee. We'll say (as ridiculous as it appears in print), "Did you hurt your knee?" Usually, the child nods and presents her knee. We'll look at it. Often, if the knee needs no medical attention, that will be the end of the incident. Tears gone, the child goes back to play. It's the recognition of her reality, and the reassurance that nothing is drastically wrong that she seeks. Body wisdom knows how to balance the painful sensations. The child certainly doesn't need us to make the pain "go away."

♦ An older child, revealing the deep hurt he feels about his parent's betrayal of a confidence, might begin to cry. Other than handing him a tissue, we just gently paraphrase what he has told us. Then, by asking, we verify that we've accurately reflected what he said. If the child indicates that we have, then we inquire, without prejudice, into the meaning behind his words. We might say, "You seem really angry that your mother told her friends about your girlfriend, after she promised she wouldn't. Are you feeling betrayed?" Then we listen, paraphrase his answer, and inquire again. By letting him hear both the impact and the import of his words, the child gains new insight into his feelings. He learns to rely on his own ability to make accurate feeling-representations of his world—the most important work for the child in Emotional-Being.

As a technique, paraphrasing takes practice. While it is easy to repeat the exact words someone has just said, it takes skill to come up with a complete and concise phrase that lets the speaker know you heard all his points and most of the meanings behind them. To practice this craft requires practicing emptiness. It's also a way to make sure you haven't mistaken any of the words you heard, a mistake that happens quite often and can have serious consequences.

Paraphrasing can have a startling effect on the speaker, especially a child. She knows she's been heard. She knows she counts and that people are genuinely interested in what she has to say. She builds her self-esteem and the ability to take control of her life.

Finally, although we've heard objections to paraphrasing from adults many times, we've never heard a child object to it. Indeed, we've seen paraphrasing improve academic skills, bring families closer together, and help in the resolution of numerous conflicts.

Listening with Intelligence

One more ingredient necessary for genuine listening is respect for the other person's uniqueness. Listening with intelligence is recognition of, and appreciation for, the individual qualities of the person speaking. Through intelligent listening we make warm, direct contact with our communication partner.

Try this experiment: Kneel down and have another grown-up talk with you while he remains standing. Discuss the same issues in the same ways you talk with children. If you're like every one of the people with whom we've done this experiment, you'll experience difficulty in both listening and speaking.

This height differential approximates the difference in size between children and grown-ups. The intelligent listener realizes that this discrepancy inhibits communication.

For Body-Being children, who so require warmth and security, the height differential threatens that security. It reinforces the discomforting sensation of being tiny in a very large world. Body-Being children greatly appreciate the elder who comes down to her level—one who makes sure both of their hearts are lined up as they communicate.

Listening with intelligence is a way of acting on one of the basic tenets of Natural Learning Rhythms: the need to connect with the uniqueness of the child while still honoring his developmental stages. There is neither contradiction nor paradox here; stage-specific wisdom exists in all of us, expressing itself differently in all of us. Let us illustrate this: every ten-year-old child is in Emotional-Being and shares certain characteristics with other children in that life stage—a new awareness of mortality, concern for fairness, a need for inspiration. All have access to Emotional wisdom. At the same time, each child is a special individual and will express that wisdom in her own way. One child, for example, may look for inspiration in religion, another in friendships, and yet another in nature.

With practice, listening intelligently gets much easier. Moreover, as adults, we have the great advantage of already having lived through all

113

the life stages of childhood. Our own direct experience can help us recall the particular qualities of those stages. In addition, we grown-ups know the unique characteristics of the children in our life better than anyone else in the world. All this says is that we already have much of the experience and equipment to do a very good job of listening. What's needed is the commitment to do so. To a child, it can make a very important impact.

At a workshop we gave in Seattle, a participant named Carlotta told us about a time when she found a good listener, and remembered the difference it made in her adolescent life.

At fourteen, an intelligent and curious Carlotta realized that she wasn't communicating with her family. Both parents worked full-time and were closed to conversations about sex. Carlotta felt her parents treated her as grown-up when it came to responsibilities but "like a kid" in relation to issues of individuality and freedom.

Around this time, Carlotta developed a close friendship with Debby, whose mother, Mary, was the good listener. According to Carlotta, Mary was "right there" with them when the three sat around the kitchen table talking. No subject was taboo, no opinion ridiculed. Mary understood that there was no contradiction between Carlotta's aggressive need to meet boys and her shyness when on a date, or between her strong interest in sex and her modesty in intimate situations. Carlotta knew Mary would never violate her confidence. When Mary gave advice Carlotta listened. She knew that Mary's intention was to support and help, and that she held Carlotta's happiness close to her heart. The special relationship with Mary ultimately allowed Carlotta to mature by exploring and determining her own values.

Integrating

We often picture communicaton as a two-step process consisting of listening and responding. But if we reconsider our interactions carefully, we notice that there is an intermediate step: *integration*. First we listen, then we *integrate* what we've heard, then, finally, we respond. Our responses arise from our integrated understanding, not directly from our partner's message.

There are five elements to remember when communicating with children:

♦ **the specific information that has been transmitted**

- ◆ **our resident knowledge of that specific child**
- ◆ **our comprehension of** *stage-specific wisdom*
- ◆ **our understanding of the context**
- ◆ **our personal repertoire of possible responses**

Integration often happens so quickly as to seem instantaneous, perhaps explaining why so many of us are not even conscious of it as part of communication. Even if aspects of integration occur during the time we are listening, the process must still occur within our mind (and heart) before we can respond. The old adage "Think before you speak" could be rephrased "Notice how you integrate before you respond."

When we integrate a child's message, we are essentially answering the following questions:

- ◆ **How did we understand the words, body language, and feelings that the child expressed?**
- ◆ **What is this child's personal history?**
- ◆ **What is she going through right now?**
- ◆ **How do I feel about her?**
- ◆ **How are the child's developmental needs fulfilled in her life?**
- ◆ **What are her developmental needs at the moment?**
- ◆ **How is her transmission a statement of stage-specific wisdom?**
- ◆ **Where is this communication taking place?**
- ◆ **Which responses are available to me?**
- ◆ **Which ones fit this child in this context?**

This is a very important juncture. Understanding the way we integrate information can radically alter the way we respond to a child, and hence, how effective we can be. We can *see* this process most clearly with very young children.

Abby, a clever and vivacious one-and-a-half-year-old, knew that her mother Kathy did not want her to bang on the computer keyboard atop her father's desk. All the same, for several days in a row, Abby would climb the chair, bang on the keyboard, then look to mother with all the sweet ingenuousness of a toddler. When Kathy would tell Abby not to bang, Abby would stop, then fifteen minutes later start again. Each time the toddler would resist Kathy's admonition a little longer. When Kathy removed the keyboard from the area, Abby acted the same way about climbing onto the dinner table.

Sizing up the situation, Kathy came to the conclusion that her baby daughter liked the power of forcing her mother to react. Believing the toddler was manipulating her as part of a "power struggle," Kathy was considering punishment. She hadn't taken Abby's behavior as a personal affront; she'd been patient and attentive, and had accounted for the fact that the toddler loved to explore. With no rancor in her heart, she had decided that Abby needed to learn that power struggles simply don't work.

Yet as Kathy contemplated further, her mind kept coming back to what she knew about toddlers' need to explore, and slowly, she realized that exploration implies the testing of limits. That single thought was a revelation for her. No power struggle actually existed. Rather, Abby was acting from Body-Being's developmental wisdom. Abby had always been active. Now, in her own home, in the proximity of a trusted parent, she was actively exploring the boundary between her movement in her world and the reactions of the people who lived there. She needed to know how it all worked together.

At this point, Kathy reconsidered her own understanding of flexibility. She had always supplied flexibility within certain boundaries, but not at the edge of those boundaries. In other words, Abby had ample opportunity to expore if she behaved as Kathy wished. Now, Kathy's revelation led her to a new response.

First, she alerted all of Abby's care-providers of her insights. Everyone agreed to offer non-coercive support in helping Abby explore and define her boundaries. When the toddler came near places that were off bounds, an older child or grown-up would join her to make sure she didn't hurt herself or damage something. If no one could watch over her at that moment, the care-provider would tell Abby "no" in a pleasant manner. Those times when she persisted by grabbing something, the toddler's hand was gently removed. If Abby still persisted, she was moved to a new locale. At no time was she scolded or made to sense that she was bad. Abby soon completed her explorations and, because of the abundance of flexibility in her life, returned to the rich, textured "child-proof" environments Kathy had created

Responding

Our society places a high premium on *response*. It is our moment in the spotlight and we are judged by how well we do. We spend much time preparing our answers, often while the other person is speaking. Our public schools grade students according to the way they respond, but spend almost no time teaching them how to *listen and integrate*.

The emphasis is misplaced. Listening is much more important than responding: We have to know as much as we can about the other person's transmission before we enter a common understanding. Integration is also more important than responding: We have to know as much as we can about how we've interpreted that transmission before we can react to it. Responding itself is a simple and straightforward act once we've listened and integrated.

One key to good, clear communication with children is to speak in direct response to the specific issue the child communicated. Answer clearly and concretely so that the child knows she is heard. If you have something to add, do it after you've spoken to the specific. Once her answer has been received, the child's mind is free to consider new information. Circuitous, abstract replies almost never work with children.

Successful response to children also depends upon choosing words, concepts, and gestures appropriate to their developmental stage. Our communication with children must reflect their level of development. For Body-Being's child, attention and respect for body language is critical: Learn to listen to your child's postures and gestures; we say much more to these young children by the way we touch and the sensations we provide than by the words we speak. When we do use words with Body-Being children, they should refer to the world as perceived through the five senses. And remember, children often play with words during Body-Being: They *don't* always say what they mean and mean what they say.

Emotional-Being communication has everything to do with feelings and the way we model justice, fairness, honesty, and caring, and has nothing to do with data transmission or lectures on ethics. Our relationships with family, friends, and community *are* our transmission as to how to decipher personal and social feelings. The child is naturally primed to accept our modeling of interpersonal relationships, for we are her models.

Use feeling words when communicating with Emotional-Being's child. You will find a list of them on the next page. By developing a feeling vocabulary with our children, we help stimulate stage-specific wisdom. When we let them know we understand them and are on their side, we

117

NEGATIVE FEELINGS VOCABULARY

MILD	MODERATE	STRONG	INTENSIVE
unpopular	suspicious	disgusted	hate
	envious	resentful	unloved
	enmity	bitter	abhor
	aversion	detested	loathed
		fed-up	despised
listless	dejected	frustrated	angry
moody	unhappy	sad	hurt
dismal	bored	depressed	miserable
disconnected	bad	sick	pain
tired	forlorn	disconsolate	lonely
	disappointed	dissatisfied	cynical
	wearied	fatigued	exhausted
indifferent	torn-up	worn-out	worthless
unsure	inadequate	useless	impotent
impatient	ineffectual	weak	futile
dependent	helpless	hopeless	abandoned
unimportant	resigned	forlorn	estrangement
regretful	apathetic	rejected	degraded
	shamed	guilty	
bashful	shy	embarrassed	humiliate
self-conscious	uncomfortable	inhibited	alienated
puzzled	baffled	bewildered	shocked
edgy	confused	frightened	panicky
upset	nervous	anxious	trapped
reluctant	tempted	dismayed	horrified
timid	tense	apprehensive	afraid
mixed-up	worried	disturbed	scared
	perplexed		terrified
	troubled		threatened
sullen	disdainful	antagonistic	infuriated
provoked	contemptuous	vengeful	furious
	alarmed	indignant	
	annoyed	mad	
	provoked		

118

establish family interconnectedness. We invite you to make parallel lists of words appropriate to Body-Being, Will-Being and Reasoning-Being.

The essence of communicating well with Will-Being children is founded upon the parent's ability to show sensitive respect, making sure not to upset the fragile balance between the child's drive to express her individuality and her insecurity at having no experience of how to do it.

The essence of Will-Being wisdom is founded upon freedom, individuality, and ideals. It is no surprise, then, that Will-Being's children respond well to conversations about their personal "space" and personal freedom. Here, listening without prejudice is crucial. If the child believes that the parent has engaged him in order to "prove a point," communication will wither immediately. If the parent shows a willingness to be fair, however, and refrains from moralism and lectures, the child will want to participate in deciding appropriate limits. Successful communication about limits can lead to exciting communications about the way the world should look and why people do what they do.

Enter in. It's the only way to communicate. Because of quickly changing perspectives, it's sometimes toughest to get involved with the child in Will-Being. Still, just like every other child, the young teenager is a living example of evolution in progress and wisdom unfolding. Thus when we succeed in communicating with him, we become part of the natural rhythm of human development. If we fail to communicate, the child suffers, as does the family, the community, and humanity.

119

As the child grows into her reasoning capability, all of time and space becomes a subject to study. She can consider the past; she can consider the future. Where did she come from? Where is she going? Why? Reasoning-Being's child hungers for data. She wants to explore, to reach out and taste the vastness the same way she reached out to taste everything when she was a baby. Words are one of her main tools for exploration. She hopes to match words with reality and thus understand both better.

We communicate with the child in Reasoning-Being through the mediums of mature recognition and co-exploration. We do it together, keeping in mind that she has chosen this investigation—be it about music, governmental policy, or coyote behavior—to satisfy a need we may not fully comprehend. If we disagree with the child, we offer the argument or data supporting our position, but we never tie that position to support of the child. The Reasoning-Being child needs to find his *own* purpose in life. As parents, we will learn more from co-exploration than we ever will from proving our point.

Brook, our neighbor, came home from college full of information about particle physics. Her father Michael, knowing very little about the subject, asked her question after question. Delighted to talk about her new interest, Brook spoke far into the night. Before they went to bed, Michael asked her to recommend a simple text, and later he read it. Subsequent conversations, which started with physics as a base, ranged from basketball to philosophy. Together, they co-explored the interconnectedness of all information. The following year, when Brook came home keen on German existentialist philosophers, her father followed the same steps. When his daughter graduated, Michael joked that they received two college educations for the price of one.

Ritual Rites of Passage

A Very Human Endeavor

Anthropologists tell us that from the earliest appearances of human soci- ety, every known culture has created ritual rites of passage for its chil- dren: the Mbuti and the Jews; Australian Aborigines and Protestants; Thai Buddhists and Inuit pantheists; Native and immigrant Americans. From deep within ourselves, we humans universally recognize that the various stages of our development must be marked and acknowledged. In doing so we fortify the child, the family, and the community, and we become conscious of our contribution to our continuity as a species.

We must therefore consider ritual rites of passage both natural and ele- mental experiences rather than supplementary occurances. These rites embody the creative process of the entire participating community. They use strength of self, family, and society to create a safe, supportive struc- ture from which to contact the very essence of self, family, and society. Indeed, rituals allow us to both transmit and transcend the wisdom of our own culture. They are a way of saying who we are, and a means to explore who we might become.

At the very same time, ritual rites of passage are accelerators: They move the entire family toward a recognition of their togetherness. Through rit- uals we sanctify the growth of the child and allow each one to come into harmony with herself and her family. Ritual reawakens us to the power and beauty of nature; it reminds us what we are doing here.

Ritual Rites in the Post-Industrial Age

Industrialized societies have, for the most part, forgotten what makes a ritual potent. Time-honored rites of passage are either ignored or made into hollow formalities that too often mock the truth they once so lovingly conveyed. In the West, many of these rites—high school graduations, military inductions, and some religious coming-of-age ceremonies, to name a few examples——have lost any vestige of authenticity: Rarely do participants come away refreshed by a well-conceived, risk-taking exploration into themselves and their world. Rather, in line with the values of the industrial world, they come away with the socially determined objectives: money, commodities, approval, or social status.

Once rites of passage guided children toward their own inner wisdom. But many present-day ritual expressions deny access to that wisdom rather than fostering it By dispensing with such rites, we believed we would be free from the constraints of tradition. Instead, without rites of passage our cultural and spiritual ties to one another are dying.

By restoring ritual rites of passage, we hope to reclaim them.

Reclamation

We can begin to honor our natural growth patterns by taking the time to expand ourselves and one another through a more authentic relationship to ritual

Children love rituals! They are so *non-ordinary*. When the ritual matches the child's development, her innate wisdom responds so readily that everyone is able to delight in its essence. Recalling her nine-year-old son Wesley's ritual rite of passage (during which the boy, in a safety harness, climbed a seventy-foot Ponderosa pine tree), forty-two-year-old Suzanne describes her unexpected awe: "Time was suspended. Everyone felt a great sense of belonging. Even tensions long harbored by one relative against another seemed to drop away. Afterwards we stood looking at each other and wondering, 'Where did this grace-filled moment come from and where can we get more of it?'" Each child we have known who has undergone this kind of rite of passage has developed a more open relationship with every member of her family, is more willing to take responsibility, and has become more socially skilled and attuned.

The Six Ingredients

The ritual must include certain basic ingredients to accomplish its manifold purpose. From our own fieldwork and study of cultural anthropologists, we have derived six ingredients neccesary for a successful ritual rite of passage. They provide the framework within which the inspiration for the ritual can develop. They also serve us as points of reference, a path we can trod upon together.

If any of these ingredients are missing or are not included in proper sequence, the ritual will lack potency. Less-than-potent rituals, or rituals enacted at the wrong time can have a deleterious effect for everyone. We have witnessed families with the best intentions fail to account for all these important ingredients, and these families have experienced the pain and disappointment of a potentially awakening event missing the mark.

1. Acknowledgment of the old self
2. Casting off the old self
3. The GAP
4. Acknowledgment of the new self
5. Celebration
6. Thanking

123

Acknowledgment of the Old Self

Who have you been, child, and who have we been in relationship to you? Using words, chants, play animals, clothes, or any object that symbolically represents the past life stage (or stages), the family collectively acknowledges the child's past, specifically those which have inhibited growth. We take the moment to acknowledge past feelings, to reflect, grieve, and rejoice.

Casting off the Old Self

It's time to let go, to empty one's self; as with a full cup, there's no room left for the new wisdom. Bury the old self, burn it, float it down the river, disavow it out loud or in writing, but in full awareness, let it go.

The GAP

It is transcribed here in capital letters, because the GAP is the hardest to understand and the hardest to do. In the GAP, reality is temporarily suspended; ideally, the child stops thinking, stops constructing reality verbally, and is swept away into a more expansive awareness.

Many parents have difficulty designing the GAP because they fear its extra-ordinary qualities: One mother, for example, gasped after her husband presented his plan for the GAP in their six-year-old son's ritual, "We're going to have *my* six-year-old walk through the forest in the dark? No way. Not my kid." After her initial fear, however, the mother saw the value in her husband's proposal. Safety precuations were set up. A small area of the woods was chosen for the ritual. Adults would be hidden in the forest all along the way, should the child need help or become scared. Because the child was well prepared, including several nighttime walks in the woods, he felt very comfortable and a powerful ritual ensued.

GAPs should vary according to the individual child and the stage he is in. Strong exertion in nature, isolation, and dancing are some ways we've seen GAPs created. Later in this chapter we describe some specific rituals, including the successful GAPs that were designed for them.

Children want to grow, they want to explore, they want to engage their parents at the peak. All the children we have worked with have loved the GAP element of their ceremony. Some, in fact, have asked why we kept this experience so mild—including in instances where we thought we were truly stretching their limits.

The older the child, the more dramatic the GAP can be. But even older children should not have the final say in formulating the GAP. Why? Because they cannot, from their present perspective, know what kind of activity will truly suspend their reality. They can have ideas and insights, but their fears and expectations will cloud their vision. It's up to us, the elders, to create the GAP. It's up to us to acknowledge the mandated separations built into the child's development process. It's up to us to guide our children to learn how to live.

Acknowledgment of the New Self

The change has occurred, is occurring, and we're here to say so. To the child we say: Did you discover a new name, child? We'll hear it and use it. Did you have an experience worth retelling? We're here to listen. Can we speak? We're here to tell what we saw, how we felt, why it's new to us. Did we lead the way up this mountain? We'll gladly follow you down. That old way *was* us; this new way *is* us, and we're happy to grow with you in it.

Celebration

Time to rejoice in our growth together. Whether it's simply with the ritual participants, or with extended family and friends, we engage the bounty of our good feelings with ceremony and festivities. Gifts, usually symbolic, are offered; food and music are served. Relax, enjoy, and share.

Thanking

Here's where the child gives thanks to all those who have participated in the ritual rite of passage, and perhaps all of those who have been influential in his life. The older the child, the more elaborate the thanking. Whether through song, poetry, dance, or a simple speech, thanking should be well planned and treated with care and reverence.

Developmentally Appropriate Ritual Rites of Passage

Not only must all these six ingredients be present, but they must be in accordance with the child and her family. What's an appropriate casting-off for one child is not for another. Also, each child grows at her own speed. Even the physical changes related to puberty are not a totally reliable guide to when to carry out the coming-of-age ritual.

So we have to go slowly here. We must examine the developmental process for indications of when and how to create the ritual. In taking on this challenge, it's as important to notice what doesn't work as what does.

125

Indications and Contraindications

Ritual rites of passage do not work well with a child who is transfering from one stage to the next. The parents must hold off until she has both feet in the new stage. Stage transitions are already full of surprises and wonder for the child. She's moving into a new stage, contacting a new wisdom, and ultimately experiencing a whole new way of perceiving the world. To introduce a ritual with its accelerated intensity only confuses rather than clarifies. In that case the ritual would be meaningless to the child and detract from family unity.

So we watch the child carefully and check our perceptions with other caring elders in his life before proceeding. "Is he truly in Emotional-Being?" we might ask. Looking for signs, we might reflect: Have there been straightforward conversations about death? What's the child's relationship to appearance? What's his response to inspirational stories? Does his understanding of drama include the feelings of the characters? When there's a consensus that the child is truly in Emotional-Being, we then proceed with an Emotional-Being ritual.

The same approach works for all of the life stages; we simply modify the questions so that they apply to the stage the child is entering.

A common mistake is to make the coming-of-age ritual which marks entry into Will-Being, coincide with the advent of puberty. Most often, puberty itself is a transit manifestation; the child does not yet stand firmly in Will-Being. Wisdom lies in being certain. Let's not hurry our children; let's not want them to be adults before their time. Puberty itself can be marked by a modest celebration. Successful coming-of-age rituals are usually very energetic and intense affairs. If we wait for the right moment we can truly give the ritual our all, meeting Will-Being's assertive energy at its own level of intensity.

Ritual rites of passage can also mark the changeover from one *phase* to another. As with the life stages, it's best to wait until the child is fully in the new phase, though not quite so critical. In the course of a phase change, the child reaches a new relationship with the resident stage-specific wisdom—that is, body, emotional, will, or reasoning wisdom. His way of perceiving simply shifts, but it does not get stripped away to be replaced by something radically different. In any case, the child will be most ready for a ritual when he has become fully established in the newest phase. That's when the child can receive the full meaning and import of the rite of passage. That's when the most complete learning, enjoyment, and family bonding occur. For both stage and phase rituals, better to err on the side of caution.

As with stage transitions, never carry out a ritual when the child is in a hesitancy. These hesitancies, you might recall, are natural moments in the development process when growth seems to slow down and even regress. In these moments the child is pausing, gathering strength for a great leap forward. Were the drama generated by the ritual to interrupt a hesitancy, the results would be chaotic and very likely detrimental. Let the hesitancy's pause occur. Critical work is happening behind the scenes.

Many workshop participants ask about the use of ritual for healing fam ily wounds. Generally speaking, within the context of Natural Learning Rhythms, we don't believe it to be a good idea. While rites of passage often have tremendous curative powers, the ritual's aim should always be to mark a passage, whether to a new stage or to a new phase within a stage. Ritual is not appropriate for children under stress, for that child has enough to integrate without the drama of the ritual. She needs support to finish her in-the-moment process, not unusual experiences to "pull her through."

If, however, there have been ongoing difficulties in a child's life and these difficulties are being addressed openly, then a healing work may begin, with aspects of the ritual designed to support that healing. This requires a high degree of refinement and skill, and works best when everyone involved in the healing collaborates with all family members.

Difficulties stemming from divorce are among the most common that can be addressed during ritual. If elders cooperate to support the child without creating the false impression that reconciliation might occur, then some of the trauma can be mitigated. Parents who are in therapy, or who follow a particular spiritual tradition, should seek counsel about whether they can truly cooperate in the ritual milieu. It is important to repeat: Ritual rites of passage are highly charged accelerators. Do use them, but do so with respect and reverence. Make certain that they serve children and the family; find other forums to work out personal troubles.

We've heard of radical rituals attempted in response to desperate situations with severely wounded children—children who have suffered abuse or repeated abandonments, or whose self-worth has been damaged by unnatural, imposed standards of achievement of behavior. At best, such rituals have had mixed success, occasionally bringing about a temporary cessation of the dysfunctional behavior, such as returning to school after dropping out. In other cases, however, such rituals have only exacerbated family problems. There is no magic cure to rebalance a life-time of neglect and despair: At no time can such rituals be considered a substitute for *long-term, committed lifestyle changes* that support access to developmental wisdom. The most effective deterrent to serious dys-function is prevention, paired with a long-term commitment to healing.

An Emotional-Being Ritual Rite of Passage

What specifically does a successful ritual look like? Debra, a mother and teacher who has been practicing Natural Learning Rhythms, told the story of a ritual rite of passage for her Emotional-Being daughter:

In May, 1989, our family created in a ritual for our nine-and-a-half-year-old daughter Chamise. We recognized that ritual forms a cornerstone of the parent-child relationship, and knew that we'd have to include the six basic ingredients to create an authentic rite of passage. So with those ingredients in mind, we began to plan our family's ritual expression.

♦ **Planning and Preparation**

I. Acknowledgment of Old Self

In the weeks prior to the ritual, we helped Chamise identify behav-iors and "labels" she felt no longer fit her. Some were labels Tom [her husband and Chamise's father] and I used. Some were old fears. Some were outgrown behaviors Collectively, these repre-sented her "old self." Throughout this process, Tom and I were given the opportunity to admit where we had made the mistake of applying labels to Chamise or demanding certain behaviors from her.

II. Casting Off of Old Self

Chamise planned to write down the names of the identified labels, fears, and behaviors on slips of paper. During the ritual she would cast them, one by one, into the fire.

III. The GAP

Chamise's ritual celebrated her passage from Body-Being to Emo-tional-Being. Only after careful observation and consideration of our daughter's personal history did the three of us create the ritual structure. Ultimately, we decided on a dramatic myth interwoven with music and dance. The central theme was to be death/transcendence. During the past several months Chamise had been seriously inquiring into death, spirit, and the unknown—a natural activity for a nine-year-old. Her cherished grandfather (Opa) had died when she was seven-and-a-half, and six months later, both of Chamise's great-grandmothers died. Thus, death had strongly affected our family life while Chamise was entering the Emotional-Being stage. So for these particular personal reasons as well as developmental ones, we felt that death should be the ritual focus.

After researching many myths, Tom and I wrote our own. We wanted it to be relevant to Chamise in her life as an child in the late 1980s. The myth we created had a tribal, ancient feeling, with details and issues important to our family. Indeed, it actually came from an event in our own lives.

The previous spring, in our garden, Chamise had found an injured kestrel, a small falcon-like bird. Although the kestrel lived only a few hours, Chamise found special significance in connecting with this fierce, wild creature. The myth we wrote for her ritual told of a young girl named Talon who finds an injured bird and bonds with it, and then the bird has to face its death. Through the bird, and with the help of a wise woman, the young girl faces the mystery of death itself.

The myth itself provided a framework for the GAP. A strenuous dance sequence was the true GAP-inducer. Chamise knew the basics of the dance sequence, but we held certain information back. She did not know how long the dance would last, or its exact rhythm, for Tom would determine that by the way he played the drum. As long as it beat, she must dance.

Two of Chamise's friends, Amber, fourteen, and Kale, twelve and a half, had essential roles in the ritual. Amber danced, acted, and sang with Chamise. She played the wise woman who guides Talon through her quest for the meaning of death and life. The dramatization of elder guiding the younger metaphorically expressed their real life sharing of three years. Amber instructed Chamise in specific classical South Indian *Bharat Natayam* dance movements, an experience that vitalized both the ritual and their friendship.

129

Kale played Talon's parent. The inclusion of Amber and Kale showed Chamise their acceptance of her as growing into their world. But the teaching was not a one-way interaction: Amber and Kale had the opportunity to give and to share—to support their young friend.

Chamise wrote the first three songs of the myth. Using her own words and feelings helped make the story hers. Tom and Chamise created a feathered mask for her wear in the dance. The mask signified many things: "trying on" new feelings and personalities, creating a new and different "face," and the presentation of a new self.

IV. Acknowledgment of the New Self

After the drama/dance, we planned to gather in a circle and individually acknowledge Chamise's new self. The ritual participants included Tom and me, Josette, Ba, Amber, Kale, Eric, and Chamise's grandmother, Oma. Eric, a family friend in his early twenties, had a growing rapport with Chamise. In retrospect, his presence seems to have brought about a deepening of their friendship. Oma, who attended Chamise's birth and had consistently nurtured her, embodied the power and grace of the beloved elder who is so revered in traditional cultures and so ignored in our own. Oma's presence also reminded us of Opa's absence, and helped focus attention on death, separation, and spirit. Thus, our gathering was small but carefully representative of different life stages. And most importantly, each person was committed to Chamise.

♦ **Chamise's Ritual**

We chose a remote part of the nearby Yuba river as the ritual site because of its association with power and renewal. We'd considered a nearby mountain top as a choice, but the weather in early May was too severe. So on the appointed day, the ritual began at the trailhead of a challenging hike to the river.

Tom and I dropped Chamise off at the head of the trail with her backpack, and a big hug. We then drove to the trailhead of a connecting path where Tom set off, also alone. Chamise hiked the first mile on her own, a act that symbolized separation and individuation. She and Tom met up where their paths converged, symbolizing a redefined sense of self and relationship.

Chamise and her father hiked along quietly. Words were few and centered on the passage that the ritual honored. At the ritual site, they worked together writing down the fears, labels, and outgrown behaviors onto slips of paper. They sat quietly, allowing any overlooked behaviors to come to mind. The rest of us arrived late in the afternoon. After a swim and a light meal, the preparations began.

We dug a fire pit and made an altar of natural objects. Josette braided Chamise's hair with flowers and grasses she had gathered along the trail. Everyone changed into their ritual clothes.

At dusk, Chamise and I walked to the water's edge. We breathed together silently, holding hands. She was vibrantly alive. Each breath was filled with anticipation. I briefly reminded Chamise that the ritual was part of her education, and not a performance. I asked only that she do her best. I also told her that she could chose a new name if she wished. Because she had taken Talon as a new middle name some months earlier, I said that we would support her if she wanted Talon to be her new name.

All too soon for me, the time came to join the others. At the fire circle Tom and I welcomed each participant. Chamise, her voice strong and confident, read the words on the first card: "Prejudgment by my parents." She cast it into the fire. A second card read, "I want to stop hiding from taking out the garbage." A third said, "No one can call me 'Baby-Boo' [a family nickname] anymore." Each of the eleven cards was read aloud, released, and burned in the flames.

The sky was dark and the fire dancing as we began the drama. While I narrated, Tom played the kalimba, recorder, and drum. The story unfolded, word by word, song by song, weaving subtle individual messages into a meaningful whole.

Then, the main dance, the GAP. Chamise opened with the graceful movements Amber had taught her. With her back to the rest of us, she put on the feathered mask. When she turned, a new person emerged—bold and ready. Chamise danced the dance of her own spontaneous creation, her moment. The drum beat, intense and inescapable. We chanted and clapped, keeping the rhythm alive, entering into the moment with her. Around and around the fire she danced, strong and committed. As she flew by her father, she called out to him, but the words were lost in the music. He guessed she was tiring. Still she danced on, and on. Finally, the drum was silent, the dance over. Soon the myth ended as well, finishing with a song.

Everyone gathered around the fire. Here Chamise left her name behind and presented herself as Talon. With offerings of words and gifts that held special meaning, each person greeted Talon. Our words centered on transformation, her coming years, and the coming-of-age ritual, and we spoke of life's mystery. Each offering was unique, yet the main message was clear: "We are aware of the changes taking place in you. These changes are profound. We are with you. We honor you." We closed the circle singing and went to sleep near the fire.

V. Celebration

The next morning everyone awoke at dawn to plunge into the cold river. We then played games in the woods and sat down to a celebratory feast. As we gathered to share food, we sang a simple, joyful song that acknowledged and celebrated each person there.

VI. Thanking

The myth's ending song was of thanks to the Great Spirit, the Earth, and all life. It was simple, clearly articulated, and the result of caring attention.

After the feast, we formed a closing circle. Speaking from the heart, Tom and I thanked each friend for the gift of their presence and caring. We, too, gave thanks to Nature, the Earth, and to life.

♦ In Retrospect

Since the ritual nine months ago, we have had time for reflection. The transition to our daughter's new name was surprisingly easy for our family. However, when anyone refers to Talon as "Talon" when speaking of the time before the ritual she firmly corrects them, "That was Chamise, not me!" Talon also says that her own first birthday is approaching. If Tom or I use a discarded label or behavior, she vehemently reminds us that the behavior is no longer a part of her. Talon says that Chamise is in a faraway place and sends word now and then. She is doing fine and never sleeps in the same place twice. When asked if Chamise will ever return, the answer is "no."

Shortly after the ritual, Tom asked Talon what she had called out to him during the dance. Her surprising reply was: "Faster!"

It is difficult to describe the completeness and correctness we felt through the enactment of Chamise's ritual. As parents and co-explorers, we experienced a depth of understanding and surrender that seemed to touch the core of our being. The ritual pierced the sentimental aspects of our parenting. We are less attached to our identity as "parent." With that detachment comes a deeper sense of connection to Talon and through it, to the whole of humanity. The ritual has allowed us to glimpse the true meaning of the parent/child dance.

Maturing in the High Country: A Coming-of-Age Ritual

Our first Natural Learning Rhythms workshop was given to members of our community, who live on northern California's San Juan Ridge. Two of the families attending had boys between thirteen and fifteen years old. After the workshop, these families decided to have a combined coming-of-age ritual for their boys.

The boys agreed, with the condition that they could each ask a friend to join. In the end, four boys and their families were ready to participate.

Over the course of three months we held a total of five meetings with the boys and their fathers to plan the ritual. They liked the idea of marking the passage into maturity, which they could easily recognize was occurring. Yet they did not know why intensive discipline had to be incorporated. None of their friends were having a ritual, and they felt singled out and odd. Many of the grown-ups' suggestions on how to conduct the ritual didn't fit the boys' preconceived ideas. For instance, the boys found themselves both attracted to and repelled by the possibility of experiencing non-ordinary reality.

Nor did the boys fully understand the intent of the ritual. Proceeding cautiously and patiently, we explained that a ritual is designed to aid the passage from one way of perceiving "reality" to another. The suggested ritual disciplines were aimed at stimulating the boys to find new resources *within themselves*. These tools would help them in dealing with a new more mature and more complex relationship to their world.

As the planning progressed, each boy, in his own way, expressed the desire to leave behind the "kid" inside. Each wanted to assure himself of his new power and maturity. As elders, it was important to point out that the "kid" had been with them for fourteen years, and was not going to simply disappear on command. Their fathers gently reminded their sons of recent occasions when the boys had acted like kids and were sorry for their actions later. These examples included relationships with girls, whining and complaining, and improper handling of valued tools.

Now eager to move forward, the boys readily acknowledged the truth in their dads' examples. We then asked the boys how they intended to transcend their "kid-ness." They didn't know. Together, we tried to solve the question. One of the dads did research on coming-of-age rites from other cultures and times. As he related his findings to the group, the use of disciplines such as fasting, maintaining silence, and long hikes—all of which inhibit the childlike part of the participant from obstructing the passage—became obvious to everyone. By the third meeting, the boys agreed that such disciplined practices were necessary.

We designed a model for the boys' ritual and explained to it all participants. In each meeting, aspects of it were modified. Though the final plan bore some resemblance to the original, every person had placed his or her unique stamp upon it. For example, a long hike from the base camp to the top of a mountain, was originally to have been made in silence. At the following meeting, we changed the silence to chanting. In the final version of the plan, we agreed to do part of the hike in silence, then have a long "sweat" when we returned.

A sweat is a Native American custom. Traditionally, sweats have had many functions, most importantly purification and spiritual practice. The sweat takes place in a lodge that holds heat; the lodge may be permanent or temporary, large or small. In a firepit outside the lodge, rocks are heated to very high temperatures, then brought inside. There, ceremonial participants sit inside sharing stories or singing songs of encouragement. Everyone behaves according to a ceremonial etiquette.

Calmly, and in considerable detail, our group discussed the possibility of experiencing non-ordinary reality in anticipation of the ritual day. "Safety nets" were devised to mitigate the boys' natural fear of entering the unknown alone. Quiet, non-moralistic statements reminded them that realizing a strong, meaningful relationship to their own individuality required some contact with the extraordinary. There was no attempt to explain the mystery at the heart of existence. Slowly, the boys saw that the ritual intended to allow access to, rather than definition of, the non-ordinary.

Over the ensuing weeks the boys' attitude changed. First, they were moved by their families' commitment to them. Also the challenge was appealing. The boys felt connected to an initiation tradition that transcended time and place. Two wanted new names. They were interested in experiencing the effects of the ritual modifications they had instituted. By the day of the ritual, a mutually supportive enthusiasm, still tinged with fear, prevailed.

The morning arrived and we were driven to the high country of the Sierra Nevada mountains. Our party consisted of myself (Ba), the four boys, and their dads. Josette was to have a special role that required her to rendezvous with the boys on the third morning.

From the head of the trail, our party climbed to five thousand feet and camped by a lake. On the way up, one of the dads instructed the boys in the use of topographical maps and the compass. Other than that, there was no formal structured activity.

After arranging camp we collectively built the sweat lodge. Using three well-placed trees, rope, and plastic tarps, the lodge was just big enough for the nine people. We would place sleeping bags over the plastic the next afternoon when the lodge was to be used. The boys went to find suitable rocks for heating, and placed them by the fire pit, along with a supply of firewood.

135

For the four initiates, this was their last day as boys. They had freedom to act as they liked. Accordingly, they chose a game to include everyone. The boys were on one team, the men on another. One team hid while the other tried to find them. The goal was to reach a centrally located base before being discovered. Everyone played with the abandon of small children.

Dinner consisted of vegetable soup. The boys tried to catch fish to feed everyone. Tired from the afternoon's climb, we went to bed at ten, the boys sleeping near each other. Excited and a bit nervous about the events awaiting them the next day, they talked long into night.

Everyone awoke at five in the morning and had tea for breakfast. By six, we were all on the way to the top of the Buttes, looming geological formations over eight thousand feet above sea level. The last hour of the climb, over narrow trails of loose rock with precipitous drops on either side, was done in silence. Upon reaching the top, each of the dads found a private niche to sit in with his son. Using a drum I had brought along, I kept a steady beat. The dads spoke about bringing up their boys, particularly noting any problems they felt had not been resolved.

They asked forgiveness of their sons. They questioned if there were any resentments the boys were holding, and asked forgiveness again. The boys also asked forgiveness for mistakes they had committed. After half an hour everyone finished. Our group sat on the top of the world, drank water, and resumed casual conversation.

The descent from the Buttes was joyful. Glissading down large patches of remnant snow, drinking from glacial lakes, and tramping through fields of wild flowers, the group arrived back in camp around three in the afternoon. We lit the fire. When the rocks became red hot everyone entered the sweat lodge.

A "round" in a sweat lodge consists of remaining in the lodge until one cannot bear the heat, then immersing oneself in cold water. During the first round, the men instructed the initiates in sweat lodge procedure. Each person felt the strain of the two-day hike, and the lack of food and sleep melt away in the dry heat.

The second round was devoted to each elder speaking about sexuality. Moralizing was minimized. Men told of the evolution of their sexual identities. They described their current sexual choices and the values they held. At first the boys were shy and embarrassed, but by the time the third man spoke they were keenly interested. For the last thirty minutes they listened with complete attention.

The third sweat round consisted of the youngsters asking questions and the grown-ups answering them. Sexuality remained the chosen topic. An hour passed, and everyone baked and finally retired for a long swim in the lake.

It was sunset. Tea was served. Each initiate searched for the spot in which they would spend the night alone. The men prepared the evening fire. We would keep it going for the whole of the night.

The dads embraced their sons. This was the last time they would see them as boys. The initiates went to their respective areas. The fire was lit, and the drumming started. The elders chanted, sang, meditated; spoke their hearts about children, family, friendship, and community. A late moon hung low in the sky. From time to time I visited those young men not practicing complete isolation.

Dawn came slowly. When the sun finally appeared the boys coming of age returned. Speaking directly to the fire each young man first stated his name; then, if he chose, his vision. When the last young man had finished, the dads greeted their son by name. They embraced, and then everyone embraced. I served tea.

The newly initiated young men led the way down the mountain by themselves. By plan, they were to meet Josette at a waterfall a short way off the trail. When they arrived each stated his name. Josette greeted them, representing Woman. She welcomed them into their manhood. For some time she spoke of the needs and desires of women, giving the young men some idea of what to expect and how to act with women as they grew older. Most of the time, however, she was answering their many questions.

When the fathers, sons, Josette, and I came off the mountain, the mothers and siblings were waiting in a field. A light meal was shared, our first solid food in over fifty hours. Then everyone headed for one of the families' homes for a community-wide celebration. There, a feast with music and dance went on for many hours. At appointed times during the night, each young man gave a short speech of thanks.

In the days following the rite, the young men did not say much about their experience beyond a general term of approval—that it was "far out." It seemed that they were a little stunned by the intensity of the previous four days. As the first in their community to undergo a coming-of-age rite of passage, they were unsure how to react to the many questions put to them by friends and neighbors.

137

Over the course of the next several weeks they revealed more of their experiences to us. One young man had shivered with fear for several hours as he went through the night of complete isolation. Sometime in the depth of the very early morning hours he willed himself to stop his fear. A calm descended. He felt the power to take control of his life. For the rest of the night he gazed at the stars, feeling interconnected with the universe as new confidence to meet the challenges of his future flooded his awareness.

Another young man spoke with gratitude about the sexual discussion that took place in the sweat, and with Josette. It relieved much of his anxiety as to how to approach his own sexuality and how to relate to women. He realized that he needn't rush into a relationship because of the status it might give him with his male friends. This young man also had a very hard time during his night alone. At first, he couldn't accept the intensity he felt when continually chanting. When I visited him in the middle of the night I had gently guided him into a state of calm and focus. He spent the rest of the night experiencing surges of energy in his body, which he liked, but he had no deep vision about his life. This frustrated him and a couple of weeks later, there was still some negative emotional residue. He believed that if he could have centered on his own, he would have been granted a vision. I visited him several times in the following two weeks. As he talked, he saw that the ritual had revealed much about his strengths and weaknesses to him. One weakness was an excessive dependence on his mother, undoubtedly due to the death of his biological father when he was young. He was able to bring this up to her, and together they redefined their relationship. Before long he appreciated the many subtle lessons in his rite of passage. To this day, four years later, he speaks of it as the best experience of his life.

A third young man had been having heart-wrenching difficulties with his entire family, especially his father. These difficulties continued during the ritual. His father had tried to alter his plan to meditate all night. Each of them had little to say during the forgiveness ceremony, though they had much to forgive one another. Disparaging looks from the father to this young man during the sweat inhibited many of his sexual questions. In later discussion, I found out he had many wild sexual fantasies of which he was both fascinated and afraid. Therefore it was not surprising that this young man spent all of his alone night agonizing over his family relationships. By the morning he decided to "go it alone" because, he said, "I can't expect my dad to do anything my way." Within six months he moved in with an aunt who lived close to the high school he attended.

The fourth young man has remained mostly quiet about the ritual. He says every part of it was valuable to him, and the night he spent in complete isolation was a mind-altering experience. The noticeable changes in his life are subtle: an increased acceptance of responsibility in school, family relationships, and household chores.

Special Features of the Coming-of-Age Ritual

Every young person needs a coming-of-age ritual. Unless her right and responsibility to be an individual is wholly acknowledged, her development will likely be frustrated. The early teens are years of Will-Being energy, of fiery becoming, of personal assertion. It is a time when ideals are formulated and explored, when a construction of reality is undertaken and defended. Turbulence dominates biologically and psychologi-

cally; it is a rapids in the river of life. Any seeds of inter-generational conflict sowed in earlier years will sprout and quickly grow unless parents
can provide ballast in these rapids. A coming-of-age ritual is an excellent
way to provide that ballast, to dance with your child as she goes through
some of the most radical changes in a human being's becoming.

The coming-of-age ritual rite of passage for the child in Will-Being has
several unique features. To honor the child's need for sensitive respect
there can be no secrets. Everyone plans together, knows what is to happen and why those choices were made. Wherever possible the young
people participate in the decisions. If they devise a way to accomplish an
aim that is different from the elder's, that way should be honored as long
as the aim is accomplished: In the previous case of the four young men,
for instance, they voted down a morning of silence in favor of a sweat.

An offering from the young people to those who have helped them
through childhood should be part of the celebration. Individually or collectively, a dance, play, song, or speech works well. This offering should
be as expertly done as possible with considerable rehearsal, perhaps
over several months: In the previous story, the simple thanking comments made by the young men at the ritual's celebration did *not* constitute a quality expression of this feature. As a result, many of their family
and community members failed to appreciate how profound the four
days had been for the young men. The celebration was merely a party.
The young men were not deeply acknowledged as young men.

Only a parent prepared to let go of the child and welcome the young
woman or man can aid the coming-of-age. Forgiveness must be at the
heart of the moment; specific forgiveness ceremonies can be included as
well. Sexuality must also be addressed, for this child is now capable of
creating children of his own. If that deep and obvious change is not acknowledged, the ritual loses credibility. Ritual rites of passage provide
the opportunity for one of the most glorious dance steps of all. In the
coming-of-age ritual, the parent has the opportunity to speak her sexual
truth, and grow from the risk that entails. Frank exposure of sexual
attitudes provides the healthy basis for future conversations on the subject for both parent and child.

Who should be present at the ritual? Should there be contact with an
elder of the opposite sex? Some say no, believing that the purpose of
coming-of-age rite is for the child to realize his manhood or her woman-
hood, and that the opposite sex only "gets in the way." In his book *Boy*

into Man, for instance, author Bernard Weiner indicates that for boys' ritual rites of passage, mothers are to be left behind.

We disagree. On what grounds? Simply, to include both sexes is more balanced. Men have a feminine aspect inherent in their nature and women have a masculine aspect inherent in theirs. Josette met the young men in the ritual context as Woman. Maintaining confidentiality, she answered their questions. She modeled and mirrored their feminine side.

There are many ways to enhance the coming-of-age ritual. Include a ceremony with a trusted teenager that focuses on the initiate's expectations of the next five years. Have the ritual guide lead a discussion on issues timely to the child's life. Use masks and costumes. After the acknowledgement of the new self, but before the initiate reenters "society," carry out the thanking ceremony.

Well-conceived gifts add to the meaning of this ritual; they both acknowledge the young person's new level of maturity and leave him with a material reminder of the ritual experience. They should always be of high quality and useful in the young person's life. Such gifts were missing at the coming-of-age ritual for the four boys, and this ultimately detracted from the value of the celebration.

In the ritual rite of passage, *cultural relevancy* is a must. It is *you* designing the ritual according to *your* place and time The language, both symbolic and verbal, should come from your life; it will never be the same for any other person in any other time, for change is a constant part of life Teenagers particularly strive to establish their identity in their culture, asserting their individuality. Meet their need directly. Let the rit ual arise in the context of their life and lifestyle

A Body-Being Ritual Rite of Passage

Our aim in this book is to empower you to create ritual rites of passage for your own family. Many people flinch when they first encounter this aspect of Natural Learning Rhythms. They've never had or participated in an authentic ritual, and they are unsure how to do so

We have studied, designed, and led many rituals, and because it may be helpful to parents, we'd like to relate the process by which a group of people at a recent workshop developed an entirely new ritual rite of passage. Their assignment was to design a ritual for a child in Body-Being,

They were free to choose this child's family and living situation. The ritual had only to be responsive to the child's natural learning rhythms.

As we've discussed, Body-Being children receive and transmit information through sensation. Their body is their primary tool of communication, and loving touch is the most important food for the parent to provide for the health of Body-Being's child. The workshop participants chose a child transiting from Body-Being's trial and error phase to competency. Any parent will recognize this moment, which usually occurs between three-and-a-half and four-and-a-half. At this time the child is capable in all the primary coordinations. She can run, get the food to her mouth, use the bathroom, and verbally interact with the general public. A burst of energy and confidence permeates all her interactions.

The workshop participants chose to create a ritual rite of passage for a child from a rural area who had some ability to swim. The ritual begins with family and close friends going into the cold river as winter turns into spring. They enter only as far as the child usually does. The parents are to say, "This is as far as you usually go into the river." This statement constitutes an acknowledgment of the old. Then, while taking a long climb to a higher part of the river, the child is told what awaits her. This begins the process of casting off the old.

At this new part of the river, they reach a rope swing. The child has been here before, but she's never used the swing. The elders enter the waters and form a circle. The father or mother picks up the child, swings her over the circle, and drops the child in the middle. The picking up and swinging constitute the end of the casting off and the beginning of the GAP. When let go, the child is in the GAP.

The circle closes quickly and the elders pick the child up. If she's small enough, they cheer and lift her over their heads. Then they all go to shore and have a feast. The child is then presented with a high-quality nature exploration tool, such as a fine compass. She is told how she will be taught to use this tool. This series both acknowledges and celebrates the new. The thanking is lighthearted and informal, for that ingredient is of minimal importance for a child of this age.

With the completion of the ritual, the child will have a much greater sense of herself as competent in her body, which is crucial since she will spend the next two to three years exploring body-as-environment. She knows she can trust her elders. She can engage the world. She is in

141

touch with her center, her wisdom. The requirements of both ritual rites of passage and human development have been met.

As an exercise, design rituals for your own children. Also, see if you can create different meaningful rituals for each of the developmental life stages. By doing so you can make the Natural Learning Rhythms' key concepts come alive for you. By inspiring and celebrating the child with time-honored traditions, we help him make sense of major changes in his life within an environment of support and acknowledgment.

Remedies

Restoring Balance

What do you do when you get sick? If you're like most people, you gather information and make a diagnosis, then assess your personal repertoire of remedies, and finally choose one you will use. You may opt for bed rest with a cup of hot tea and lemon, a change in diet, or a long ocean cruise. You're trying to restore balance to your system according to the remedies you know.

Our personal repertoire of remedies for illness is a result of what we've learned from our family, friends, school, independent research, and our own experience. When these resources do not work and our health does not seem to be returning, we usually turn to a physician.

What is a physician? A physician is a human being who possesses wider knowledge than we do in three main areas: She knows more about physical symptoms of diseases, understands their underlying causes, and has a larger selection of responses to illness.

Expertise notwithstanding, more and more physicians now recognize how important it is for each individual to take as much responsibility for his health as possible. They know that when the patient is actively involved in the healing process, the chances of a successful treatment are much higher than when he accepts a passive role, expecting to be healed by the doctor. This is not so surprising: Anytime we, as individuals, consciously focus our energy on a goal, the chances of achieving it multiply.

From healthcare manuals to magazine features and television documentaries, we are surrounded on all sides with information intended to increase our store of responses to illness. We add this data to our present knowledge to compose the best remedy.

By the very same method, we can refine our prescriptive capabilities and increase our personal repertoire of remedies in restoring balance to our own children or troubled families. For parents and teachers, Natural Learning Rhythms begins with a basic diagnostic insight: The child who displays a "dysfunction" is actually a child who has not had his developmental needs met. When these children aren't "heard," their inherent stage-specific wisdom resorts to more desperate behaviors to make their needs known. In our years of working with families, we've never encountered a behavioral "dysfunction" whose purpose wasn't to point out some critical need of the child.

Because these behaviors are not dysfunctional at all, but rather are indicators of a state of malaise in the family, we prefer to call them *manifestations*. More often than not, the child's manifestation points us to an imbalance in someone else, or it indicates the way other family members are relating unsuccessfully to her or to each other. As we shall soon see, rebalancing must occur in the whole family to be effective.

Manifestations are analogous to medical symptoms; they indicate the existence of a disease. When we increase our understanding of the causes, as well as our knowledge of remedies, we can make great strides in healing ourselves. As an analogy, consider the current interest in the fiber content of our diet. Until recently, it was not commonly known that a lack of fiber was one of the main causes of cancer of the colon and heart ailments. Now that the news is out, we've expanded our set of remedial responses to include the intake of high-fiber foods. Indeed, there's a plethora of new foods and cookbooks aimed at making high quantities of fiber readily ingestible. This said, there will still be a number of people whose health cannot be remedied by a high-fiber diet. These people have been too long without a healthy diet and must now turn to medical interventions. Nevertheless, the fact that some have passed the point where high-fiber intake might have been a help does not invalidate the importance of fiber, and ought not to dissuade us from including more of it in our diets.

We've learned to make lines between diet and disease. We must look at behavioral dysfunction in children in the same way.

Threats and lack of security in Body-Being are two of the underlying causes of excessive stubbornness and submissiveness in very young children. If we eliminate threats and increase the child's experience of security, many children will have no need to manifest these behaviors. Knowing this, the next natural step is to design a remedy. This chapter is intended to help all of us to do just that.

To reiterate, there are indeed a small number of children so off-balance due to lack of security that our expanded prescriptions will not help. Their families will need to find professional help. Still, the number of severely damaged children is far fewer than one might imagine, so gently try the remedial steps you read in this chapter first. Time and again, we've seen impressive instances of healing that occur right within the family.

Parents as Practitioners

We acknowledge that certain types of imbalance may call for more professional help. We make part of our living providing that help. But we are certain that aware parents, practicing Natural Learning Rhythms alone and in groups, can expand their repertory of remedies to the vast majority of what are commonly labeled "childhood dysfunctions."

How can we be so certain? For more than a decade we have worked with thousands of parents, teachers, and children, alone and in groups, who have clearly demonstrated to us their ability to restore balance. It is these parents and teachers and children who have expanded our own repertoire of remedies. With this book, we try to pass on to you what they have made available to us through their collective experience.

A Healing Attitude

A remedy's efficacy greatly depends upon the attitude of the person administering it. In his excellent book, *The Healing Brain,* Robert Ornstein shows that a person's expectations determine her responsiveness to any medicine—pharmaceutical or psychological. If we believe a healing method will work, the possibility of it working increases dramatically.

For children, parents and respected elders are the single most important factor in their environment. If the parents demonstrate a healing attitude, the child will acclimate to the healing atmosphere; she will be receptive to the remedy. The proper remedy must be chosen, and that depends primarily on the parents' developmental understanding and observation of the child and family. A healthy attitude on the part of the parents means, first and foremost, that we meet the "dietary" require- ments of the child.

Good communication is a major component of that attitude. It supports the idea that "we're all in this together." Taking in and passing on infor- mation about the problem in a respectful way boosts the effectiveness of any remedy. Besides good communication, a healthy attitude has four more facets: inclusion, creative conflict, humility, and humor.

Inclusion

An *inclusionary* life-style—one that acknowledges the child's vital role in family harmony—reminds all family members that the problem belongs to the whole family, and not solely to the individual manifesting it. A remedy administered in such an environment has an excellent chance of working. The child who believes she is integral to the well- being of the family knows that remedies are intended for the good of all.

It's important to include children from as early an age as possible. One family gave the job of emptying the plastic recycling container to their two-year-old, Owen. Of course, a parent always helped the toddler with his job, but the container was rarely emptied without him. If Owen was sick or otherwise occupied, his parents brought in more buckets to hold the recyclable material. When Owen was able to do the job again, empty- ing the buckets was a celebration of his return.

Many parents also fear asking their teenagers to participate in family decisions and responsibilities. Confronted by Will-Being's dynamic assertiveness, defense of personal space, and attachment to peers, the parents may lose confidence in the child's ability to make decisions— and lose out on the value of Will-Being's wisdom. They may see the child's idealistic assertions as "immature" or "unrealistic," even as they note the child's dramatic physical changes and new-found strength. Other times parents may believe their child to be grown and, intimi- dated by the fact, back down when the child resists their inclusionary efforts. Unwilling to "fight" their child, they simply leave her out, thereby letting resentment build on both sides.

But Will-Being's child loves to be included. She just doesn't want to be told what to do, and she has to resist in order to experiment with individual freedom. Neither of these reactions need be fatal to inclusion.

We learned this one summer when we lived with two fourteen-year-old girls, our daughter and her friend. Because school was out and the girls were responsible, we set a midnight curfew, feeling we were being quite generous. Be that as it may, not long afterward, the girls broke the curfew and sneaked out of the house. When we later inquired why they had done it, they answered, "Just for the thrill." We were perplexed. "What's the problem?" we asked. "We weren't included," they replied. The message was clear. We realized we had to start all over again. "What would be a fair curfew?" we asked them. Surprisingly, the girls replied, "Eleven o'clock." And they kept this curfew for the rest of the summer.

Creative Confrontation

Making humble, straightforward contact with our children in a moment of distress reminds all family members that they are connected to each other and to nature. Through our words and actions, we keep the focus on the bonds between us. It might be through regular family meetings, or by maintaining contact during a child's tantrum, or with a simple inquiry such as, "How does your action affect other family members?" But one way or another, we don't let expressions of separation and disconnection pass.

Lack of balance, what we sometimes call "wobbling," manifests itself in, among other things, a sense of separateness, abandonment, or lost connection. Children find this sense of isolation particularly scary, since they are dependent on their family for both physical and emotional security. Without a sense of security, it is difficult for the child to experience the fullness of his inherent stage-specific wisdom. Creative confrontation keeps this sense of separateness at bay. The child's fear of abandonment finds no room to grow. Feeling connected to his family, he is eager to participate in the restoration of balance.

To bring attention to a problem, the child sometimes provokes confrontation in the family, either consciously or unconsciously. Usually he is trying to allow the family to reconnect in ways that nourish his own development. Giving his perceptions a "voice" representation makes them more manageable. Because confrontation itself is loaded with risk—the child may make himself vulnerable to the displeasure of his parents—clearly, he must perceive himself in dire need of connection. The parent's task is to honor this expression by attempting to discover the need that prompted it. The parent needs to create appropriate responses to the need, not punish the child for being confrontive.

As parents, we cannot step out of boundaries of gentleness when practicing creative confrontation: Harshness will only ruin the process. Children easily digest consistent, low-key reminders. The aim in the guidance we offer is, as always, empowerment. For a child, to say "I did it myself" is the most empowering statement of all.

The tools for communication gained in the last chapter apply to the practice of creative confrontation as well:

♦ **Vocabulary that is developmentally appropriate works best.**

♦ **Undivided attention and listening without prejudice revitalizes the commitment to each other, in the midst of confrontation.**

♦ **The integration aspect of communication—keeping in mind the child, her message, and that message's effect on us—keeps us in the present moment, directly leading us to the most creative way to engage the child during the conflict.**

Humility

The fastest way to become friends with a child is to let her knock you over—literally. It's quite all right to fake the fall. For the child, the important thing is the grown-up's willingness to *come down to her level*. That indeed is the definition of humility; to see oneself as equal in wisdom and importance to the child.

The parent's or teacher's ability to admit he is wrong and correct his mistakes is a key component of humility. We all make mistakes. By surrendering our self-importance in our relationship with the child, solid understanding grows.

Remedies ought not to be mystical concoctions handed down by revered authorities; they should be natural acts shared by the whole family. Implemented with an attitude of humility, these remedies honor the child as opposed to those that simply "happen" to the child. While severe psychoses may require a cure "handed down from on high," most of the problems besetting families do not. We can heal our own injuries, and see to it that they not recur.

Humor

When applying remedies, humor has special significance. A light-hearted, playful approach brings a sort of light and spaciousness into the gloom of family difficulties. By reducing logic from a religion to a tool, humor opens us to seeing balances we never considered. When we laugh, we want to join. When we join the people with whom we laugh, we are willing to explore and grow together, and to find remedies to our collective problems.

Different people approach humor in different ways; what's funny to one is not funny to all. I (Ba) tell teaching stories that bore everyone, but occasionally they produce laughs. Other people are avid punsters. Still others embellish comical stories from their childhood. Here's a teaching story that I used to break the ice in a rigid public school classroom where I came to speak about discipline and cooperative learning environments.

149

> Mullah Nusruddin, a Sufi teacher, was said to have lived in Persia in the eighth century. One day, Nusruddin was hired to drive ten donkeys to a neighboring village. He rode one and drove the rest. About halfway along the dusty road, he decided to count the donkeys to make sure none had wandered away. Counting only nine, the Mullah panicked. He jumped off the animal he was riding and counted again. This time there were ten. Muttering to himself, but relieved, he remounted and started off. Further down the hot dusty road he grew suspicious and counted again. There were only nine donkeys. Angry, he dismounted, counted, and sure enough, the donkeys again numbered ten. This time he decided he would not be fooled. He walked, driving all the donkeys in front of him.

> Arriving at the village covered with dust, the animals' owner asked Nusruddin how he had fared. "Just fine," the Mullah answered petulantly, "as soon as I got used to those blasted donkey tricks."

When the children hear such a story, I am no longer a distant authority, and they are freer to express their views about my talk that follows.

In summary, each group and family has a natural, unique expression of right attitude. A mix of inclusion, creative confrontation, humility, and humor works best. Because each of these facets generates great health and growth, finding the right blend is an enjoyable experience for each member of the group or family.

The Remedies Chart

On the next page you will find a comprehensive chart describing some of the remedies we have classified. We have based them on actual successes with families and children in our fieldwork.

This Remedies Chart presents very specific responses to many of the troubles children and families experience. Please study the chart carefully while reading the following sections. Among them you may find familiar remedies—ones you have already come to on your own. The manifestations (or symptoms) described in the chart are some of those observed by parents and teachers practicing Natural Learning Rhythms. The remedies prescribed for particular manifestations represent only some of the options available. In every workshop, new remedies come to light.

For the parent or teacher, developing appropriate remedies depends first on observing the child and second on fully understanding the family environment. The Remedies Chart is intended to be a guidepost in that search. Understanding Natural Learning Rhythms means knowing that every situation calls for a unique combination of remedies. Each family can discover the ones that best apply to their own dilemmas.

The Character Traits

The human heart looks very different in a four-year-old child than in a forty-year-old adult, yet its basic form remains recognizable. As with the physical organs of the body, the human psyche undergoes radical changes over time, yet its overall components and form remain intact. We call these components *character traits*. Each child is born with her own unique blend of these traits, and each child's character traits respond to the unique circumstances of her life.

We have identified six principal character traits, which are listed in the left-hand column of the chart. The balanced expression of each trait will

REMEDIES

MALFUNCTIONING CHARACTER TRAIT	BODY-BEING – Loving Touch		EMOTIONAL-BEING – Right Modeling		WILL-BEING – Sensitive respect		REASONING-BEING – Mature Recognition	
	Manifestation	Remedy	Manifestation	Remedy	Manifestation	Remedy	Manifestation	Remedy
BELONGINGNESS *Strength*	Major Breakdown— Stubborn, wishy-washy. Over-territorial or under-protective of body, family, or home.	Restructure the environment. Reorganize family relationships. Gardening, pets, scheduling, eliminate threats of all types.	Jealousy, sullen attachment to organized religion, hero worship, abuse of body.	Charity work, inspirational teenager or elder; improve parental models, supply non-romantic sexual information.	Holding on to childhood. Violent attitude toward objects and institutions, self pity.	Challenges in nature, apprenticeships. Connection with global politics.	Body disease, obsessive interest in specialized area (usually of expertise). Complete identification with peer group; defensive of body, attitude, and/or country. Inability to evaluate social and/or economic situation.	Expose to new or experimental environment. Explain and compare study of body, attitude, frank conversations about sex.
REPPESCTIVE *Discrimination*	Repeated life-endangering incidents. Lack of awareness of effects of contacts.	Non-threatening challenges, observation and interaction with animals, supervised peer play, coordination games.	Disrespectful of people and things, senseless flash moods, inability to listen.	Inspirational stories of wise people. Elder accepts restriction for disrespect shown by the child, i.e., older fasts if child forgets to feed pets. Supervised peer play, modeling assessment of situations.	Domineering, bravado or bullying. Careless in nature.	"Hard tasks" within the realm of success, nature, charity work. Engage project of child's ideas.	Major Breakdown— Loneliness, general impotence, unable to see value of investigation or to consider lifes meaning.	Travel, undertake extensive examination into area of difficulty, i.e., loneliness, if possible, contact with intelligent elders, placing child in situations in which he must make critical choices, stimulation of the child's ideals.
AUTONOMY *Humility*	Unable to explore. Unkind to peers and siblings. Unable to find right place. Exhibitionism.	Guided exploration. Contact with sensitive, older child. Rearrange flexibility parameters. Share responsibility. Building Activities.	Over-attachment to parents (especially mother); attempt to limit peers, afraid of nature. Wishing for a power (or to give up to a power) that will cure all ills, exhibitionism.	Inspirational exploration stories, guided exploration by a trusted teenager; travel.	Excessive need to prove independence, arrogance, wimpishness. Defensive attachment to institutions, hero worship.	Grounded apprenticeship, challenges in nature or athletics. Making space safe and then encouraging individual or small-group exploration.	Lack of initiative, concern with the dull and repetitive, repulsed by the breadth of human endeavor and the investigation thereof, day-dreamer, flights of unrealistic or even harmful fantasy.	Direct experience of the deep guide within through contact with a consciousness accelerator, travel, charity work, examination of psychology, of nature and/or the human race in nature.
INCISIVENESS *Fearlessness*	Restlessness, ineptness in relationship to own body and objects, unsure in nature, cruelty.	Check role models. Nature and animals, right peer stimulation. Supported exploration, hugs and physical support	Hard to make friends, unable to trust oneself or others, lying, cruelty.	Check role models, nature, clarity work, controlled peer group, respected elder.	Lying, patriotism, attachment to symbols, infliction of punishment, ineffectual definition of personal space, self pity.	Strong challenges, or few challenges, (depending on the individual and situation) adventure, travel, charity work.	Unable to search for meaning in life, unable to follow through on investigation began, undue submission to peer group, uncomfortable with the opposite sex.	Charity work, travel, examination of human potential, encouragement and guidance in sexual encounter, simulation of the decision-making process, intellectual or idealistic project mutually engaged by child and elder.
ECOLOGY *Interconnectedness*	Unprotective of own life, clumsy and fear filled in nature, not in tune with everyday environment	Lots of quiet nature time, cooperative games, pets, allow contact with infants.	Major breakdown – Lack of feel for glory and wonder and beauty, insensitive toward animals, overly egocentric.	Pets, lots of time in nature, quiet small-group nature games, infants, music, constant reminders of the cycles of nature, nature films. Cooperative games.	Self-righteousness, delight in conquering, identification with predator or prey, immature sense of balance and justice.	Time in nature with adventuresome naturalist, charity work, travel, exploration of grandest natural natural wonders.	Superficial and self-centered, immature perspective of the meaning of nature, fear of nature and the future, obsessive toward specially rather than interest in the whole system, weapon-oriented.	Science, music, art, cybernetic, time in nature with rigorous examination thereof, deep inquiry into self, caring sexual contact.
HONESTY *Humor*	Lack of enthusiasm, unwillingness to explore, defensive, not wanting to be touched.	Nature, pets, hugs, caressing, engagement of the body at all times, care-filled scrutiny and interaction. Tells lots of jokes.	Suspiciousness, morbidness, sarcasm, sneakiness.	Charity work, situations of trusted elders & peers, cooperative games and endeavors, increased supervised responsibilities, tell lots of jokes and expose to humor.	Sarcasm, very defensive of personal space, cruel, loneliness, lack of faith in self, society, and life, humor at the expense of others.	Apprenticeships, nature, challenges, care of the young, care of animals, continued modeling of friendship, support child to find own humorous situations, engaging entire peer group in project that accords with their ideals.	Sarcasm, uncomfortable with self-animation, suspicious, believe rather than examiner, humor at the expense of others.	Exploration of the value of honesty, repeated exposure to genuinely funny situations, travel, lovers, insistence on risk-taking, contact with intuitively awake people.

Vertical text in central column: STRONG PUBERTY RITUAL

vary from family to family, from child to child, and from stage to stage. There are, however, certain constant qualities in each trait that give them each a unique value and meaning:

♦ **Belongingness/Strength:** The child's being in a secure relationship to all aspects of her world. She is where, and with whom, she is supposed to be. She is aware of and actively engages her natural talents and abilities.

♦ **Perspective/Discrimination:** The child's adeptness (within her developmental capabilities) at "seeing" the way her world works, and then "acting" on that seeing in a healthy way.

♦ **Autonomy/Humility:** The child's proficiency at interacting in a way that is respectful of herself, others, and her environment. She is comfortable being by herself and with others, and possesses accurate self-perception.

♦ **Incisiveness/Fearlessness:** The child's skill in appreciating the critical aspects of a specific event or environment. She can choose behaviors unencumbered by unnecessary fears of personal consequences.

♦ **Ecology/Interconnectedness:** The child's knowledge that she is part of a larger whole and what one part does affects all other parts.

♦ **Honesty/Humor:** The child's frank and sincere perceptions of the incongruities and peculiarities in life. When this trait is balanced, the child acknowledges the limitations inherent in her own development and those placed upon her by the culture.

Manifestations

Balanced character traits allow the child to access the deepest parts of her stage-specific wisdom. When the character traits fall out of balance, stage-specific wisdom contracts to defend the child's physical security; it can no longer serve the full developmental needs of the child.

Manifestations, commonly known as "problem behaviors," appear when a character trait is out of balance. The nature of the manifestation varies depending on the developmental stage of the child: During Body-Being, for example, a damaged Belongingness/Strength trait might manifest itself through extreme territoriality; during Emotional-Being, it might show up as jealousy; in Will-Being it might appear in the form of a violent attitude toward institutions.

On the Remedies Chart, a "malfunctioning character trait" refers to fairly severe manifestations. The classification "severe" depends on several factors: The behavior either appears to be extremely inappropriate to the child's context; a particular manifestation surfaces repeatedly; or several manifestations appear together. A manifestation is dysfunctional only when it inhibits growth or access to wisdom.

If we're unsure whether a given manifestation is indeed a malfunction, we must first attempt to correct the difficulties by restructuring the child's psychological diet. Is the Body-Being child, for example, getting an appropriate blend of warmth, security, flexibility, and nourishment? If the manifestations persist, we proceed to the remedies.

In our view, there are three necessary links to understanding the underlying causes of dysfunction in children:

♦ An appreciation of the character traits (through which we perceive the manifestation)

♦ A recognition of manifestations

♦ A knowledge of human development

153

Together, knowledge of the manifestations, the character traits, and human development lays the groundwork for determining the causes and origins of the troubles that beset our children.

Remedy or Therapy?

The remedies we've described on the chart are highly effective for many, many family problems. There are times, however, when therapy is appropriate. Everyone, for example, needs professional counseling in cases of child abuse, excessive violence, or when parents have exhausted all family-generated options. But as with surgery or high doses of antibiotics, therapy is often chosen prematurely out of desperation and ignorance

Many times therapy is not only unnecessary but adds to the family's problems through expenditure of time and money. In addition, therapy places a stigma on the child as the cause of the problem. Caring parents can do a lot to remedy family problems before jumping to therapy. Parents are the natural keynote for the consistent, long-term life work that true healing demands. Developmental stages unfold over the course of years. There is room for trial and error, and time to steadily bring the family into focus and balance.

Major Breakdowns

During each developmental life stage, there is a particular character trait whose balance is vital to the child's growth. If this critical trait malfunctions, all the other character traits become unbalanced as well. The traits particularly important to the four life stages are:

- ♦ Belongingness/Strength during Body-Being
- ♦ Ecology/Interconnectedness during Emotional-Being
- ♦ Autonomy/Humility during Will-Being
- ♦ Perspective/Discrimination during Reasoning-Being

Malfunctioning Honesty/Humor is a major breakdown whenever it occurs.

As we know, during Emotional-Being, the child's main challenge is to become aware of her own feelings and the feelings of others in her life. She expands into the marvel of nature. If she cannot *feel* nature or other people—if she loses her sense of interconnectedness—she cannot accomplish her primary task. As a parent or educator, what remedy would you use to help this child get back into her own natural learning rhythm? Let's make a detailed examination of the chart.

Know the Child's Personal History

The Natural Learning Rhythms system always works with the whole child, and so this must be the approach when considering remedies to family troubles too. A thorough familiarity with the child's personal history and present environment helps us know which remedies to choose and how to apply them. The child's family therefore possesses one of the most important tools for healing, for these immediate family members know the child's personal history better than anyone else.

Experiment

Go ahead and experiment. We've never heard of a case of a child being damaged because of a remedy attempt by his family. The fact that every remedy offered in this book is healthy for the child should give you the confidence to try out new ones. One remedy, for example, charity work, will awaken valuable feelings of interconnectedness in the child, even if it fails to dissolve the child's manifesting self-pity. One way or another, remedies based on the child's natural learning rhythms attune themselves to family harmony and empowerment.

As we experiment, our appreciation of the problem becomes more refined. Be prepared to modify or completely change your diagnosis. New remedies can then be created with increasing exactness. Be patient. Every attempt at restoring balance yields valuable clues into the nature of the malfunction and the best response to it. Careful observation of the remedy process and knowledge of the child's rhythm of growth will soon put you on the right track.

Though they do occur from time to time, don't expect overnight cures. Patient experimentation over time combined with knowledge of the child's personal history yields a rich portrait of the child as an individual and as a family member. Remedies, applied within this encompassing context, become a family expression.

A warning: Don't mistake *hesitancies* for *malfunctions*. Hesitancies are part of the child's natural developmental process. Remedies often meet resistance when applied to a hesitancy. Go slowly. If your child is at a prime hesitancy age, before calling her behavior a malfunction, take a look at the possibility that a hesitancy is occurring. Continue to experiment until you arrive at a satisfactory diagnosis.

Work from Strengths

The notion of constantly correcting a child in her "weak" areas is barbaric and cruel. Work from the child's strengths. Those areas are weak because of underlying problems. Picking at weaknesses reduces the child to unhelpful behavioral classifications: Some behaviors are labeled "good," others "bad." For the perspective of the child's growth, however, *every behavior has value and meaning in the context of her motiva-*

155

tions. A "why" exists for every action, no matter how unusual that behavior might seem to the parents.

Michelle, a mother of two, has a great respect for nature and found a brilliant solution to a problem with her ten-year-old son, Marcus. The boy was repeatedly cruel to animals. He drove the family dog crazy by tying objects to its tail, tried to drown the family cat, and trapped and mutilated birds. His mother was justifiably concerned, especially because her son's behavior pointed to a breakdown in Ecology/Interconnectedness during Emotional-Being.

Michelle's solution derived from her incisive consideration of her son's personal history. Marcus was very attached to other people. He always wanted to be with anyone with whom he could get along, especially relatives and friends in the community. So, Michelle recruited a trusted teenager, Terrance, to help. She explained the situation and asked Terrance to spend time with her son to help him rebalance. She never believed her son was "bad," and so this idea was not a part of her explanation to the older boy. Terrance grasped the situation quickly and was honored that he'd been asked to help.

Throughout the time he spent with Terrance, Marcus knew what his mother was doing. He had some reservations, but finally acceded to her requests. He also appreciated the teen's companionship. Michelle communicated frequently with Terrance and learned some of her son's frustrations centered on her divorce with his father, his feelings of rejection from his older brother and father, and his shyness in school. Keeping the teen connection alive, Michelle also enrolled her son in a small private school and several wilderness expeditions. Within a couple of months Marcus's manifestation was remedied.

Go through the Open Window

When applying remedies, work within the rhythm of the dominant developmental stage. Go through the open window; direct yourself to the current stage-specific wisdom, for it has the information necessary for the restoration of balance.

The genesis of Marcus' difficulties happened in Body-Being. His Belongingness/Strength trait was severely disrupted by his parents' divorce, and by the subsequent rejections by the older males in his life. Gardening, caring for pets, or reorganizing family relationships—some common remedies for Body-Being children—would have had only minimal impact on Marcus now that he is ten. As we've established, Emotional-Being works through feelings and is primarily concerned with "I and other": How do you feel about me, and how do I feel about you? Inspirational guidance in nature and contact with a respected teen will therefore speak much more directly to Marcus's inherent wisdom.

With its powerful appreciation of past and future, Reasoning-Being provides a last great opportunity for the young person to heal the wounds of childhood.

In a workshop in San Francisco, we described one powerful means of taking advantage of this precious moment. It is an event we call the Recapitulation Ceremony. In it, the parents and the nineteen-year-old child seclude themselves together for an entire weekend. The parents then explain to the youth the reasons for every important decision they made for the past nineteen years. They answer all the child's questions.

In the midst of our description, Gilberto, a thirty-year-old man, started crying.

> Don't worry," he assured us. "I'm crying from happiness. Five years ago I returned to Guatemala to see my family, probably for the last time. I had many resentments toward my father. When I told him of my feelings, he took me to a cabin in the mountains. For the whole weekend we shared in the way you just described. It was beautiful and my heart knew peace. Last month he died. I'm crying because I am very happy we parted with understanding.

Peter's Lesson

Eleven-year-old Peter, following the lead of his alcoholic father, behaved abusively toward females. He took pleasure in teasing and hitting his younger sister. When with other boys who were his peers, he would encourage them to exclude or put down other girls. When angry, he'd yell at and hit his mother.

Peter's mother, now divorced, sought to remedy the situation. She and her new boyfriend belonged to a Natural Learning Rhythms support group. After considering her history, the support group advised setting up situations in the home in which she and the boyfriend clashed. The boyfriend would then model non-abusive resolutions. To speed the process, the support group suggested discussing the clash and resolution immediately afterward with Peter.

This remedy and variations of it heal Perspective/Discrimination malfunctioning during Emotional-Being. We call it the Modeling Remedy. Peter's case shows one specific use for this remedy. And indeed, within a month, Peter's untoward behavior toward his mother and sister had dramatically improved.

Read the other remedies listed on the chart. Remember to give lots of support to your child while using the remedies. Don't expect too much. If she's displaying a manifestation, her consciousness is off balance. Include yourself as part of the malfunction and part of the remedy. A unified family accepts responsibility for the acts of each of its members. When we acknowledge that responsibility, we can move toward wholeness.

The parent support group was a tremendous help to Peter's family. By and large our culture lacks genuine community connection and intimate extended families. Much of the time we are expected to go to "experts" to restore family balance. Unfortunately, no matter how well educated or well intentioned, experts cannot supply the personal and confidential caring that informed community members can. When a community defines a child's family as that set of people actively working to supply her developmental needs, it instantaneously creates the requisite atmosphere of caring. Natural Learning Rhythms' support groups provide an ideal forum to voice our family concerns, and then to constructively engage in remedial actions. Such groups offer models to help rebuild our culture.

A Remedy Exercise

Here's the case history of a neighborhood child considered during a recent Natural Learning Rhythms support group meeting. Read the case carefully. Then, using the Remedies Chart and all the Natural Learning Rhythms information you've taken in thus far, devise a plan, as they did, to help the troubled child reconnect to deep stage-specific wisdom. Two hints: Try to ascertain which traits are malfunctioning, and work through the dominant developmental stage, even if the manifestation originated during earlier stages.

The group's remedy follows. Write your answer before reading theirs. Remember, by providing a healthy atmosphere through the use of the principles of a healthy attitude, there are no "wrong" answers.

The Case to Consider

Susan is ten. Her father and mother divorced when she was two and she went to live with her mother. Ostensibly taking her away on a visit one day, Susan's father kidnaped her and kept her for two years. Then her mother kidnaped her from her father's home and took her to live in the country. The father finally accepted this arrangement. He has come to visit a few times, but always agreed to return Susan to her mother.

Susan had an older brother, Kevin, who went through the kidnapings with her. Two years ago their mother remarried. Susan likes the new man, but her brother never did. When their father came to visit last summer, her brother decided to leave with him. Susan became an only child.

Susan is brash and adventuresome. She lies and manipulates her friends, constantly turning one against another. She is also quite partial to cliques. Her peer relationships are extremely unstable and unfulfilling for everyone including herself.

Susan does not achieve at academics and avoids them whenever possible. Her great love is animals, and she willingly does every chore that involves them. Her new dad likes her and spends some time with her. But he is a full-time businessperson and has a number of time-consuming outside interests. Susan keeps trying to arrange things for them to do together, but she is usually unsuccessful.

Susan's mother, often brash and loud, has a habit of telling everyone how healthy and "together" her daughter is. She acknowledges some of Susan's shortcomings but feels, all in all, that the child is doing very well. Now, imagine the following: When the stories of Susan's lies and the hatred she displays in peer groups reach her mother's ears, the mother finally seeks help and comes to you. What would you advise? Go into detail and be specific, writing your answers down before reading the next section.

159

A Natural Learning Rhythms Response

The support group sat in a circle with their Remedy Charts open on their laps, considering remedies for Susan's troubles. First they went over Susan's personal history. Here are their conclusions and final suggestions:

Due to the kidnaping events in her early years, Susan has experienced a serious breakdown in Body-Being—a complete disruption of the character trait of Belongingness/Strength. By the time we meet her she is firmly rooted in Emotional-Being, and malfunctionings are occurring everywhere.

As might be expected, Belongingness/Strength remains unbalanced (as evidenced by the manipulative relationship to her peers). Her mother refuses to see Susan as she really is. The mother has also chosen a man who does not provide the time and attention Susan needs. Now her brother Kevin, whom she had grown close to during the period of the kidnapings, has opted to leave home, abandoning her as well. Where and with whom does Susan belong?

When the support group reached this level of understanding a lively dialogue ensued. Each person seemed able to empathize with a different aspect of Susan's experience. At first they tried to pinpoint the imbalance of the character traits. Said one man, "If you don't know where you belong it is awfully hard to be balanced in Autonomy/Humility. Her exhibitionism and desire to limit the activities of her friends tell me she is grasping for security. That means fear, and fear means the loss of incisiveness. Where is the trust? Why *should* she be kind or tell the truth? How can she possibly see her healthy options?"

"She's crying out for help," a mother of two girls said. "Her mother and new dad cannot hear her, so she must cry that much louder." If the group were responsible for devising a remedy, how could they empower Susan? How could they activate her stage-specific wisdom?

Maria, a long-time Natural Learning Rhythms practitioner, spoke next. "The only way I know of is what we do in our own family. First, the foods for Emotional-Being must be considered. There is neither justice nor fairness in Susan's life. No one talks to her about death. Any remedies we chose must make up for these deficiencies.

"Even though the her sense of belongingness in Body-Being has been trashed," Maria continued, "and even though it is probably the cause of many of Susan's problems today, we have to approach her through her present stage-specific wisdom—Emotional-Being's. It looks like Incisiveness/Fearlessness is showing the severest damage at the moment. Susan has lost her ability to see what's most important. She is reacting with great fear of loss of status with family and friends."

"You're right," said the man who had spoken first. "We need to start by working with Incisiveness/Fearlessness. Susan's lying is not so much a breakdown of honesty as a breakdown of fearlessness. She lied because of a fear of telling the truth, not because of "meanness" or morbidity. The sneakiness in relation to her friends indicates a wobble in Honesty/Humility, but not a full malfunction."

All support group members seemed satisfied with this analysis. They turned to their charts. The Remedy box for Incisiveness/Fearlessness during Emotional-Being says: "Check role models; nature; charity work; controled peer group; respected elder."

"Well, the role models are completely skewed," said a woman who hadn't spoken before. "The mother is lying to herself about her daughter, and the new dad is not giving Susan the necessary time and attention. So, our first job is to find someone to break the news to Susan's mother. Since I'm friendly with her, I'll do it. Not the most fun job in the world, but there's a child at stake so I'll take it on."

"The fact that we live in the country has been a saving grace for Susan," said Maria. "At least she has some contact with nature and a chance to express her love of animals. Only animals accept her uncritically. She seems to feel she belongs with them. I think we should use this love. Then we'll be working from Susan's strengths."

Maria's ideas excited the mother of two girls. "Let's go all the way for her. How about new friends, with supervision, around activities involving animals. We could try 4-H clubs, horse groups, and field trips to wildlife refuges. We could probably even work in some academics during these activities, too."

As possible solutions appeared the conversation became animated. Everyone had something to say. "Academics can be taught around animals, too. And if we can tie all that in together and give her a feeling of competence, her self-esteem will shoot sky-high."

"If it does, she'll right her behavior with her peers."

"And also, animals also lead naturally to discussions of death and justice."

"But I wouldn't recommend trips to the zoo. The caged animals may remind her of her own despair and frustration."

"Public service work might help. To work with disabled humans, especially children, may remind her of the indomitable human will striving to overcome all obstacles. She'll have a chance to break through her self-pity."

"Public service work stimulates inspiration. Inspirational stories, including those with animal heroes, is good medicine for Susan."

"Maybe I can get my teenage daughter Jessie to help. She's been a go-between for others."

"Our children's class would be a fine place for Susan. She desperately needs guidance in how to be a friend. That's what they learn there."

"I know," said the woman who had taken on the responsibility of talking with Susan's mother, "that Susan's mother realizes how painful the kidnaping was. She'll be honest as to why Susan's brother went back to live with his birth father. If the brother still feels close to Susan, let's get him back in the picture. We can suggest ways they can communicate and at least give her one male who's still on her side."

Are the Remedies for Grown-ups?

In every workshop we've had, adult participants who study the Remedies Chart find descriptions of unresolved aspects of their personal history. Frequently, they ask if they can use the indicated remedies to help themselves.

There is no definitive answer to this question. If the remedy strikes you as meaningful, try it. More likely it will take some sort of therapy, such as counseling or body work, to pry open windows long closed. For most grown-ups, the open window is Reasoning-Being's particular wisdom. Use reasoning to assess your situation. Afterward, create the remedy you need; it may focus on the body, feelings, or cognition.

The Joy of the Remedies

Once accepted, these remedies save time, health, and effort, and create a great deal of joy. They take time to learn, as does the system of Natural Learning Rhythms. But once learned there is an exponential increase in freedom for all family members. An atmosphere of natural grace and harmony prevails; there's more free time for everyone. Every family who has assiduously practiced Natural Learning Rhythms attests to this kind of simple transformation.

What, after all, can be more debilitating to a family than the physical and psychological pain of dysfunction? The time spent worrying about children saps the energy of every family member. On the societal level, a cry of suffering can be heard everywhere. A terrible waste of human energy is represented by that cry. Appreciating our natural learning rhythms helps us prevent that terrible waste. With these skills, we can hear the cry, recognize its causes, and respond with a viable remedy—an efficient, ecological, sane, and humane way to live.

Authentic Education

Educating the Whole Child

How much of the world's suffering is necessary? What part of it can be altered by the behavior and ideals of human beings?

How can we explain the gap between human intellectual and societal development—that the same creatures who have crafted ingenious machinery and sophisticated logistical strategies are also capable of behaving with rude insensitivity toward their own children, spouses, people from other cultures, and different forms of life? What inhibits us from *envisioning* a way to live that will allow a judicious, non-destructive relationship to natural resources and living things?

In pondering these questions, we run headlong into the debate over the essence of human nature. Does the human ability to be wantonly destructive serve some divine purpose? Some evolutionary purpose? Is it due to our genetic make-up, or to the fact that we have yet to activate the full power of our brains? Natural Learning Rhythms begins with an even more fundamental consideration: What is the consciousness of the person asking the questions? Has his education left him whole enough to be able to truly reason?

The answer may be surprising and more than a little unsettling: Most of us *have not been educated* in a way that allows us to tap into our natural wisdom. Indeed, our essential nature has been largely hidden. Bad education—that which denies stage-specific wisdom—obscures inquiry into human nature. It limits the definition of intelligence to a function of the intellect only; curriculum specifics, data storage and retrieval, and symbol manipulation are the principal aims. By demanding that the child deny body wisdom, emotional wisdom, and will wisdom, a painful schism is created in her consciousness. Knocked away from her natural learning rhythms, the child loses touch with essential aspects of her being. Authentic reason consequently fails to surface.

As an educational system, Natural Learning Rhythms has just the opposite effect. By allowing stage-specific wisdom to come to consciousness, the child becomes aware of himself holistically. He is not so cut off from his body wisdom that he becomes capable of needlessly destroying other bodies. And later, having access to his own emotional wisdom, he will not need to view others as competitors or less worthy than himself. As a teenager, he will be able to assert his freedom and individuality without deprecating peers. And as a young adult, with the earlier stage-specific wisdoms properly developed, he will reason with clarity and humanity.

We were all children once, including the chemical manufacturer willing to pollute the river to make a profit; somewhere in the course of his education, that individual lost connection with his natural learning rhythms. With them, he lost the innate knowledge that the future will be determined by his actions in the present.

A generation educated in accordance with their own natural learning rhythms could begin to remedy the social and spiritual ills that burden our society. With that ideal in mind, we offer the following examples of particular academic and social means by which parents and teachers can incorporate Natural Learning Rhythms into a holistic plan for the education of our children.

Natural Tendencies

Human beings possess an enormously varied range of talents and abilities. From the basket weaver to the astronaut, from the psychologist to the farmer, from the poet to the long-distance runner, we fill every occupational and geographical niche on the planet, combine every element with every other element, find things that cannot be seen and have wildly different understandings of how the universe works. We are an awesome creation.

Howard Gardner's theory of Multiple Intelligences, which he describes in the book *Frames of Mind, The Theory of Multiple Intelligence*, offers excellent insight into the nature, formation, and growth of human tendencies. Gardner defines seven clearly distinguishable arenas of human accomplishment: linguistic, musical, logical-mathematical, spatial, bodily-kinesthetic, intrapersonal, and interpersonal. Staying strictly within the guidelines of traditional scientific observation and testing, Gardner uses detailed cross-discipline research to show the independence and interdependence of these inherent intelligences.

It is vital to the health of the child and society at large that we appreciate and celebrate her unique tendencies. These tendencies are an integral part of who she is. By ignoring them, we move toward a monolithic or, at best, a minimally pluralistic society. We lose the diversity that is the wonder, as well as the evolutionary advantage, of humankind.

Honoring the child's tendencies is more difficult in a society that values one or two specific capabilities more highly than any of the others. Contemporary Western society, for example, places an extraordinarily high value on one particular type of intelligence: the ability to manipulate symbols, to store and retrieve data. The ability to access *inner wisdom,* or to negotiate friendships, or even to compose music does not fit into this narrow definition. If a child has a tendency to excel in these areas (indicating other types of intelligence), he must exhibit these abilities outside the school environment and somehow garner support to develop it.

167

For proponents of Natural Learning Rhythms, the right to develop natural tendencies is part of the child's birthright. Inherent tendencies are a sacred gift that allow each child to fulfill her own natural destiny. Education that fails to honor tendencies is toxic.

We've all seen what happens to a child's self-esteem when the rest of the world around her values forms of intelligence that are different from her natural tendencies. She's consistently seen as unimportant by peers and teachers, and even, at times, by her family.

Some say that the "glue" that holds a given culture together is the specialized form of intelligence that it supports. Others consider this most-valued form of intelligence the very definition of the culture itself. Through these lenses, the United States is seen as the scientific society, with a scientific culture. And the ability to turn raw materials into finished products using scientific methods gives us the strength to maintain that culture.

But the society that accepts such a view of itself nurtures but a fraction of its human potential. It sets one person over another, one inherent talent as more important than another. Part of our human heritage, represented by the undeveloped tendencies, dies of neglect. Like a tree with all its roots on one side, society become unbalanced. In our case, the glut of lawyers, politicians, soldiers, computer engineers, and spies is proportionate to the lack of peace-makers, mathematicians, futurists, and philosophers.

Holistic education creates another kind of culture. Everyone makes his contribution resulting from his own natural tendencies. Each individual is valued and integrated. All of us possess a valuable piece of the puzzle, and we all get the chance to help put it together. This society is like a tree with roots spread out in all directions, one that will not uproot in high wind or perish in drought; it is stable with a powerful hold upon the earth.

The numerous attempts to systematize and label human tendencies indicate that they are of great interest and importance. These methods include the Buddhist samskaras, astrological systems, the character types of Jung and the temperament types of Rudolph Steiner. In each system, the names and descriptions have definite, specific meanings within their own particular context.

In our own work as educators, we have found it most useful to begin with Gardner's work on Multiple Intelligences, which provides a supporting framework for observing and analyzing tendencies. Combining Gardner's theory of multiple intelligences with a knowledge of children's natural learning rhythms (such as the fact that Body-Being's child expresses her truth instantaneously through her body), parents and educators have a remarkably unfettered technique for discerning the young child's tendencies. From the child's earliest years, parents and teachers can begin to identify and nurture the child's tendencies in an unpressured, natural way.

Varied, Safe, and Sensual: Educating the Child in Body-Being

Many years ago we ran a small preschool for four and five-year-old children. To implement our early childhood curriculum, we used the great Indian epic, *The Ramayana*, as a focus. This story was especially suitable for young children because of the important role assigned to the animals—especially the monkey Hanuman, the vulture Jatayu, and the bear Jambhavan. The children lived through these animals as they leaped oceans, faced perils, laughed and cried together, uprooted trees, and flew through the air.

The children came for six hours a day, three days a week. Each day began with a new installment of *The Ramayana*. The telling of the story aroused many feelings in me (Ba), which I neither denied nor exaggerated. At no time did I try to be expert in my rendering. I did not imitate voices or animal sounds. I often hesitated and always asked the children many questions, even during the most exciting moments. Our storytelling circle was close and intimate.

Singing and elementary use of the recorder was interwoven throughout the day. A particular favorite was a song honoring Hanuman, as the children sang they would reenact many of Hanuman's fabulous feats of daring and strength.

After the story came Arts and Crafts. Each child's project had to relate to the story, preferably the installment they just heard. They could chose any medium and work individually or collectively. The time remaining before lunch was devoted to cooperative games and activities, which were carefully selected in accordance with the needs of Body-Being children.

Lunch was a cooperative affair as well. Without pre-planning, each child brought one part of the meal, and then all the parts were combined into one dish. Inevitably these dishes turned out to be a surprise and a source of great fun. The children never failed to eat full portions of their own creation.

Acting and "academics" occupied the afternoon. The installment heard that morning provided the theme for the acting. Each child played several roles each day. Gender was no indicator of which roles were chosen; often a boy played Sita, the beautiful heroine. Usually the children played the parts as they remembered them, often supplying their own dialogue. Teachers helped only when the children were confused and uncomfortable about it.

Academic activities mostly consisted of learning the alphabet and the numerals. Using sandpaper, soft woods, clay, paint, and dough, the children shaped the letters and numerals in dozens of different ways. A favorite game involved the children using their bodies to make letters, simple words, animals, and numerals. There never was any factual teaching. The natural curiosity of the children kept their attention focused and brought forth a thousand questions. Soon they were using their letters to label their art.

Every creation relating to *The Ramayana* was saved. At the end of the year they were put on display and the parents and friends were invited to an open house. As the children walked their parents through their creations they spontaneously began to recount the epic tale. Then one child picked up the recorder and they all sang the Hanuman song. Finally, to the amazement of all and with no direction from the teachers, they acted out the story for close to thirty minutes.

How Much is Enough?

Three days a week is an adequate amount of school for Body-Being's children. Parents and family are their primary support system and almost every need can be addressed within the family. The value of school is to supplement and enhance the learning taking place in the primary family. Preschool is the spice, not the stew, for children in this stage. Social needs are minimal outside the family.

Body-Being works to establish a firm knowledge of body-as-environment. To accomplish this, Body-Being's child exchanges information with her environment via sensation. She uses imitation as an important learning tool. Neither sensation nor imitation provide good discrimination when interacting with peers. While there is great value in their playing together, five-year-old children only need to do so for a limited time each week. At Ramayana preschool we therefore kept school time to a minimum and class size small.

Every aspect of the storytelling contributed to a healthy sensation environment for the children. The emphasis was on allowing the children to contact stage-specific wisdom rather than be entertained. The unhealthy sensation environment of expectation was minimized by simply recounting the story in my natural way, without attempting to be a performer. Including the children through the use of questions also helped. All the principles of communication described in the previous chapter were consistently employed. The children had continual access to me. Loving touch was present throughout.

Free-form guidance focused our activities. The class had a central theme, but the many variations on that theme allowed Body-Being's egoism ample room to express itself. There was no predetermined goal, no objective we were trying to reach. It was the learning process rather than the product that was most important. The children often had to make choices, yet the absence of a rigid goal and the specific daily scheduling prevented those choices from becoming an infringement on any individual. In this way the food groups of security and flexibility were provided.

Because the children were in Body-Being, retributive justice prevailed during controversy. Often the children solved their own problems, and when necessary the teachers suggested solutions. The collective and cooperative activities, and particularly the acting, allowed the children to appreciate one another without competition or put-down. Their respective talents manifested in a safe place and in a safe way; they could be themselves without fear or threat. Everyone accepted the boy who wanted to play a female demon or the girl who needed to be king of the bears.

The acting, of course, did not have much to do with empathic role playing. These children simply chose the part that most directly related to that aspect of themselves that needed expression. The rich variety of characters in *The Ramayana* provided ample fare.

Creating and sharing the meal together added a great amount of warmth to the class. We discussed a wide range of topics at this time, often with excellent humor. The animals also added warmth as they personified the exaggerated sense of self common to the competency phase of Body-Being. The story spoke as the children and the children spoke as the story.

171

Creating Learning Environments for Body-Being Children

For children in Body-Being, parents have a number of fine, established curricula to choose from, whether at home or in a school setting.

The Montessori Method uses excellent sensory teaching tools in an atmosphere free from high-pressure expectations. The classrooms include children of mixed ages. Though the quality of the teaching greatly depends upon the skills of the individual teacher, the Montessori Method recognizes Body-Being's fundamental needs.

In either setting, the best learning environments are designed in accordance with the child's natural learning rhythms. At home, spend ample time exploring and playing, use communication tools, such as using stage-specific vocabulary and integrating what you hear, and incorporate ritual rites of passage. Through these activities parents can easily teach the social and academic skills required for children of Body-Being age.

Our curriculum chart lists a number of options to begin with. Let's use math as a model: If baby animals are born in the household, the parent and Body-Being child can weigh them every two days. Together, they can make a simple color-coded bar graph that tracks the animals' weight gain; the child can color the bars. Parents can also use "manipulatives" such as simple scales and Cuisenaire rods to teach math. Whether measuring flour or board feet, both cooking and building projects also provide excellent hands-on opportunities to understand math as a part of daily life.

Especially with Body-Being children, don't be overly concerned with solving math problems or learning facts. Allow the child's hands and eyes to relate to proportion, speed, depth, and weight. It is the experience of math as part of the environment, known through the body, that will stimulate Body-Being wisdom and lay the foundation for more complex mathematical knowledge.

Children can hear the properties of sound best at approximately four years of age. This means it is time to listen to music, not necessarily to play it. True playing, like true acting, requires sophisticated feeling. Learning to play an instrument serves Body-Being only when the family atmosphere is not loaded with expectations. Do not expect or demand discipline or expertise. As we know, there are all too many stories of children turned off to music by eleven or twelve because parents, delighted by their child's sense of pitch or her ability to imitate body movements at five or six, pushed too hard. There are exceptions, of course, and a child who willingly puts time into learning to play a musical instrument shouldn't be inhibited.

When should a child learn to read? Observation of the child and demands of the environment supply the best clues. Three-year-old Linda, who lives in the city, began quite early. Reading was useful to her in learning to cross busy streets safely; it also helped her connect to her mother's experience as they drove through urban thoroughfares whose scores of signs literally determine the rhythm of human behavior. Seven-year-old Jason, on the other hand, was still happy cooking with his mom, caring for animals, and tending to a garden plot of his own. There was no need to disturb his natural rhythm. At eight, Jason made a new friend who excited him with stories of how fun and adventurous reading can be. With this incentive, Jason quickly learned how to read.

For parents as well as teachers, reading and telling stories to children is an excellent way of teaching. Pick the stories carefully. Young children do use stories to compensate for their sense of being small and dependent in a large and mysterious world. Some identification with the conquering hero is natural and necessary; still, much of the violence can be minimized. When I (Ba) recounted *The Ramayana* in the daycare center, most of the epic's rather explicit "gore" had been eliminated.

Through unstructured time in nature, the child is free to explore at her own natural rhythms, fundamental to the education of the child in Body-Being. The textures of dry grass or river silt, the rasping sound of a bluejay's call, the flashing image of a redwing blackbird in flight, the muted colors of sand and clay and rock, the cool smell of the eucalyptus—all textures, tastes, sounds, sights, and smells of nature— stimulate rich awareness of body-as-environment and call forth Body-Being wisdom. In nature, Body-Being's child continues the lessons begun even earlier, during the highly sensitive moments of birth and conception, transitions that need to be treated with the utmost care.

Honest, Fair, and "There": Educating in Emotional-Being

So many children have been damaged by insensitive care during the birth of Emotional-Being! With the onset of Emotional-Being, adults often interpret the child's new, more sophisticated mode of perception as a sign that the children can simply be turned loose with one another. Consequently, we often *lessen* adult guidance of the children during social interactions (transforming it into authoritarianism later, if the child does not meet our expectations), and this at a time when the children are the most vulnerable they've been since infancy.

173

No wonder aggressive territoriality describes the "law of the land" in many school playgrounds. The situation from the perspective of Emotional Being's child? He is vulnerable, yet curious and desirous of social interaction. He is looking for guidance and protection. At school, he's suddenly thrown into the midst of thirty strangers. Someone acts in a way that feels "strange" to him, or worse, hostile. The child concludes: "They're not like me. They don't like me or they would not have done that." Looking to grown-ups for help, he frequently finds little of it; only rules and expectations about how he's supposed to act. These edicts he interprets as a second round of hostility, coming from the very place where he sought guidance. He then takes the only option left: He looks toward his peers and finds a few kindred souls with whom he can congregate, each often alone in his own world. He knows something's missing, for he genuinely wants to interact. But under such circumstances, the chance to do so is rare. His experience: a vague emptiness quickly covered up by what meager interactions he can engage in.

Emotional-Being children need to be taught the art of communication. It is their most important task, for without communication skills, children have no way to relate their feelings to one another. Resentments fester when there is no communication. Violence among children—and grown-ups—begins when resentments fester.

Many of us may actually need to go out and learn communications skills ourselves, if we adults are to pass them on to our children. To interact with others in a balanced, harmonious way every human being alive needs to feel good about herself. For a child of nine, self-esteem is precious and delicate. She'll need support and guidance in the development of her feelings. She must have conscientious models who demonstrate and teach techniques for non-violent expression of resentment, for non-embarrassing expression of inter-gender friendships, for non-intimidating interactions with people of other ages, races, abilities, and cultures. Only then will the full richness of emotional wisdom come to the child's consciousness. Only then will each child access her resident knowledge of how to be friends—so crucial to a peaceful and pleasant existence in human society.

Cooperative Games:
For Emotional-Being and Beyond

One day, a neighbor dropped off ten-year-old Marty for a family counseling session at our home. His parents had not yet arrived. Because the child was visibly nervous, we started a simple two-person hand game to loosen up. Within minutes, Marty was engrossed in the game.

As Marty played, he began to talk fluidly about his life at home. We were surprised by his behavior, and later we scanned the literature on cooperative games, looking for any reference to the use of cooperative games to ease tension and allow equalization between counselors and children. Though we searched thoroughly, we came across no mention of that application; yet with Marty, and on other occasions with other clients and children, cooperative games worked perfectly. In a session with a different family, for instance, we found that a simple animal acting game allowed angry and distrustful family members a good laugh. Friendliness increased. Conversation became easy and relaxed. Playing cooperative games often created a natural bridge to discussion of family dynamics. Because the breaking down of stigma and the building of trust are such important ingredients in successful counseling, this phenomenon commanded our interest.

We deepened our investigation in Friday Class, that wonderful laboratory where, each week, we met with Emotional-Being children and went out into nature to explore, act, and tell stories. It was the natural place to introduce cooperative games and activities. What effect would playing cooperative games have on the children? Would the games bring them closer together? Would they stimulate healthy communication? Could they be used to resolve conflict? Could they aid the children in conscious connection to emotional wisdom? We had some pretty weighty questions about a group of simple games.

In researching and sampling scores of cooperative games, we found that cooperative games had three essential ingredients in common:

♦ Everyone wins; there are no losers.

♦ Everyone's best effort is more than sufficient to make the game enjoyable.

♦ The game is successful when participants support one another because they want to.

And that's it. The games themselves were as varied as the many cultures from which they originate: Mexico, the United States, Bolivia, Japan, Fiji, Tanzania, Zimbabwe, the Ukraine, and the Netherlands, to name a few. They can all be adapted to different ages, skill levels, and environments.

Cooperative games and activities can be adapted to serve the dominant stage-specific wisdom, and they can be used to teach academics. They also help improve communication, build self-esteem, resolve conflict, and help bind a disjointed group into a close community. On top of that, these games are fun and challenging and accommodate individual styles.

One game played we all loved in Friday Class is called "The Web." This game can be played as an ecology game, as a moving sculpture, or as a way to clarify values. It's quite simple: The group chooses a subject. A ball of yarn is tossed from player to player. When a player has the yarn she is the speaker. When she finishes, she wraps the yarn around a finger, and tosses the ball to someone else. A web forms.

On different occasions Friday Class used "The Web" to speak about death, home schooling, pets, toys—in short, everything of interest to any of us. One day in Friday Class using "The Web," we talked about how to

175

act in class. Initiated by three children in response to one boy's continually disruptive behavior, this startlingly candid conversation brought forth apologies, strategies for minimizing "rudeness," and feelings of cohesiveness and strength.

Cooperative games work well in other contexts as well: They have the power to dissolve cliques, help strangers grow closer—and even entrance teenage boys.

A group of half a dozen thirteen-year-old boys came to a cooperative games picnic in Sacramento last year. They had an air of arrogance about them, disdaining cooperative games as "wimpy." We observed them attempt a few games. A definite hierarchy existed in their small clique. As the games tend to undermine hierarchy and cliques, two boys who acted as leaders grew increasingly impatient. The four followers liked the games but could not risk the disapproval of their friends.

In a quiet way we isolated the six boys and began to play "Co-op Juggle." In this game, the players form a wide circle. A ball is thrown around. Each player catches and throws once. The last player throws it back to the first player. A pattern is established. Player 1 always throws to player 2, who throws to player 3, and so on. In this group there were eight players, so 8 threw back to 1.

More and more balls are introduced. The record is seven balls juggled by a group of eight. A high degree of cooperation and communication is necessary to match that achievement.

These young men loved the challenge. At first they attempted a fast tempo and ridiculed those who couldn't keep up. Then they realized they needed a collective rhythm that could accommodate their differing skills. When they finally juggled seven balls, a cheer went up. They actually crowded around the "worst" athlete to congratulate him for his excellent efforts.

Spontaneously, we asked them if they would help with some of the activities of the day. We explained what was needed and gave them their choice of jobs. They accepted this responsibility, even though they had to split up to do it.

Nowadays, we instruct teachers, parents, home schooling collectives, playground supervisors, and psychologists in the use of cooperative games and activities, for resolving conflict and enhancing communication. We have also published a book, *Everyone Wins,* with over 160 games best suited for these purposes.

Cooperative games can work for everyone. Because many of these games can be played by people all ages, they are especially useful at extended-family gatherings. In one such game, the group simply sits on the ground with a circle of rope in front of them and then, pulling together, hoist themselves up with no other support. The need for mutual sensitivity to the right amount of tension on the rope creates an atmosphere of interdependence and trust.

Nature Class

Our Friday Class, still ongoing—though now renamed "Nature Class," and run by our colleague, Debbie Weistar—provides an excellent model for allowing Emotional-Being children to gain an understanding of their own feelings and the feelings of others. This challenge, during their Emotional-Being years, is their primary task.

Eleven girls and boys, ages six to twelve, make up Nature Class. Boys and girls interact in a natural, comfortable way with no stigma or separation. Despite the longtime cultural myth reinforced by the toy industry and the public school system, which contends that boys and girls of Emotional-Being age do not like to play together, we find great examples of friendship and cooperation in every class. Small class size (most days we average eight children) helps trust and friendship develop and endure.

Throughout the day we tell short stories. Near the end of the day, when everyone is ready to quiet down, we have a special story time. Sometimes the story is part of a continuing tale, whereas others are completed in one sitting. Each story includes two important attributes: First, it is usually a *teaching* story—one that stimulates the listener to question, wonder, and seek. Second, the story is *participatory.* Either the group actually creates it or each person is drawn in, with carefully timed questions. Nature Class gives children the chance to hear myths and act them out.

The children in Nature Class love circles. A circle is strong, an expression of its own unity—there is no beginning and no end. The whole class gathers to open our day with a circle. We end our day with a circle, and we use circles during the day to work out conflicts, decide how we're going to spend our time, and express our feelings. Circles are safe; they honor everyone equally.

When all these elements are combined, each child will, at sometime during the day, have a secure moment to contact and express his feelings.

Community Education and Home Schooling

Nature Class satisfies an important part of the curriculum for the education of Emotional-Being children. To it, we must add academic schooling and the arts as well. As a matter of fact, our Nature Class grew out of a broad-based home schooling program in rural North San Juan, California, called Community Education. This program gives parents of the local community the opportunity to teach the children the skills they know. Computer literacy, German, Spanish, English, Art, Herb Lore, Wilderness Skills, and Field Trips are a few of the courses that have been offered through North San Juan's Community Education program.

Community Education's aim is empowerment of parents, teachers, and children. Learning occurs in small, mixed-aged groups. Along with teaching in their area of expertise, the adult in charge makes the commitment to address interpersonal issues as they arise. Parents come to know different types of children with varied learning abilities. Because so many different neighborhood sources offer meaningful educational opportunities to its members, the community becomes a comfortable, safe repository of knowledge.

Home schooling, in which a child's education is a family responsibility, is the heart of the Community Education. How can Natural Learning Rhythms bolster the efforts of the home schooling parents? Let's take a particular teaching sequence as an example: Through Natural Learning Rhythms we've learned that Emotional-Being children love rhythm. At home, parents can take advantage of this knowledge to devise a more creative and effective lesson plan. Math or spelling can be taught while playing catch with balls or bean bags, or by tapping out rhythms with foot-long dowels. With rhythm as a vehicle, these kinds of spelling and math exercises can lead directly to writing poetry. Drawing or painting can be used to illustrate writing themes, and then return to rhythm by setting the entire project to music.

Through the Emotional-Being years, Natural Learning Rhythms guides parents to build upon the strengths of Body-Being. If the child has been well educated, she will already have a working knowledge of body-as-environment. Now is the time to use that knowledge. The new awareness of feeling in the Emotional-Being child allows a finer focus and openness to gentle discipline. Dance and gymnastics, which emphasize rhythm, also integrate feelings. Singing comes from the body and summons the emotions. It is a bona fide Body-Being to Emotional-Being bridge.

Caring for pets or farm animals can give Emotional-Being's child a first opportunity to distinguish her own feelings from the feelings of another living thing. For country children, horses provide a unique and worthwhile challenge: The horse becomes an extension of the child's body yet remains a significant other whom the child must feel.

Emotional-Being is the time for drama. Let the actor out, for through his performance emerges a myriad of feelings yearning to be acknowledged. Simple plays in the home provide great fun, teach concentration, and enhance appreciation of literature and literacy. Plays depicting different epochs teach history and geography in unforgettable ways. In our community, a group of ten-year-olds, who adapted the Greek myth of Persephone in a classroom play, brought the ancient story to life in their outdoor games as well, never tiring of it all spring. In world history classes, dramatizing the future has been a fascinating and uproarious way of focusing on contemporary social and scientific events.

Because of their great ability to feel, for Emotional Being's children empathy with other cultures is the surest route to an understanding of geography. Writing pen pals from other countries, visiting community members of foreign ancestry who have maintained strong ties to their mother country, and making clothing or cooking meals in the same way as people of other cultures lets the child imagine how she might feel if she were to meet the diverse demands of different physical and social environments.

By the end of Emotional Being, most children need basic literacy and math skills in order to meet the demands of Will-Being. How this should be accomplished is the parent's key challenge.

The relatively recent resurgence of home schooling has had an important influence on public education. A number of communities now offer independent study programs along the lines of the public school curriculum, guided by an accredited teacher. Some of these programs support natural growth and learning patterns, others do not. Parents need to choose mindfully.

The same careful stance should be taken in investigating the many curricula marketed for the home schooling community. Parents can use Natural Learning Rhythms, along with their own deep appreciation of their child, as guides in deciding the best combination for their own family.

Fortunately, public school teachers can adapt many of these options suggested in the Curriculum Chart for use in their own classrooms. Incorporating cooperative games into the traditional physical education curriculum would represent a giant step toward educating the whole child. Initiating cooperative learning activities, such as those described in the *Tribes* manual (see bibliography), could mean another great advance. Designing a curriculum sensitive to all seven types of human intelligence, and guiding children through interpersonal interactions, would represent another major qualitative improvement in the public school classroom. And if, on top of these advances, a real working understanding of developmental psychology were mandatory in each teacher's own education, the public school system could come very close to offering a genuine holistic education.

Waldorf and Unicorn

As established models, we would like to profile two other approaches to educating children in Emotional-Being. One, the Waldorf school, is internationally known; the other, called Unicorn, is a unique educational experiment conducted by six families in our local community.

In Waldorf schools, each class of children stays with the same teacher for the first eight grades. This arrangement provides the children with the consistent modeling so important to Emotional-Being. In Waldorf classrooms, myths are interwoven with the teaching of history, and rhythmic exercises aid the learning of math. Developmental psychology, as formulated by founder Rudolf Steiner, is taught to each teacher. Drama, instruction in art and music, and eurythmy (a discipline in which the student expresses sound through body movement), are integral to the curriculum. Notably, these subjects are imparted in ways intended to stimulate feeling. Parents are expected to support the school and keep in close contact with the teachers.

These observations are not a blanket endorsement of Waldorf Education; they simply highlight areas in which Waldorf Education corresponds to the natural needs of the child. In a number of other ways Waldorf Education runs contrary to natural growth and learning patterns. Among these are large class size, a lack of attention to interpersonal interactions, teachers who are frequently overworked, and excessive academic expectations of students.

Unicorn, the second school we mentioned, is a refreshing example of a group of families that has created an educational collective to meet the needs of their children, with none of the usual institutional considerations. There is no attempt to attract other students to the school, and very little energy is spent on worrying whether the school will exist in the future.

The families who organized Unicorn designed the basic curriculum, then hired a teacher they felt could meet its unique requirements. Parents also assist in the classroom. A part-time tutor teaches Spanish. School meets three days a week, six hours a day, in a building on the land of one family. Such subjects as music and art are given the same importance as writing and math. Learning is never competitive, though it is often individualized according to ability. Grown-ups set aside adequate time for attention to classroom problems and conflicts. The teacher and some parents have studied child development.

The Unicorn group takes a thematic approach to learning a range of subjects. For instance, when a large forest fire occurred near the school, they used the event as a focus for drawing pictures, making music, writing stories and poetry, and running a relief program for the fire victims. Afterward, the children gave a public presentation combining all the mediums they had used when studying and responding to the fire.

181

Justice and Ecology

Many classrooms institute a type of student government, but few incorporate any sort of student-run judicial system. At home or in the classroom (public or private), all educational systems need to work hard to provide honesty and fairness for the Emotional-Being child. When the child's feeling for justice is not activated, he becomes bored and often disconnected from the learning process. The attempt to educate him fails.

Summerhill school in England, and the Korchak orphanages in pre-World War II Poland (see bibliography: *Summerhill* and *The King of Children*) represent excellent examples of schools that allowed children to genuinely express their feeling for justice. They published their own newspapers that ran candid opinions of the students without censor. At both Summerhill and the Korchak orphanages, children, well-advised by elders, determined what was an offense and what kind of punishment it deserved.

Given the opportunity and the right context, children in Emotional-Being and the later life stages know what justice is and how it can be administered. We cannot expect children to learn humanistic social skills if their models, especially parents and teachers, administer justice with a totalitarian or capricious attitude.

Ecology, the understanding of the relationship between a living organism and its environment, awakens feelings of balance and interconnectedness in Emotional-Being children. But the study of ecology *must* echo the Earth's own natural learning rhythms. Our local public school's third-grade curriculum includes some nature studies. One year the students wanted to learn about insects, so, according to the teacher's instructions, children were to collect bugs, bring them home, and freeze them. This way the bugs would be "fresh" (though also, obviously, dead) the next day when the children would study them under the microscope.

This is not the way to teach or study ecology; it models a manipulative, at-our-convenience relationship to nature. The instructions left many of the children confused and disturbed. In Emotional-Being's terms, treating bugs as disposable objects lacks humility and fairness. Ecology can be taught properly in the simplest of ways. Through drawing, films, gardening, geography, picture books, and observation outdoors, the child in Emotional-Being can learn about—and more importantly, *feel*—nature's interrelated systems. Both fictional and real-life animal stories stimulate the precious imagination of the child in Emotional-Being.

In Nature Class, we often include time for reading aloud, such as James Houston's writings on life in the Arctic, or Robert Franklin Leslie's books on the North woods. Besides being a powerful way to teach ecology, camping, tracking and wilderness skills (see the Tom Brown books in the bibliography), such books supply adventure, an important nutrient for these children—particularly in Emotional-Being, predator-prey relationships, which exist everywhere in the natural world, sparking the consideration of life and death, allowing the child to discover the deep wisdom of the present life stage.

Challenges and Apprenticeships: Educating Children in Will-Being

How can we educate a young person consumed in the fiery assertion of a first attempt to declare his own individuality? What type of curriculum can possibly satisfy the simultaneous needs for personal space and increased peer sensitivity? How can the educator blend the pure expression of ideals with the awkwardness that accompanies the onset of puberty? What kinds of activities are challenging and adventurous, and also allow the student to perceive himself as successful?

The educator must devise a curriculum responsive to these issues. Then she must meet her students zealous challenges to her position as teacher—challenges to the subject matter, the educational philosophy of the school or home, and to the teacher herself as a person. Now, were the core of these challenges to remain consistent, the educator might have an easier time coping with them. But the nature of the child's challenges are forever changing, for Will-Being's child is changing so rapidly that what was of life-or-death importance today becomes trivial tomorrow.

183

As an additional source of vexation, many Will-Being children have been subject to poor education during the Body-Being and Emotional-Being life stages. In the Remedies chapter we explore ways to remedy the damage children have suffered by the time they reach puberty. Many of these methods can be incorporated into formal education. Here, we will cover the most important considerations for choosing the curriculum for the young teen.

Carrots and Sticks

The public schools' attempt at educating Will-Being's child can only be described as ignominious. Having addicted the child from a an early age to rewards and punishments, the school must intensify the "fix" to gain the teenager's mercurial attention. This means introducing more competition, along with more failure. It means breaking the will of those who do not fit the system. Alienation grows. Most young people are faced with the choice of sublimating their will to the institution or becoming outsiders. It is not a fair match: The inexorable power of social institutions grinds the individual down. How can this be changed?

The Zen Buddhist master Suzuki Roshi once said, "To tame a bull, give it a large pasture." When the child begins to reach for responsibility via strong idealistic assertion, the curriculum should meet her head-on. Even though there is a lack of substance behind the student's insistence, the teacher must be sensitively respectful. Here's how:

- ♦ **Include the student in the decision-making process.**
- ♦ **Encourage peer interaction when decisions need to be made.**
- ♦ **Provide a forum where students communicate their ideals to one another.**
- ♦ **Guide the process and help set boundaries.**
- ♦ **Do not fill the role of central decision-maker.**
- ♦ **Turn the responsibility back to the students with gentle guidance.**

The public school teacher can employ these guidelines in her own classroom, even if they are not part of the standard curriculum. Neil Postman and Charles Weingartner's excellent book, *Teaching as a Subversive Activity,* describes how to use the method of *inquiry* to decentralize authority in the public school classroom. The teacher become questioner and clarifier. Students meet their own academic and interpersonal goals, from raising money to support an environmental organization to creating a student government with real power. Such goals come with built-in challenges, many of them difficult. Yet few students fail to attain the goals they themselves have set.

As the inquirer, the teacher helps the student articulate his goal as precisely as possible, then offers a "reality check," making sure that the strategy for achieving the goal is in accord with the student's personal aims. The teacher garners as much support as possible for the student She refers him to other teachers, resources, organizations, or funding sources that could be of help to him. In addition, the teacher might offer special instruction in skills that pertain to the student's goal—anything from computer use to fly-fishing to how to ask a funding source for financial assistance in a polite and effective way.

Almost any goal set forth by the child in Will-Being will involve a learning challenge. We've seen this phenomenon occur with Will-Being children who have concentrated on such varied fields as mechanics, photography, world game simulation, and champion chess. In these cases, reaching their own goals meant acquiring language and math skills or mastery of the body or spatial composition. Time and again, the students met the challenge.

The attitude of the inquiring teacher is one of humility. She cannot claim to know the meaning of life or what each person ought to be doing. She does testify that the inquiry into self is the basis of real wisdom and personal fulfillment. By practicing humility, the teacher offers just what the student needs: room to admit he is not yet fulfilled and inquiry as a way to actualize self-fulfillment.

Apprenticeships

Today many home schooling families are leading the way to a more intensive kind of education experience for their teenage children by turning to apprenticeship programs. Recently, in fact, the National Home Schoolers' Association established a clearing house in Tennessee to place apprentices with willing teachers.

In the area where we live in rural California, Community Education has fostered a number of part-time apprenticeships. Tenth grader Jesse learns botany and wilderness skills with Tom, a forty-year-old naturalist and outdoor educator. Sixteen-year-old Elizabeth apprentices at a nearby onion and strawberry farm that practices sustainable agriculture. Several children learn veterinary skills and computer programming with local professionals. And there are others as well.

We've known Ian, now a strapping, quiet sixteen-year-old, from when he was a small boy. Not long after he entered high school, he began doing poorly there. He frequently missed classes and eventually teetered on the brink of dropping out. When a caring school counselor confronted him with his truancy, Ian admitted he was having difficulties, and suggested calling in both his parents and us to see what could be done.

Because Ian had always shown a strong interest in cars, we suggested an apprenticeship with Barry, an auto mechanic acquaintance who had taken our workshop. Barry asked Ian to work with him three days a week; Ian would attend high school the other two days. Over the next year, Ian and Barry became close friends. Ian was able to talk over his personal concerns with Barry, and the older man's insights gave Ian a deeper perspective on his life. In addition, Ian's reading and math skill improved dramatically during the year, since they were critical to completing his tasks as an apprentice mechanic. By the end of his apprenticeship, Ian had decided to take

185

the high school equivalency examination and to enter a community college to learn more about the world.

The early feedback has been positive on Community Education's apprenticeship placements, from students and teachers. Still, the number of apprenticeships that exist is still quite small. There are many reasons for this, all solvable. One is the strong pull of society's educational directive for young teens that tethers them to formal schools or trade programs; as old a tradition as apprenticing is, it is new to today's educators. Another factor that must be contended with is the need of Will-Being children to conform with the activities of their peers. Students will have nothing to do with a situation they consider even remotely "weird."

Adults who wish to act as mentor to a young apprentice need not be state-certified teachers. To do the job well, they must simply be willing, financially able, and aware of the young person's needs. The financial pressures on would-be mentors—the need to earn a living and complete their own work while teaching an apprentice at the same time—is the most formidable block to actualizing a broad-based apprenticeship program. Currently, there is simply no support for the mentor position in our society. We need support from the school system, parents, and community. In the case of Ian, his auto mechanic mentor solved the financial obstacle early on by teaching Ian skills that would genuinely contribute to running his shop.

Contrary to popular myth, the young person in Will-Being does *not* want total autonomy. She easily accepts limits if she has participated in setting them and if, to use the words of Suzuki Roshi, the pasture is large. Firmness, when accompanied by flexibility and fairness, is welcomed by the child. She needs those limits. Yet what Will-Being's child cannot accept—and there are sound developmental reasons why she cannot—is any behavior that resembles the absolute parental control that characterized her first twelve years. With an understanding mentor, meaningful limits can be mutually created. Knowing the limits and sharing a personal relationship with the mentor, the student experiences a new freedom. She's guided and safe, with room to roam.

The adolescent's realization that he will have to take his place in the world marks the beginning of the acceptance of personal responsibility. The task looks exciting, if sometimes daunting. Naturally, he is unsure if he can meet this responsibility. Through apprenticeships he learns a trade that will allow him to gain a livelihood. It need not be his "career." Having learned such a skill, he can explore Reasoning-Being and beyond without the fear that he may go hungry. This lessens the pressures of personal responsibility, while yielding greater freedom to explore himself and his world.

A Curriculum of Ideals

A group of thirteen- to fifteen-year-old children in our community believe very strongly in the principles of nonviolence. We have incorporated these ideals into their school curriculum as thoroughly as possible. Reading, field trips, history, and geography are investigated with respect to their value for promoting peace. Because peace studies are the focus of the curriculum, neither promise of reward nor threat of punishment is required for these children to do their work. The same is true for Will-Being children anytime the curriculum follows their ideals.

In other areas as well, our curriculum matches the ideals and interests of these teenagers. Whether those inspirations come from the world of rock music, business, philosophy, or sports, a curriculum that allows exploration of authentic interests evokes the child's natural curiosity. Students learn quickly and easily. Here's how to go about it:

187

- ◆ **Engage ideals to the fullest. Allow children of Will-Being to believe they can shape the world according to their desire.**
- ◆ **Join them in the experience. They will find the truth for themselves and become much better decision-makers in the future.**
- ◆ **Enter their perspective. In due time, the value of their actions will be learned through their own direct experience.**

Living History

Another exciting curriculum approach we call "the history of consciousness" includes the additional advantage of bridging the gap between Will-Being and Reasoning-Being. Workable in both traditional and alternative school settings, this multi-subject approach divides history into four distinct epochs:

- ◆ **The Stone Age**
- ◆ **The birth of agriculture through the Pythagorean era**
- ◆ **After the Pythagorean era up until the Renaissance**
- ◆ **Modern times**

Each of these four historical epochs make up a year's study: First-year high school students study the Stone Age, seniors study modern times, and so on. Everything about the epoch is studied interactively. Whenever feasible, students enact achievements in math, language, art, literature, and religion as human beings of that era did.

Using this curriculum, we explore the ideas and achievements not simply of the West, but from many different regions of the world. In doing so, students discover that ideas and understanding know nothing of national borders. In studying modern times, for instance, students might investigate Chaos Theory by witnessing the Belousov-Zhavotinski reaction, in which chemicals, placed in a shallow dish, spontaneously self-organize into recognizable shapes. They learn that this reaction was discovered in the early 1950s in the Soviet Union, but was rejected until Western scientists could make use of it thirty years later. In the same way, when we study the historical epoch that includes the fifth century B.C., students come into contact with the great philosophers and religious leaders of the era: Socrates in Greece and Gautama Buddha in India, as well as Persia's Zaruthustra, and Lao Tzu in China. In doing so, students gain a broader perspective on human nature and achievement.

Along with meaningful historical study, and a focus on their ideals, Will-Being's children need *real life* to be an integral part of their curriculum. Human physiology and sexuality, general psychology, money management in the real world, and full disclosure on alcohol and drugs and their effects are crucial subject matter for young teens. Well-researched, easily readable books that state their biases frankly satisfy their questions best. Books such as the excellent series on drugs by Harvard's Lester Grinspoon and James Bakalar offer the thorough, objective information a teenager needs. Such a medium meets the child at her own level of development and brings the information home in clearly digestible form. Offered with sensitive respect, she will be able to hear and assimilate it. With such information at her disposal, Will-Being's child will be in a better position to make careful decisions about her own health and well-being.

The Teacher as Inquirer

Let's explore ways to impart knowledge of a particular subject to a young person in Will-Being. How can a given subject—say, psychology—be made meaningful and important to the young teen?

From the beginning, a teacher cannot impose his values on the child. Lecturing, moralizing, and arbitrary limit-setting quickly block communication. Because the child is only partially aware of the importance of her own psychology in her life, it importance to her must be illustrated. To do so, the teacher starts by practicing self-inquiry right in front of the students. By revealing his own thought process——how he comes to decisions and conclusions——the teacher demonstrates the way in which attitudes, preconceptions, feelings, and thoughts influence an outcome. Through self-inquiry the teacher also models risk-taking and imagination, thus setting the stage for her students to do the same. Also, because the inquiry was self-contained, at no time has the teacher violated the students' need for personal space, interfered with their peer relationships, or challenged them beyond their abilities.

Following the self-inquiry, the teacher begins asking about the students' thinking on a given aspect of psychological theory or practice. Remember, the basic rule is that the teacher asks, and keeps asking until he understands the "why" behind the students' thinking. Teaching loses potency when the teacher judges the validity of the students' reasons. If the teacher approaches the inquiry with a set of expectations, the process simply won't work. In general, the inquiring teacher does not supply answers, only the questions. In the course of answering his inquiries, the students come an understanding about their reasons for their actions—and *that* is the object of the educator's job.

When intellectual or interpersonal problems arise, the teacher asks the students to solve them for themselves. Give their individualization a chance to express itself as problem-solver. Set up the environment so the students can explore their difficulties *with each other.* Inquire about the difficulties and the solutions. Whenever possible, move ahead according to the students' resolution. Feel free to offer alternatives, but try to wait until you are asked.

In terms of helping teens understand practical psychology, teen support groups are very effective. Support groups examine common problems from all spheres of adolescent life—everything from pressure to take drugs, to conflicts with parents, and anxiety about unfamiliar emotions and physical changes. In addition, support group members often do research on topics of great interest, call in outsiders for advice, plan parties, share confidences, and provide moral support for one another.

In our work with one such support group—this one for disabled teenagers—the members were able to put into words powerful feelings that they'd never had the chance to express before. For example, some teens with minor disabilities admitted that they felt uncomfortable around teens with greater disabilities. Other group members spoke of the anger they felt toward a caregiver for not being sensitive to feelings or desires. Many of these teens felt a great longing to have sexual activity as part of their lives. Expressing repressed feelings in an atmosphere of mutual support and respect is the beginning of empowerment. As a result of group discussions, a number of teens in this group were able to release the tensions from feelings they'd kept inside, in some cases for years, and to make important changes in frustrating situations in their daily lives. Several group members confronted caregivers with their dissatisfactions, and a number of members went out and formed romantic relationships.

Curiosity and Challenge: Meeting Will-Being

What sort of special activities meet Will-Being's need for exciting challenge? In developmental terms, challenges in nature are of vital importance to the child in Will-Being. As the teen has the chance to surmount nature's abundant, impersonal challenges, she comes to believe in herself. "I can face my fears," she learns, and self-confidence grows in leaps and bounds.

The Ropes Course, a special program founded with such challenges in mind, grew out of the Outward Bound program and was further developed by Project Adventure. The Course is made up of a series of "elements"— combinations of cables, ropes, and wooden platforms. Some elements are a hundred feet high, up in the trees; others are on the ground, and most are in between. Participants walk across some, jump from others, and climb others. A harness and a belay system (similar to the system used by rock climbers) insures safety. Some elements call for individual courage and skill; others require precise cooperation by a group of people.

The Ropes Course combines challenge, individual effort, peer connection, and a thrilling sense of acomplishment. There are now hundreds of Ropes Courses throughout the United States, and we operate one at the Pathfinder Learning Center and use it as an integral part of our curriculum.

Developmentally, challenges in nature are of critical importance to the child in Will-Being. Take these children to the wilderness! In nature fiery assertions can be tested, ample space is available, and each Will-Being child can find challenges that suit her unique level of skill and need for adventure.

Today, in the 1990s, as we rediscover the wisdom and power of nature, we are simultaneously pushing forward brand-new uses for modern technology. Educational applications are among the most exciting. Computers can easily be programmed to provide innovative academic challenges appropriate to the child in Will-Being. At our Community Education facility, a computer program with a history database invites the student to become a famous historical figure, say, Illinois Senator Steven A. Douglas in the 1860s. Using the data base to reconstruct Douglas's viewpoint, students delve deeper and deeper into the issues of the American Civil War.

Another computer game concerns the architectural designing of a house, where players must learn the principles of engineering. If, for instance, the wrong beam is put in the wrong place, the whole house crumbles and the player must begin again. A third program with a legal database allows the child to assume the role of a particular Supreme Court Justice. The student proceeds to hear a case and try to give an opinion as the Justice would.

191

Another fascinating learning program with a history database involves cooperative problem-solving by groups of students at several terminals, each terminal representing a cabinet post of the United States government. A historical dilemma is presented, for example, the rearming of Germany prior to World War II. Students formulate international policy by plying the information in the data base. Intelligent questions yield access to more important information.

The curriculum of the Will-Being student should include the best of the popular media. Films and videos in particular often provide an entree into difficult-to-discuss issues. Watching the controversial film *The Good Mother,* (in which a child's confused loyalties lead to accusations of child abuse) with two teenage girls led to a two-hour conversation about child abuse, marital and parenting responsibilities, and the role of sex in a happy relationship. In a classroom of ninth graders, the movie *Stand By Me* (concerning the experiences of four young teenagers coming into manhood) inspired an earnest discussion on the subject of ritual rites of passage.

Allowing the student or young person to choose the film to watch or CD to listen to gives her the chance to develop a personal aesthetic. The inquiring teacher can help guide this process. Rather than dismissing the child's choice, engage it. After viewing or listening to the chosen video or CD, elicit the student's responses and the reasons for their reactions. Use the video's "stop" and "rewind" modes both during and after the movie to ensure comprehension and to review controversial issues.

The curriculum for Will-Being's child must also honor his need for ample peer contact. Inside the classroom, group the students to minimize put-downs and the forming of cliques. Cooperative learning in small groups is optimum. Outside, large gatherings of young people such as ball games, dances, and political rallies offer opportunities for socializing, and through it, the child's necessary individuation.

Finally, when considering the education of Will-Being's child, remember to incorporate the coming-of-age ritual, which we explored in depth in the Ritual Rites of Passage chapter. It is so important for the child to have the opportunity to "burn off" childhood, and to acknowledge the immense changes she is experiencing. If she fails to do so, aspects of the child will remain, impeding her progress and fulfillment. This is why the coming-of-age ritual is, in many ways, the most important educational moment during Will-Being's reign.

Investigation and Analyses:
Educating Children in Reasoning-Being

The young person in Reasoning-Being exudes curiosity from every pore in his body. He needs to *know*. His time and space perception expand to include the whole of the physical universe. With this expanded sense of time comes that most metaphysical of questions: *"Why?"*

As soon as the child asks this question, his mind's floodgates open: How does the universe work? What methodologies yield the most pertinent information? In what ways do attitude and experience determine perception? Are spiritual and scientific investigation mutually exclusive? Is there life after death? Do other realities exist besides the one we perceive through the five senses? What constitutes a just government? What does one do remedy an unjust one?

Indeed, the question "Why?" is the sound of Reasoning-Being awakening.

University Life:
The Right Idea

Out of the confusion and doubt which occurs at the end of Will-Being, Reasoning-Being is born. During Reasoning-Being's receptivity stage, the student must learn how to access information. No arena of human inquiry or talent should be left out. Students can choose subjects relevant to their search and, at the same time, intelligent educators can guide them to investigate cross-discipline connections. During the trial and error phase, the student picks one particular subject for detailed investigation. Interest in other subjects remains important, but committing to a specific student-selected line of inquiry is key. Intense specialization marks the shift to Reasoning-Being competency. Expertise is the midpoint of competency, but not its pinnacle; genuine mastery occurs only when the student knows her topic so thoroughly that she can see it as microcosmic example of universal principles.

University life provides more than study. There the student encounters people from all walks of life, from many parts of the country and the world. The exciting exchange of customs, ideas, behaviors, and social and political insights is one of the healthiest features the university has to offer. Each exchange broadens the student's perception of the world and herself. Being forced to deeply consider—to reflect—awakens the reasoning capability.

Yet to be quite frank, present-day university life often undermines reasoning wisdom in several ways. First, the homage required by a number of college professors often destroys the dance of mature recognition and coexploration. Instead of being treated as a welcome guest at the feast of knowledge, the student may find herself treated like a poor relation. Demands placed on the student for the reward of good grades may set up a system of bribes and coercion that demeans the student's maturity.

In addition, the dependence on the military, government, and private corporations for funding may compromise the university's status as a haven for free thinking—sometimes dangerously. Many students eventually realize that they will not find totally objective, impartial information in schools that answer to special interests and thus have little to do with the student's own ethics and goals.

Colleges and universities make powerful tools available that can assist our children in contacting reasoning wisdom. Let's support those schools that put the student first, and supply the fundamental Reasoning-Being needs. These young people will one day be society's decision-makers. Their actions will determine the future of life on the planet.

Travel Study

Traveling is an infinitely deepening educational choice for the young person in Reasoning-Being's late teens and early twenties. Wisdom gleaned from contact with other cultures, economies, and ways of communication force the traveler into new behaviors and produce valuable, unexpected revelations. Some of these revelations are directly linked to his new surroundings, but just as often his new insights are reflections on his own society back home.

Simply taking in the famous sites pictured in the tourist guidebooks, or trying to live as inexpensively as possible off the local people will not give the young person in Reasoning-Being the kind of quality experiences he needs. In traveling, the young person will be sure to incorporate fun and adventure. Along with the adventure, he will gain the most lasting satisfaction when, as often as at all possible, he becomes a productive, contributing guest. He may participate in the local economy in farming, cooking, building, or caring for children in the community he is visiting, or he may share skills, such as welding or photography, that he acquired back home. This is the kind of traveling that enriches both the host society and the guest.

For young people coming from modern post-industrial societies like the United States, sharing life with the people in the developing countries radically alters the mind. Our estrangement from the production of basic goods—paints, dishware, flour, cheese, brooms, tools, lumber, paper, textiles, clothing, and so on—has made their origins and manufacture nearly exotic. Relearning these lost crafts leave Reasoning-Being's child closer to himself and his own origins, as well as the earth and its resources. He feels the joys (and restrictions) of close-knit, traditional societies, and the freedom (and alienation) of modern life.

The traveler learns other important lessons when he compares aspects of his own country with similar aspects of other industrialized countries— say, labor laws in Australia, or social welfare and children's rights in Sweden, or contraceptives, marriage, and divorce law in Japan. He discovers that there is more than one way to run a modern, developed society. And when he assumes his place back home, these memories may influence him in working for progressive change or preserving what valuable rights and resources that still exist.

Face to face experiences with representatives of various religious and spiritual disciplines throughout the world often sheds light on metaphysical questions Reasoning-Being's child is so anxious to explore.

Paul, who grew up in Cleveland, and Martha, originally from Los Angeles County, do not know each other, but each spent time in Asia in their twenties, at the end of Reasoning-Being. Like many who have been to the Far East, both Paul and Martha's lives changed greatly from contact with Hindu pantheism and the non-theistic approach of Buddhism, which inspired each of them to begin practicing meditation. As a result of her travels in the East, Martha now feels she is able to maintain a more balanced attitude during personal crises, such as her mother's severe stroke last year. She also believes that her familiarity with the Eastern ways of thought has made it easier to see more than one side of an issue with her children, and to have more confidence in her own inner strength. Paul thinks of both the poverty and the spiritual perseverance of the people he came to know in Asia when he explains what led him to a career in community service. Upon his return to the United States, he decided to work with teenage single parents in the inner city.

195

International exchange student programs between universities in different countries offer the student the chance to experience travel and university life simultaneously. During Reasoning-Being, not only is the young person open, questioning, and highly tolerant, but her ability to absorb and assimilate new ideas is at its zenith. Through cultural exchange, the student learns respect for the wisdom inherent in other peoples and cultures, just at the moment she is most able to receive it. Because of this, the exchange of ideas between the world's young people during Reasoning-Being is an enormously important influence on global peace and conflict in the future.

The journey Martin Luther King, Jr. made during his Reasoning-Being years—to attend theological seminary in Pennsylvania—might have well been from one country to another, for it crossed a line between two radically diverse cultures. King grew up in the shadow of the plantation, his childhood rooted in a strict but very closely-knit religious community. As a young adult seminary student, he found himself in the more fragmented, if "liberalized" North, being exposed to the ideas of Hegel, Gandhi, Thoreau, and Emerson. At the seminary, King excelled, receiving highest marks in his chosen majors of religion and philosophy. There his peer group also expanded to include men and women of all colors and educational backgrounds—a number of whom would become his most dedicated supporters in the tumultuous Civil Rights years to come. In this milieu, King committed himself to universal brotherhood as a specific response to racial prejudice. Dr. King's ability to combine the best ideas and ideals from both his worlds, to complete a detailed examination of the information he considered critical to his understanding of the world, and to commit to his own approach to civil rights is an exceptional example of the way an individual in Reasoning-Being organizes his world as the miracle of his own powerful intuition emerges.

Specialized Interests

Besides travel, pursuing her specialized interests—be it particle physics, furniture making, health care, or photography—can be a valuable part of the curriculum for the child in Reasoning-Being. Seventeen-year-old Stephanie, whose family we spoke of in the Reasoning-Being chapter, started with an interest in river pollution. From there she went on to study the ethical considerations of environmental law, eventually becoming a legal activist. One of her classmates, a young man named Matthew, pursued an interest in waste disposal by traveling to other countries to find out how each country managed garbage. The study of art through the ages, the path taken by nineteen-year-old Justine, demanded consideration of other cultures and historical eras. Her search led to volunteer work with a team of artists restoring a medieval church in England, and later back to her hometown in Massachusetts to work on the restoration of a colonial meeting house there.

Still, focus on a special interest may sometimes lead to over-specialization: The receptive and trial and error phases of Reasoning-Being can be artificially shortened by an inordinate attachment to a particular interest. When the emphasis on one subject becomes extreme, social needs, especially contact with the opposite sex, may be sublimated or ignored.

Reasoning-Being is a time of reaching out, of exploration. When the specialization leads to a narrowing or a withdrawal, then the young person's motivations bear a closer look. Is she using her attachment to a particular interest as a way to hide from other, possibly painful interactions? Is it a cover-up for prior developmental deficiencies? Is the specialization an ego-istic identification, disconnected from a deep understanding? When we ask the child about these questions in an open, supportive way, we can help her explore her motivations and continue her true journey with confidence.

Intuition: An Important Reminder

Guiding the student toward an awareness of *intuition* rounds out the Reasoning-Being curriculum. As you will discover, young people in Rea-soning-Being have the startling capability of organizing their own lives to allow intuition's ascendancy. These young people can, by themselves, set up the conditions by which they can transcend reason itself.

Because intuition makes its appearances in many parts of life, the educator need not solely restrict himself to lecturing on the subject. Essays, philo-sophical and religious treatises, quality films, conversations, stories, art, music, architecture, poetry, fasting, rituals, wilderness journeys, and meet-ings with people consciously awakening intuition in themselves and soci-ety remind the young person in Reasoning-Being that intuition—something beyond reasoning—exists. In the service of *wholeness,* and as caretakers of her education, we allow the student to make as conscious and complete a contact as possible with all manifestations of intuition.

❦

A Final Note: Using the Curriculum Chart

Combining Harvard educator Howard Gardner's insights on the seven types of human intelligence with Natural Learning Rhythms produces hundreds of specific curriculum options. The chart on the next page lists a variety of choices. Many are suitable to any educational environment. Others center on special outings such as archaeological exploration, spe-lunking, or a day in the city; still others require special equipment, such as telescopes, computers, canoes, or a drip irrigation system on a farm.

As we read through the curriculum suggestions for any of the seven types of intelligence, we can see a microcosm of the Natural Learning Rhythms system itself. As an example, let's look at the column on verbal-linguistic intelligence: In Body-Being, the child's verbal-linguistic intelli-gence is engaged by creating textured letters, listening to stories, and practicing "tongue twisters," all sensation-based activities. In Emotional-

CURRICULUM

- O Each child is an individual – therefore, each child will progress according to his or her own blend of intelligences
- O Meet the rhythms of each child – all have strengths and weaknesses
- O Time in nature serves all learning modes

The Seven Types of Human Intelligence	Body-Being	Emotional-Being	Will-Being	Reasoning-Being
As derived from Gardener in *Frames of Mind.*	Involve the body in the learning! Be flexible in attitude, expectations, and use of teaching tools; include tools/environments which allow safe testing of boundaries; Most Important: Textured exploration opportunities; No threats; minimum confinement; no need for formal education, especially before four.	As you model so you teach! Involve the child in the fairness of curriculum choices; Most Important: Opportunities to safely explore feelings of self and community. No hypocrisy.	Fire those ideals! Honor the search for individuation – Involve the child in creating her own destiny. Most Important: Challenging events that stimulate awareness of freedom. Never ridicule.	Recognize the Childs Maturity! Honor the ability to comprehend the fullness of space/time; Most Important: Opportunities to absorb data and guidance in organizing that data into systems. Eliminate condescension.
Verbal-Linguistic *Awareness of the sounds, rhythms, inflections, meaning, order, and functions of words*	Textured letters, *i.e.*, from dough, sandpaper, wood, *etc.*; singing together; opportunity to link objects and names; clear communication with elders; gentle humor; tongue twisters; looking at books; hearing stories; Montessori teaching tools	Reading and listening to books and stories, particularly inspirational ones; acting and all performing arts; opportunity to classify things; writing without excess constraint, *i.e.*, poetry; dialogue with friends and close elders; Eurhythmy; foreign language	Public speaking; grammar; creative and academic writing; reading in all subjects; foreign language; debate; world affairs; history; media	Etymology; advanced debate and public speaking; study of original sources in all disciplines; history of language; all social sciences; research papers; general semantics; influence of language on culture; inquiry
Logical – Mathematical *Creating and operating on strings of symbols that represent reality*	Cooking; building; balancing scale; gardening; beginning Cuisinaire rods; measuring growth of living things, *i.e.*, height of plant, weight gain of baby animals, own height and weight; manipulatives for shapes, *i.e.*, pattern blocks; Montessori teaching tools; games which use the childs body to make numbers, letters, *etc.*	Continuation and expansion of manipulatives, *i.e.*, Mortensen; continuation of home–based math in cooking, building; cooperative learning, *i.e.*, rhythm games; beginning abstractions; simple word problems; lots of music, *i.e.*, beginning relationship to scale, chords and notes, as well as sophisticated listening to compositions	Computer skills; genuine abstraction, *i.e.*, algebra and up; biographies of great mathematicians; hands – on surveying and engineering; beginning hard sciences; beginning logic; physiology; farming; practical calculation skills; nutrition	Higher math; formal logic; advanced science; the history of math and time; the philosophy (including ethics) of math and science; computer science; business and economics; farming
Musical *The controlled movement of sound in time*	Many opportunities to listen, touch, and dance; rhythm sticks; playful instruction, with contact with skilled musicians, especially the precocious	All the music the child's willing to engage; lessons where appropriate but minimum pressure to perform; dance; singing; music from all times and cultures; some reading notation	Individual's preference—support for intensive skill development; beginning musical theory; dance; opportunity to listen and play and participate in all types of music	Musical theory; the math of music; opportunity to specialize and practice intensively; public performance; cultural value of music; relationship of music to dance

The Seven Types of Human Intelligence	Body-Being	Emotional-Being	Will-Being	Reasoning-Being
Bodily Kinesthetic *Mastery over motion of the body and the ability to successfully manipulate objects*	Major component— Continuous support to explore handwork, dancing uninhibitedly, running, swimming, jumping, *etc.*; minimize instruction; rough and tumble; free time in nature, parks, and home; games which encourage full body participation; kites; much texture in the environment	Cooperative play; increased skill training, some team sports, but minimize winning and losing; rhythmic exercises, especially dance; team nature/wilderness exploration, *i.e.*, canoeing; drama; Eurhythmy; lots of free time	Strong challenges in nature, both individually and in cooperating groups; wilderness skills; ropes course; support for intensive skill development in area of preference, including crafts and fine handwork; disciplined movement, *i.e.*, ability to move silently, martial arts, miming, massage	Opportunity to specialize and practice intensively in both gross and fine motor activities; fasting; challenges that test limits and require strength and coordination; sitting still and silent; linking breath to movement and concentration, *i.e.*, modern dance, pranayama
Spatial *The capacity to accurately perceive, transform, modify, and recreate aspects of the visual world*	Lots of colors, *i.e.*, in room, outdoors, paints, learning tools, games which place shapes into holes; lots of movement; activities in wide open spaces and in close spaces; climbing; coordination games, clay sculpting; rough and tumble; gentle verbal reminders of physical boundaries	Painting, drawing, building, sewing, opportunity to explore rhythms of seasons, plant and animal life from cell to whale; beginning astronomy; model-making; journeys to skyscrapers, caves and the ocean; varied movement modes, *i.e.*, horseback, bicycle, motorboat, roller skates; advanced Cuisinaire rods; sophisticated use of patterns and shapes and blocks	Major Component Exotic experience, *i.e.*, spelunking, using high-powered telescopes, space camp; computer modeling; travel, especially in varied landscapes; hands-on creations, *i.e.*, carpentry, mechanics, pottery; drawing to scale; navigation; control over personal territory; introduction to computer geometry	Emphasize correlations, *i.e.*, the music of architecture, the science of painting, the dance of logic, chaos theory as poetry; travel; extended journeys to exotic events, *i.e.*, the Taj Mahal, Himalayas, Amazon, pyramids, Empire State Building, Tokyo sewer system; detailed scale drawing and model making; electron microscope to huge telescope; archaeology to futuristic simulations; landscaping
Interpersonal *The ability to notice and make distinctions among others, and oneself in relationship to others*	Opportunities to express oneself in modest public performances and daily life; cooperative games with peers which emphasize the body; interest in the childs interests, including conversation; no put-downs; no excessive praise; minimize social expectations	Major Component Acting and all performing arts; safe space to explore feelings with friends and close elders; cooperative activities which emphasize values; chance to exercise justice, *i.e.*, deciding chore responsibility for all family members, full participation in class government; ecology; helping the less fortunate; conversations about death	Forums for expressions of Ideals, *i.e.*, U.N. Simulation, activist marches; apprenticeships; peer contact; supervised challenging group activities with processing, travel, especially to non-industrialized countries; projects that engage a cause; mutual setting of boundaries with family; caring for toddlers, the less fortunate and animals	Simulation of all types of government; travel; intimacy; exchange student; special interest activism; interaction with peers and people of varied cultures; inquiry
Intrapersonal *The ability to know oneself*	Enter child's imaginary world through playing together while following the childs lead, *i.e.*, being bears in the woods, then comment, Boy, we're really cuddly today, huh?; humor, chance to touch both live and dead creatures; acknowledgment of feelings, some control over own life, *i.e.*, letting child direct play for half-hour	Acting, myth, support to understand personal feelings through inquiry and humor; time with trusted teenager; honoring the mystery Window by simulating inspiration; conversations about death; non-lecturing exploration of elders feelings; inspirational environments, *i.e.*, cathedrals, mountain tops	Psychology; apprenticeships; introduction to philosophy and religion; Vision Quest; cultural and physical anthropology	Major Component Philosophy, contemplation; meditation; prayer; Vision Quest; all branches of psychology; inquiry

**Major Component means that the Stage-Specific Wisdom thrives on that particular intelligence. If that intelligence is not educated well, all other learning is adversely affected and can occur in only an incomplete way.*

Being, reading and listening to inspirational tales, acting and learning to classify objects are the teaching vehicles that stimulate verbal-linguistic intelligence. Public speaking, creative and academic writing, and use of the media simultaneously honor verbal-linguistic development and Will-Being's need for individual expression. Reasoning-Being, with its expanded sense of time, can engage etymology, semantics, and influence of language on culture. The same rhythm of matching curriculum to stage-specific wisdom can be seen in the suggestions for each kind of intelligence.

At the top of the curriculum chart we have included some brief notes on each stage. They are designed to help you remember the key concepts in each of the life stages, so that you can design your own Natural Learning Rhythms-based curriculum.

We know that many new curriculum options incorporating natural learning rhythms will be devised by parents and teachers, as each creates the best education they can for their children. We look forward to hearing about how other educators and families chart this infinite, fascinating territory.

Conflict Resolution

Preventative Tools

Eleven-year-old Nadine and her brother, nine-year-old Daniel, were preparing for their ritual rite of passage. The children's parents recognized that Nadine had been in Emotional-Being for some time, and they also believed Daniel had recently established himself in that life stage. Consequently, they decided to have one ritual rite of passage for both children. The couple felt that, logistically, one ceremony would be easier. They also believed it would foster a deeper bonding between the two children, also lending each child more courage during the ritual's more demanding moments.

On the appointed day, the car was packed and the family ready to go. At the last minute, the father noticed that Daniel had taken along his favorite stuffed animal. He explained to Daniel that leaving stuffed animals behind was part of the ritual. Daniel could sleep with it again in the future, but it did not belong on this camp-out.

Daniel complied and brought the stuffed animal back to the house. As he put it down on the kitchen table, he broke down and began to sob. Here is an excerpt from the father's letter describing the parents' reaction:

> My wife and I discussed whether to take a hard line on this or
> not; we realized that it was our own expectations about Dan-
> iel's readiness that were at stake. In contrast, we were getting
> a simple, clear sign from him that he was not ready. We
> looked at our own reasoning for including him in the ritual in
> the first place. Daniel seemed to be pretty solidly in
> Emotional-Being, and it was more efficient to do them both at

once; we felt we could design the ritual to address each child's needs. But those reasons seemed valueless when compared with Daniel's reaction.

So we talked with Daniel down by the creek. We let him know we had made a mistake—that as his teachers, we had misjudged his readiness. We asked for forgiveness and told him we would make his ritual at a later time. He said that was OK, and that he wouldn't quit sleeping with his animals until he was sixteen. We really gave thanks for being able to release our expectations and recognize the clear signs involved, and being flexible enough to make the best of it without causing more hurt.

Practicing Humility

In a word, Daniel's parents practiced *humility*. When they saw their son's reaction, they stopped and reevaluated their own actions. The couple didn't punish their son for his reaction. When they understood their mistake, they shared it with the boy and made a new plan that accounted for everyone's needs.

Imagine if they had insisted on their original plan: Daniel would have had a very difficult day. Without intention, his needs might have siphoned off family energy that was needed for Nadine's rite of passage. Conflict probably would have erupted between Nadine and Daniel, and between Daniel and his parents. If the eruption had occurred at a delicate moment in the rite of passage, the conflict would have severely limited the ritual's effectiveness. Daniel might well have been seen as the cause of the ritual's failure, and a foundation would be laid for future conflict.

Daniel's parents perceived him as firmly established in Emotional-Being, but the incident on the morning of the ritual undermined that perception. Because of it, they were forced to recognize that he was in fact just entering into Emotional-Being: The flexibility requirement of Body-Being was still of great importance.

So many parents, anxious to mark the progress of their children, make the same mistake. Confusing the first signs of a new growth stage for an indication of its permanence, they overestimate the child's capabilities. When the child acts naturally, it is seen as a reversion to "outgrown behaviors," and conflict often ensues.

The Cost of Labeling

Daniel's parents later admitted that they also saw their son as "independent." Now, practicing humility, they had to drop that label.

Labeling leads to conflict. When parents insist on labeling a child, inevitably the child will try to live up to their expectations. She doesn't want to disappoint her parents. If they need to believe that she is an academic failure, she will fail at school rather than fail at supporting her parents' opinions. Internal conflict, in the forms of tense striving, cynicism, and obsessiveness, proliferates when the child continually tries to live up to the dictum.

Later, when the child realizes the label is a lie, she will actively begin to distrust her parents. During Will-Being, this distrust may well explode into rebellious rejection of all family values.

Often, this child does not know that her unhappiness comes from trying to live up to a label. Indeed, in four out of five cases we have counseled, an important part of parents' conflicts with other family members stems from unconscious reaction to their own childhood labels. One mother, attending a parent's support meeting, told of the constricting environment she experienced as the "baby" of the family. Her problems at home centered on her inability to communicate effectively with her youngest child. She was overly blunt and unforgiving with this child, echoing her obvious disgust with being babied herself.

Positive and negative labels are equally harmful. It is as hard to overcome the label "neat" as "sloppy," of "beautiful" as "ugly," or of "friendly" as "loner." A teaching story from the Sufi tradition illustrates this point very well:

> When the Master Salim, the great Sufi master of Isfahan visited the town of Haidrabad, people vied with one another to be chosen as his disciples. Some were rich, others had a faultless knowledge of the Traditions, and everyone wanted to sit at the feet of Salim. But when his visit was over, Salim left nobody to guide the people, and he took with him only the son of a beggar.
>
> More than ten years later his deputy, Muzaffar, arrived in Haidrabad and resumed the Teaching there. Only when people realized his great worth did he reveal that he was the son of the beggar, chosen by Salim. When this story became current, people marveled and regarded it as a lesson, but they saw only one side of it.

One day when he was at his open Court, someone said to Muzaffar: "How poetic and just that the humblest should become the leader of all! Was it not painful to live in the atmosphere of the Master as the son of a beggar, and to endure the trials which come before one is transformed into a Sufi Sheik?

Muzaffar said: "For me it was somewhat painful. For one of my companions, whom I met there, however, it was really painful, for he was experiencing a greater change.

They asked: "And what were his origins? He must have been some sort of heretic."

Muzaffar said: "He was the son of a king."

For our purposes, the rich boy is the one brought up with "positive" labels and the poor boy is stuck with "negative" labels. Both can reach self-knowledge but it is a hard task. Just as it's harder to let go of riches than poverty, it is harder to give up positive labels than negative ones. The rich boy therefore has it harder than the poor boy.

A critically important tactic to prevent conflict is to search and destroy all labels. Spouses can work together to identify and eliminate the labeling of their children. Parents can be specific in praise and blame. Say: "Johnny spilled the milk today," and not "Johnny is a slob." Children try to please their parents. If his dad labels Johnny a slob, Johnny won't let him suffer the embarrassment of being wrong. Say: "Johnny ran fast today," but not "Johnny is such a fast runner." Johnny might not be interested in "being fast" when he is older. It would be a shame, and a source of conflict, were he to spend the rest of his life trying to catch up to his label.

In terms of the past, one way for parents to destroy labels is to remember their own. Bring the labels to awareness and then try to understand how they have influenced your life. Consider seeking therapy if the labels bring up childhood traumas. An understanding family can help tremendously. Two techniques for recalling labels include keeping a journal and setting aside quiet times for contemplation. The last fifteen minutes before sleep is ideal for this contemplation. To search and destroy labels in oneself and one's family is an act of humility. It is a way for stopping conflict before it ever begins

Humor

In laughter's lighthearted give and take, unnecessary conflict subsides and fades away. Humor breaks superficial moods and surface tensions.

We are not suggesting you use humor to avoid anger or deep-seated conflicts; we're advocating the use of humor as *preventative,* conflict-resolution tool. By including humor as part of the family atmosphere, we prevent less important irritations from feeding on themselves. Instead they wither, exposing the genuine conflicts that need attention. Later sections of this chapter offer tools for working with such conflicts.

Here's a story from the Sufi tradition that we often tell to children in the difficult transition between Emotional-Being and Will-Being. In a swift, enjoyable way, this story lets them know we can find humor in their newly emerging assertions. The children get the message that we are on their side—no matter how often that side switches:

> From his childhood, Nasruddin was known as "contrary." His family had become so used to this habit of his that they always told him to do the opposite of what they wanted him to do.
>
> On his fourteenth birthday, Nasruddin and his father were taking a donkey-load of flour to market. As dawn broke they were crossing a rickety rope bridge, and the load began to slip.
>
> "Quick, Nasruddin," his father shouted, "heave up the load on the left, otherwise the flour will be lost."
>
> Nasruddin immediately raised the left-hand sack on the donkey. The whole lot of flour was unbalanced as a result and fell into the torrent below.
>
> "Ridiculous fool!" said his father. "Don't you always do the opposite? Did I not specify the left-hand load—meaning the right-hand one?"
>
> "Yes, Father. But I am now fourteen years old. As from dawn today in our tradition, I am considered to be a rational adult, and therefore I am complying with your orders."

Inclusion

When the child sees herself as vital to the family, she feels connected to her parents and family. This *inclusion* makes it more difficult for her to fall into the mental rut of "them against me." She'll be more likely to ask for reasons for family decisions before supposing malicious intent. She'll be more open to explanations and more willing to examine her part of the problem.

Ginny, fully established in Will-Being, wanted increased freedom in her life: She wanted more choice about where and how she spent her time. Her father Franklin, wondering if Ginny was truly equal to the responsibilities that go along with freedom, began watching her very closely. As his presence became intrusive, Ginny bristled. She told Franklin to "quit nagging" her. Franklin said he had concerns about responsibility and didn't want to be labeled a "nag."

"You're not a nag," Ginny answered immediately. "That's not what I'm saying at all. It's just that you are bothering me and criticizing me about things that I'm already taking care of."

Ginny's answer reflects the response of a child who has been included. She was not labeling Franklin in an attempt to push him away. When the label "nagger" came up she immediately rejected it. She did not feel the need to compartmentalize him to prove her own individuality. She simply needed attitudes and practices of communication restructured to account for her new capabilities. Qualifying her statement acknowledged family unity and brought her closer to her goal.

Children who do not experience inclusion tend to exaggerate their statements, feel frustrated when they cannot justify the exaggerations, and fall into conflict. "You're always yelling at me," or, "Jimmy never has to take out the garbage" are two simple examples of exaggeration. By melodramatizing their position they seem to be forcing the parent away.

For parents, this is a test. Will they take the bait of exaggeration and argue with the child about the exact meaning of his words? Or will they see the exaggeration as a plea for inclusion—and create deeper connections with their child? If they take the bait, the child comes to believe her own perception of the family as disconnected individuals with mutually exclusive goals. Such a feeling gives license to pent-up resentments being expressed in anti-family ways; in other words, this perception leads to conflict.

Creative Confrontation

Often we can prevent conflict by gently confronting our children with reminders of her connection to family, nature, and intuition: to wholeness.

Creative confrontation—honest, gentle, and straightforward—works like this: The parent becomes aware of alienated thoughts and emotions in the child. She challenges him, using kindness and developmental understanding. She might hold the child and speak about family unity, or of the way nature supports all living things. Firmly maintaining connection, the parent brings the power of interconnnectedness to the child. In this way, alienation is dissipated by creative confrontation before it can putrefy into resentment, sarcasm, or cynicism.

Practicing creative confrontation shows the child that disagreeing is acceptable, and it supplies models for how to do so constructively. By providing healthy channels for expressing and resolving feelings of estrangement and disconnectedness, creative conflict allows room to be loving while disagreeing. Occasionally startling to the child when it is unexpected, creative confrontation reminds her to drop indulgences and isolationist identities, and expand into her own stage-specific wisdom.

The case history of Quinn illustrates the sudden way creative confrontations bring families together.

Quinn hated doing dishes and often sulked when asked to do so. His behavior miffed his parents, since the allocation of chores had been decided by consensus of all family members.

One night Quinn's father, Kent, noticing the slumped shoulders and downcast eyes that often presaged his son's sulking, stood right in Quinn's path as the boy moved toward the sink. Quinn tried to step around his father, but Kent stepped in his son's path. Quinn pushed against him. His father stood his ground. Gently, he took Quinn by the shoulders and said, "Hey, son, your sulking affects everyone. It's like living under a dark cloud. What's up?"

Quinn hesitated, then gave an evasive answer: "Nothing." His father persisted. At last Quinn said, "You talk about how we're all connected, but I do the dishes and everyone leaves and has fun. It's hypocritical." Quinn's statement and his father's understanding broke the tension. They agreed to pair up to do the dishes in the future. Family harmony won out.

❦

The four preventative conflict resolution tools we have just examined— *humility, humor, inclusion,* and *creative confrontation*—are the components of a healthy or "right" attitude, which we described in the Remedies chapter. If right attitude is not present in parent or teacher, neither

207

remedies nor conflict resolution tools will be effective. When it is present, right attitude prevents conflict from arising and encourages children to be amenable to remedies when conflict does come up. A healthy attitude in the parent or teacher creates the atmosphere in which children can reestablish connections to their own natural learning rhythms.

In the following story, we talk about how to put conflict resolution techniques into action.

The Cherry Festival Story

Every year in June, our part of Nevada county holds a cherry festival. It attracts many people from all sectors of the local community. As a result, everyone visits with townspeople with whom they are friendly but do not ordinarily socialize with.

For children, this can be confusing. A child may meet a friend with whom he'd like to play, and that friend may have another friend with her. While they become acquainted, another child may arrive with two new friends. One of the new children may be close to the friend who was with the original child. A large amorphous group forms. More children show up, and some leave. At the same time, almost all the parents are socializing with one another, so the children have to work out any interpersonal relations on their own. Sometimes they run into trouble.

Josette, Amber, and I attended the festival in 1985, when Amber was ten. Amber usually attempted to work out social relationships on her own, and if she ran into difficulty we were available to help. Generally, she preferred not to call us in, but she felt no stigma when she did.

As community members arrived at the festival grounds, a constantly changing mass of children gathered in a dry, grassy field. Amber was one of them. We sensed such an unorganized grouping might lead to conflict. Several times during the day we checked in with Amber. She told us, "It's a little crazy, but I'm handling it." We continued to observe from time to time but decided to allow her the experience she desired.

Sometime after lunch, Amber came to us and said that Shelly was crying and Brad was fighting. Several of the other children were taking sides. A genuine brouhaha seemed moments away.

When we got to the field, Shelly was crying and Brian was facing off with Brad. Several boys and girls were encouraging them to punch each other. Jennifer and Cleo, off to the side and behind some bushes, were whispering to each other and watching the fight. Kristen, Jennifer's six-year-old sister, was running across the field, crying and shouting, "I'm going to tell Mom!" Cleo jumped out from behind the bush, grabbed Kristen, and dragged her to Jennifer. Kristen cried as Cleo tried to quiet her by threats. Finally, Jennifer cajoled her into silence.

I stepped up to Brian and Brad. Kneeling, I looked each in the eye and asked them to end the fight.

"I promise we'll try to work this out so everybody gets a fair shake," I said. "Let's just gather together. There's no need to fight now, OK?"

Each boy hesitated, the urge to fight still strong. I stood my ground between them.

"OK, I'll try," said Brad. Then, without warning he turned on his heels and took off running as fast as he could. It took a moment to sink in, then we realized he was chasing Jennifer, who was trying to slip away among the bushes. I caught up to them just as Brad was grabbing Jennifer.

"She stays or I fight," Brad shouted. "She's not getting away with it."

"Let me alone," Jennifer spit the words out. "Let me alone or I'll kick you in the nuts."

"If I let you alone will you stay?" Brad demanded.

"Enough," I said. "Brad, please let her go. Jennifer, please stay."

The other children and Josette were now crowding around Brad, Jennifer, and me. Brad let go of Jennifer's arm. Jennifer looked hard at Cleo for a long moment, then stared at her feet.

"OK, here's what we are going to do," I said quietly. "Everyone will get a chance to speak. Everyone will be listened to. We'll try to come to the best understanding for everyone. But we'll also work to know the truth."

"Oh yeah, what about Amber?" It was Cleo speaking, and mockery and challenge permeated her words. "You'll favor her in this argument and we all know it."

"How do you know that?" Josette met her challenge, but kept her voice calm. This was the first we'd heard that Amber was involved. Josette didn't flinch.

209

"Our aim is to help clear up the bad feelings. We'll work to the truth to do that. If Amber's participation has fueled the problem let's find out about it and do what has to be done."

Cleo looked sullen but she really had no choice. If the conflict was as bitter and involved as many children as it appeared, each child would face harsh consequences when her parents found out. As many of the children attended public school, there would be dues to pay on the playground as well.

"Listen," I said, "no matter what happens right here neither Josette nor myself will tell your parents unless it is absolutely necessary to protect someone from getting hurt. Does everybody understand what I am saying?" I looked each child in the eye until I received some sign of affirmation. "Do you know what confidentiality means?" I continued. One child did and told the others. "Well, Josette and I will practice confidentiality with everyone here.

"And we're going to come to the best understanding for everyone," I said, looking straight at Amber. "Let's sit down in a circle and try to get to the truth and see what we can do about clearing the air."

Amber was familiar with the practice of non-favoritism, but all previous experience with it had been with close friends. Now her face reflected her concern. She did not know many of these children, and felt vulnerable without her parents on her side "no matter what." But those previous experiences had always come to fair conclusions. So she called on her courage and managed a weak nod in my direction.

"OK, where should we start?" I asked. Silence. "OK, let's start with what I actually witnessed. Brad, you were grabbing Jennifer, and Jennifer, you tried to run away. What was happening, Brad?"

"She's always picking on the other kids," Brad said. "Her and her stupid friend Cleo."

"Wait," I interrupted. "No name-calling. None. You can be angry but you can't call names. If you do it's just going to be endless bickering and we'll never get anywhere. OK?"

Brad nodded, then continued. "These two were picking on Shelly by telling lies that she liked Carl as a boyfriend."

"We did not," Cleo said "You weren't even there!"

"No interrupting," I said. "Everyone will get a chance to speak, OK?" Cleo just glared at Brad.

"That's what Amber told me," Brad said. "And it's mean because Carl is so shy and they just wanted to have fun at his expense."

"That's what Kristen told me," Amber said.

I cut her off. "No good. No interruptions, Amber. You'll get your turn."

Carl, in the background cluster of children, stayed well hidden but was following the events with great interest. I made eye contact with him so as to acknowledge his involvement in the process.

"Anyway," Brad continued, "Carl's my friend. And Jennifer and Cleo are always so mean. So I came and told them they were mean. And they called me ugly and dumb. And then Brian stepped out from the bushes and jumped on me. And we were going to fight when you came and she ran away like a coward."

"No name calling, Brad." I said. "OK, Jennifer, what have you got to say."

"He's lying. We never said anything about Carl and Shelly. Everybody hates Brad and here's *why:* He's always making up excuses to fight. So he came over and cursed us, and Brian told him to stop cursing, and Brad challenged him and they were going to fight."

"Are you saying you never said anything about Carl and Shelly?" I asked.

"Well, we talked about them, sure. But we talked about everyone else, too. And we weren't being mean and we didn't tell Amber to talk to Brad."

"What did you say about them," I persisted.

"Oh, just that they would make a good couple and stuff like that."

"Why was Kristen running away?"

Jennifer's innocent, factual reporting dropped away. Spite and malice came into her voice.

"Because she's a brat and won't do what she's told to do. Even my mom says so. She's just running away to cause trouble, so I stopped her."

"Was not," Kristen said.

"Wait your turn," I said to Kristen. Turning to Jennifer, I repeated, "No labels. Don't call her a brat, OK?" Then I asked Cleo to speak. She repeated Jennifer's story, almost word for word.

Josette asked Shelly why she was crying. Shelly said that she was afraid Brad was going to get hurt and she didn't know what to do. There had been no direct conversation between her and Jennifer and Cleo.

Brian spoke next. He'd been playing some distance away when he heard Brad cursing Jennifer. He came to help because Brad had hit Jennifer before. He didn't know anything that happened earlier. He was sure that Brad was the antagonist because "Brad's always sticking his nose in where it doesn't belong."

It was Kristen's turn. "My sister and Cleo were making fun of Carl and Shelly. They said Shelly loved Carl but Carl was too stupid to do anything about it. They said Shelly deserved Carl because she could never have him. Then they called her a dumb bitch."

"You liar!" Cleo shouted.

"Just wait until we get home," Jennifer threatened. "You're going to get it."

"No way," I said. "I can't get into your home to stop you from hitting her, but I will go to your mother and tell her if I have to. Remember, we said confidentiality, but not if it meant someone was going to get hurt."

Cleo jumped to Jennifer's defense. "Her mother won't listen to you anyway. Besides, Jennifer and I can get Kristen when no one is around."

Kristen started crying. I looked both girls in the eye. I spoke softly, but with exacting directness. "You can, I'm sure. But it's only going to lead to more trouble. I'm on your side. Listen, let it go. Kristen can be a great friend in your life. Make it better, not worse. If you care for her, she'll care for you. How would it feel if you had an older sister who was threatening you?

"My mom threatens me all the time," Jennifer said. "I live with it. Kristen can take it, too."

"How do you feel when your mom threatens you?"

"Bad, but it doesn't kill me."

Jennifer's mood changed with this admission. She seemed depressed and withdrawn. Her anger was no longer directed at Kristen, Brad, or Amber.

"Did you tell Amber what you heard?" I asked.

"Amber asked me what they were talking about," Kristen said, still sniffling, "so I told her. I didn't know what she would do."

"I didn't exactly ask her," said Amber, whose turn to speak had now arrived. "We were just talking, and she said Jennifer and Cleo were talking about Shelly and Carl, so I asked her about it and she told me."

"What did you do next? Did you tell Brad?" Josette asked.

Amber looked down, trying to figure out what to say next. I prodded. "Well?" I asked.

"I told him," she said in a small voice.

"Why?"

"Because I was mad at Cleo and Jennifer for making fun of me last week. I didn't know what Brad would do. I just wanted a friend who was on my side." Amber started to cry.

"Are you saying that you felt hurt and left out and thought that if you told Brad then he would feel sorry for you and be your friend?" I asked. I did not attempt to comfort Amber.

Amber nodded through her tears.

"Did you get what you wanted?"

"No," Amber said. "I didn't think he'd bother them. I thought he'd just play with me."

"We didn't say anything bad about her last week," Cleo said. "She's so damned sensitive she just took it wrong."

"I did not. You're always saying bad things about everyone. You think it makes you look better."

Cleo's anger erupted. "You bitch!" she shouted. "All I said was you're always running to your parents for help 'cause you think they're so great. You're just chicken to be without them. And here they are, protecting you again."

Several children started to argue with Cleo, defending us as fair. After a moment everyone realized that Jennifer was defending us, too, and quieted down.

"They are being fair," Jennifer said. "They are. They got her to admit she turned Brad against us."

"Well, you said it about Amber too," Cleo told Jennifer, looking both sullen and depressed.

"I know and I do think they protect her too much. But right now they are being fair."

A quiet ensued. After a full minute, I spoke.

"OK, let's piece it together. I'm going to say what I heard. If I'm speaking of you and I say it wrong please interrupt to correct me. Don't let any mistake get past you. It's very important for this to be an accurate summary of all that's been said.

"Last week Cleo and Jennifer made a comment about the way Josette and I treat Amber. Amber took offense. Today Cleo and Jennifer made a comment about Carl and Shelly. Kristen heard it. She believed they were making fun of Carl and Shelly. Amber asked Kristen about the conversation between Cleo and Jennifer. She told her. Amber told Brad, who became angry at Jennifer and Cleo. He believes they are mean and make fun of people. Brad yelled at Jennifer and Cleo. Brian heard and came to defend them because he believes Brad is an aggressive troublemaker. Is that it? Does everyone agree that that's what happened?"

Everyone agreed.

"Well, what do we do now?" I asked. "Can anyone see a way to leave this field with better feelings about each other?"

Silence.

"How about you, Amber?" I asked. "Can you see anything you did that you wouldn't do again? Do you owe anyone an apology?"

Silence.

"Was it right to get Brad involved?"

"No."

"Did you know that Kristen was telling the truth about Jennifer and Cleo?"

"No. OK, I should have checked out Kristen's story and I am sorry, Brad, for dragging you in."

"That's all right, Amber," Brad said. "I do want to be your friend." He looked at Cleo and Jennifer. "I guess I get angry real quick. I only wish you guys wouldn't talk about us."

"I get angry quick, too," Brian offered. "You're stuff just does it to me, Brad. Maybe we should stay away from each other."

"Or find a grown-up to help when you start to get angry," I interjected. "Get help. You're not supposed to have all the answers at ten years old."

Silence.

"Jennifer?" I asked.

Silence.

"Jennifer?"

A rueful smile crossed Jennifer's face. "OK, so we had our part, too. Maybe we should be more careful when we talk about people. We didn't mean it to blow up into such a big mess."

"And Kristen?"

"OK, so she just made a mistake cause she was mad at me."

Kristen smiled. "I did try to get back at you, but I won't ever do it again. I promise."

Jennifer smiled, then gently said, "Oh sure, you little monkey." And they hugged.

"That leaves me out, as usual," Cleo said. Everyone was uncomfortable. A minute passed.

"I'm your friend," Jennifer said.

"Even if we don't talk about other people?"

"Sure. We don't do it all the time, you know."

"I know. I'm just not sure I want to give it up."

"What did it bring you this time?" Josette asked

"Trouble. But it didn't start that way."

"What did it feel like when you started?"

"It was fun. I felt close to Jennifer."

"How does the trouble feel?"

"No good. Everybody's hurting."

"Were the good feelings worth the bad feelings?"

"No, but if the bad feelings did not turn up I would have liked the good ones."

Everyone had been listening to Cleo. I had nothing more to ask her. After waiting a few minutes to see if anyone else had anything to say, I spoke.

"Let me tell you all a story. It comes from the Jewish tradition. In Jewish villages the Rabbi is a very important person. Not only is he a man of religion but he is considered wise on every matter that affects the lives of the people.

"One day an older man came to the Rabbi. 'Rabbi,' the man said, 'I have a problem. All my life I have gossiped about other people. Now I see the pain it has caused. What can I do to make up for my mistake, Rabbi?' The Rabbi thought for a while, then said, 'Come tomorrow to the center square of the village and bring a feather pillow with you.' The man could not believe his ears. He repeated the Rabbi's instructions to make sure he understood them correctly. When the Rabbi assured him that he had, the man left to do as he was told. The next day the man came to the square with the feather pillow. The Rabbi met him there. 'Do you still want to make up for the trouble you've caused by your gossip?' asked the Rabbi. 'Yes,' said the man, 'I do.' 'Very well,' said the Rabbi. He looked around the square. A high wind was blowing. 'Break open the pillow,' said the Rabbi. The man did so and the feathers flew everywhere. 'Now go collect the feathers and the trouble caused by your gossip will be fixed.'

"So, it's a rare event," I summed up, "when gossip doesn't turn out badly."

The children, worn out by the day's events, smiled and began to leave. The conversation had lasted for almost two hours The conflict energy dissipated, most of the children offered one another friendly words of parting.

Five minutes later I went back to the field to retrieve the sweater I forgot there. Carl and Shelly were standing there, talking

On Conflict Resolution

It can't be said too often or too plainly: *The single largest inhibitor to the resolution of conflict is the parent or educator who takes the child's conflictive behavior as a personal affront.*

Conflict is impersonal. It is a cry for help. When children are unable to access the resources they need to live harmoniously, they turn to conflict to express their suffering. The deeper intent of the child is to draw attention to pain she is experiencing, not to single out an individual as the object for an act of vengeance. Parents and educators that are aware of this intent are freed from identifying themselves as the "victim" of the child's action.

Consider this parallel: When a child is physically ill most parents do not feel attacked by the changes in the child's behavior. Few would punish a child for waking them up in the middle of the night because of a fever. The parent understands that the child is calling for help, not spitefully destroying his parent's sleep.

In the same way, conflict is a call for help the child employs when she is beset by stress and psychological imbalance. She is not maliciously upsetting family unity, but drawing attention to a family imbalance as it manifests in her. Indeed, she is acting wisely by reaching for help, and she is doing the family a favor by showing where additional care is needed. In the face of this desperate act, many children are punished. At that moment, the seeds of personal and social disease are sown.

Reacting personally to conflict behavior borders on the ridiculous: We've all seen a five-year-old child trip over a toy, stand up, and kick the toy. Experiencing frustration, he attacks the most available person or thing. Are his actions a personal affront to the toy?

Consider this: Meg is a high school student angry with the tedium of school. She's been sitting in classrooms since Body-Being. Now it's the spring of her sixteenth year, and her unalterable desire is to be in unstructured contact with her peers. Meg begins to talk in class. The teacher reprimands her and she is rude to him in turn. Should he take it personally?

When he does, he aggravates the problem: Insulted, he will increase the punishment. If the student insists on her position, the punishment will increase again. At some point either her will breaks and she capitulates, or he keeps on insisting, becoming abandoned and isolated. In neither

217

case is the original conflict—Meg's need to socialize and his need to follow the lesson plan—actually resolved.

An *impersonal* reaction helps the teacher to see the cause of the behavior. Many options then present themselves. He might give her an option other than staying in class that day, thereby gaining her trust and saving everyone time and effort. By modeling trust he creates the conditions that will lead to his being trusted in the future. In a talk after class, he might acknowledge her needs and work out a solution acceptable to both of them. Or he might start a class discussion on the effect of the seasons on behavior. One way or another, he brings a moment of natural sanity when he drops his identification as the "teacher who the student is trying to get" and answers the students real needs with meaningful solutions.

Resolution, then Healing

The intensity of the moment of conflict often precludes long-term healing efforts, which work best when the air is cleared. When conflict arises, the aim should simply be to resolve. Allow each individual adequate time to come to as broad and open a position as possible. With the immediate conflict cleared away, you can begin working on the deeper issues that beset children and family; only at the deeper level can long-term healing occur.

Treating the dissolving of momentary conflict as an end in itself is like picking a weed by the stem, leaving the root. It will only grow back more strongly and be more difficult to eliminate later. In "The Cherry Festival Story" obvious issues such as Jennifer's relationship with her mother, Cleo's fear of abandonment, Brad and Brian's need to violently compete, and Amber's insecurity were not addressed. That work must be done in a different context. The hope is to resolve the conflict to the extent that this more fundamental work can be started.

While conflict is dramatic and grabs our attention, resolving it is actually the more superficial aspect of connecting with children. Conflict is simply the least subtle of the behaviors used by children to draw attention to their more serious needs.

Many parenting techniques, especially those that favor "reward and punishment," stake their claim on their ability to resolve conflict. Unfortunately, making such a claim is similar to concluding that a cough drop is a cure-all because it temporarily alleviates the symptoms of an illness.

Such a conclusion ignores the biological cause of the disease. Perhaps more importantly, it ignores the child's true condition, which left her susceptible to the virus.

Natural Learning Rhythms pays attention to the whole child. Even at first, when conflict precludes the deeper healing work, the developmental needs and inner wisdom of the child are honored. The next sections describe how to keep developmental awareness at the forefront while engaged with the heat of conflict.

Approaching the Conflict: Stage-Specific Word Choice

Developmental appropriateness is the foundation for all conflict-resolution tools. Parental guidance and discipline that falls above or below a child's developmental capabilities causes mistrust and confusion in the child: Many times a ten-year-old will walk away from a parental reprimand with a sneer of disgust, "She treats me like a baby!" Or a six-year-old, listening to a lecture on how he "misbehaved," will say "yes" in the appropriate places— then behave the same way an hour or a day or a week later.

Vocabulary is one important way to let the child know you are in tune with her. In "The Cherry Festival Story," a mixture of mostly Emotional-Being and some Body-Being vocabulary provided a medium through which each person could communicate. When Josette talked about clearing up the bad feelings with Jennifer and Cleo, she was using Emotional-Being vocabulary. We used no words that would force any child to process the conflict within a conceptual framework beyond their stage-specific recognition capabilities. More subtly, the words guided the way in which issues were *perceived*.

I set firm limits on Jennifer's threat toward her younger sister by exercising my natural authority as elder. I did not attempt to reason with Jennifer. I neither used threats nor felt threatened. I did not coerce Jennifer into an agreement to leave Kristen alone. I did not take her attacks personally or see myself as protector of a "sweet, younger child." After stating the limits, I simply switched to an Emotional-Being question: "How would you feel if it happened to you?" This established a precedent. Limits would be set. The child could respond within her capabilities. The child's response would then be treated with respect and courtesy.

Later, when Cleo was speaking, the conversation, following the guidelines, turned solely to exploration of her feelings. Cleo mentioned she felt "left out, as usual." Tangential issues did not arise. Everyone was focused on the central issue of Cleo's feelings. Her expressions of vulnerability touched everyone there.

When parents and teachers are able to use stage-specific vocabulary, they keep everyone in the same circle of communication.

Offering Appropriate Alternatives

Children in the midst of conflict feel trapped and confused. They often cannot see the way to resolution. Many children gladly accept alternative courses of action when those alternatives account for the roots of the conflict, and the needs of each child.

During the Cherry Festival conflict we were continually searching for alternatives we might offer the children. To Jennifer, I suggested a healthy way to feel about Kristen. I offered Brad and Brian the option of contacting a grown-up when they felt anger toward each other. In other cases we've presented as many as five or six alternatives to each child embroiled in a conflict.

Such suggestions, *because they are suggestions,* empower the child through the exercise of choice and by telling her you are on her side. They should not be insisted upon. When we insist, we force the child to take her attention away from the conflict at hand.

Supporting Each Child

When approaching conflict remember: You are the model. As you model, so you teach. In the Cherry Festival case there was no good to be gained in raising my voice when limiting Jennifer. Arguing with arguers yields more argument. Instead, the aim should be to allow each child to reach as broad an understanding as possible without violating the truth. Modeling an open, fluid approach shows the child how to achieve this aim.

Come to the conflict prepared to listen. Drop expectations. Careful listening will stimulate the right choice of words. The ability to *paraphrase,* as described in the Communication chapter, is one of the most important conflict-resolution tools. Paraphrasing is possible only when the individual trying to resolve the conflict knows how to listen.

Each child has something valuable to contribute to this world. The educator's job is to create the conditions that can bring forth this contribution. No matter how difficult the moment, keep in mind that each child is profound and worthwhile here and now. The child does not have to do anything to prove her existence meaningful; her mere presence is sufficient. Each child embodies *stage-specific wisdom.*

Accepting the worthiness of each child destroys favoritism. In dealing with a group of children, the mindful parent knows that his child's—and society's—best interests are served by finding the healthiest outcome for each child.

The educator's demeanor is also key. Come to the conflict with the courage to act. Try to work through your own feelings of intimidation before engaging the children, because these feelings only get in the way of a resolution. In the conflict at the festival, we came to the field with an intent on reaching the truth. We did our very best to follow through on that intent.

A word of caution should be added: You'll do best when you don't adopt too rigid a moral stance, because great moral expectations will prevent resolution. At the Cherry Festival, the Body-Being children would not have sensed flexibility and warmth, and the Emotional-Being children would not have felt fairness and adaptability if we had insisted on rigid standards of right and wrong.

In the Heat of the Moment

Children in conflict are children in trouble. Their life has not yielded the results they expected. Frustration has set in. They intensify their conflictive behavior, only to find themselves further than ever from their desired goal. Their frustration either may boil over into physical or psychological violence, or decay into apathy, depression, or alienation.

A resolution requires compassion on the part of the grown-up. It will take patience, honesty, completeness, diplomacy, gentleness, dependability, appropriate action, and the elimination of "put-downs." These tools can be applied in the heat of any conflict to help bring resolution.

In the field at the Cherry Festival, Brad claimed he didn't curse at Jennifer and Cleo. The two girls, and Brian also, claimed he did. Patience means: Go slowly. What was a curse to Jennifer, Cleo, and Brian may not be a curse to Brad. The grown-up must ascertain: Was the distinction between cursing and yelling crucial to resolution? Only by using patience could we find out. The issue of cursing was not forgotten, just put "on hold." As it turned out, the distinction was not important. The time and energy saved through patience was then reinvested in the crucial issue: the interpersonal relationships among the children.

Two hours—the time that was needed to resolve the conflict at the Cherry Festival—is a long time to maintain focus and intensity for both children and grown-ups. Yet only through commitment to finding out the whole story, no matter how long it takes, can each participant experience inclusion and have a meaningful stake in the outcome.

This commitment to patience served everyone during the delicate moment when Cleo and Jennifer redefined their friendship. Had there been any sense of rush, had another person intruded in their dialogue, the girls could not have redefined their friendship there. Part of the conflict would have gone unresolved. The other children would not have witnessed Cleo and Jennifer's kindness and concern for each other.

Completeness also builds a sense of inclusion. By paraphrasing and answering every question, the conflict is presented as a whole. Each participant has a chance to see her part in it. At the same time, she can also recognize the interrelationship of all the players, how they co-created the conflict. Immediately, each person's fear of being blamed as the sole cause of the trouble falls away. They are in this together. They probably need to work it through together.

Grown-ups must practice total honesty during conflict. The pressures of the situation leave no room for "white lies" or half-truths. The children need to know your values in order to risk their truth. When the resolver exemplifies honesty the children sense a way out. The light of honesty shines at the end of the dark tunnel of conflict. The children are naturally drawn to it.

Honesty bears direct relation to dependability. Being dependable means to always keep your word. We promised no favoritism, and a we made consistent attempt to uncover the truth and preserve confidentiality within certain limits. By carrying through on these promises, dependability made its appearance. The children came to trust us. They felt trust. They began to turn to us for mediation. By the time Cleo, in her desperation, accused us of favoritism not one child believed it. Forced to abandon her attack, she had to face her own contribution to the conflict.

Total engagement is critical. No interruptions are allowed for anyone, by anyone. If a parent had come into the field to play with one of the principles of the conflict, we would have explained the situation and asked her to either participate or leave. When indoors, pull the plug on all electronic interrupters.

Total engagement also refers to complete attention to all facets of the conflict: being there for the children, listening, asking them to be there for each other, modeling concentration, and keeping the focus, especially through the use of paraphrasing. When attention wanders, the grown-up can use paraphrasing to quickly and easily bring both individual and collective attention back to the point.

Josette and I have a button that says "Imperfect yet Sacred." As grown-ups, it is our natural role to act honorably and straightforwardly with our children—even though we may not understand everything about the whole universe. So, when the time is right, take appropriate action. In the field at the Cherry Festival, I assessed what was needed, then acted. Modeling strength, I stepped in the middle of the fight between Brad and Brian. Later, modeling quiet wisdom, I told the teaching story.

Never allow a "put-down" of any kind, not even as a joke. Stop name-calling as soon as it occurs, as I did with Brad at the beginning of the conflict. The resolver cannot become involved with violence or pejorative without dragging down the children with him.

In all cases, be gentle. Be slow to threaten and slower to punish. Jennifer claimed not to have gossiped about Shelly and Carl, then admitted she had done so. It is not necessary to punish her once she's spoken the truth. The lie indicates underlying problems to which remedies should be applied, but in the heat of the conflict the simple revelation of truth is a great victory. It means she felt safe enough to risk. To punish her would destroy her safe space.

The aim is to reach relative balance, not to prove a point. Brad is not "bad" for fighting. He is wounded and crying out. No sane parent would punish Brad for catching a flu. Instead, he would nurse Brad to health. When he recovered, he would keep Brad from getting over-tired and remind him to eat.

Finally, use diplomacy. Don't try to make excuses or explain from one child to another. Be the facilitator, the medium in which all parties can express themselves freely. I helped Amber understand why she told Brad about the conversation between Cleo and Jennifer. I did not try to explain Amber's position to the other children. If I had I would have been seen as defending Amber. Then, the other children would risk no more that day.

Some Additional Conflict-Resolution Tools

The Tao Te Ching, the ancient book of Chinese wisdom, tells us, "Take care of problems while they are small and they will never become big." Because harsher expressions of conflict appear when the more moderate forms are ignored, a child merely turning his shoulder sharply or muttering under his breath gives sufficient reason to stop and investigate. Both harsh and moderate forms of conflicts stem from the same root cause. By meeting the problem in its early stages, that cause is more easily accessible. It is not buried under all the pain and confusion that develops over time. In the classroom or the family, a rule can be made to act upon conflicts as they arise. Consequently, rarely does violence erupt, or do conflicts involving many children arise.

Again, when approaching the conflict or acting in the midst of it, refrain from labeling. In the gathering in the field, we never accepted the idea of Brian and Brad as "violent troublemakers," or Cleo and Jennifer as "mean." By remaining focused on the specific events of the conflict, the facts were uncovered. Had such labels been accepted, litanies of past transgressions from whence the labels originated would have surfaced. And like gray clouds blocking the sunlight, these labels and stories would have obscured the truth.

When interacting with a family unit, remember that any and all problems originate in the family, rather than the individual. Children who lie, for instance, generally feel badly about themselves. How has their self-esteem been destroyed? Why hasn't the family taken the actions necessary to empower the child? Some of the more common situations that lead to children lying include envy between siblings caused by parental favoritism, anger at material rather than heart-felt expressions of love, and the desire to explore "forbidden fruits." There are others, and they need to be uncovered and remedied by the family as a group.

Grown-ups gossiping about a child exacerbates conflict. Whether the child is a member of your family or not, to idly or spitefully speculate on a child's character or behavior isolates that child from the grown-ups in her extended family and community. In no way does it empower the child to learn how to resolve her conflicts.

So many parents wish to hang on to peaceful times that they avoid recalling the nasty moments. In so doing they neglect one of the golden rules of conflict resolution: Use the good times to speak about the bad times. While conflict is at bay, a state of relative balance exists. The child can review her behavior and perhaps accept the need for improvement. She's open to trying out new ideas. In addition, speaking of conflict during the good times establishes continuity within the family. Yesterday's conflict is a symptom of "dis-ease"; the more that can be known about its cause the healthier the family will be. This is not a call to badger the child with guilt and blame: The intent is to create a family history—a relationship through time—throughout which responsibility is taken for the whole of the family's interactions.

If the grown-up cannot resolve the conflict, she can reach an agreement with the children to call for help, an option that is particularly valuable when interacting with Will-Being and Reasoning-Being children. The person or people called in must be acceptable to all parties. Children often fill this role with excellent results; they frequently translate both the words and the feelings of other children more skillfully than an adult can. Don't place too much pressure on the helping person. If she cannot help, gracefully release her from any obligations.

The tools described thus far apply to any conflict. Used often, their wide range of practicability becomes apparent. From sibling rivalry to conflicts over chores to fights between peers, these tools allow adversaries to take a breath and renew their perspective.

225

Three Challenges for Families

In workshops and in counseling, the following three problems are presented to us over and over again for resolution. Many different parents have reported success when approaching these problems in the following way:

♦ **Tantrums**

When a child is having a tantrum, the parent applies the conflict-resolution tools, always staying in contact with the child. If possible, especially with children in Body-Being, the parent touches and hugs. Even if the child is violent or extremely antagonistic, the parent keeps feeding her loving touch. If the child absolutely will not let herself be touched, the parent stays as close as possible and maintains eye contact.

Always gentle, never taking the child's behavior personally, the parent speaks from his heart: "I love you and know you are upset. I'm just waiting patiently for you to return so we can work this out. It's safe to return. I am not going to punish you. I love you." If the parent cannot maintain calmness, she can call in others to help. Siblings are often a healthy influence, if they are inclined to take on the problem.

As soon as the tantrum stops, the parent thanks the child and tries to address the problem. If the child does not want to discuss it, the parent drops the matter. He attempts to bring it up later. If the child resists, the parent simply mentions the fact that the tantrum did occur.

Much the same methods can be applied to sulking. Sulking is the flip side of having a tantrum, just as being wishy-washy is the flip side of being a bully. Here again, gentle contact leads the child back to a state of balance.

♦ The "Bad" Peers Predicament

A different type of conflict—often concerning teenagers—arises when the parent disapproves of the child's peer group. What can be done when the child runs with a "bad" crowd and refuses to consider the parent's position?

Developmental awareness is key: Beginning in Will-Being, the child begins to assert her independence. She also becomes very sensitive to peers. One common way of expressing these natural inclinations is the development of a self-defined peer group. Recognizing how likely this development is to occur, the parent prepares by maintaining friendly relations with her child's peers at all times. When the child phases into a new peer group, the parent is an unobtrusive part of the process. Sometimes the parent determines that the new peer group holds her child back. In these cases, she then engages the problem while it is small, at the beginning.

If the parent hasn't been part of the phasing process already, she can still adopt an "enter into it" attitude. Gentle and patient, she interacts with the whole group during her contacts with them. She listens and paraphrases. Without insistence or pejorative language, she honestly explains her opinions and positions. She asks the group to paraphrase her comments. She only objects to the truly objectionable: Making a fuss, for example, over a hairstyle takes away from important issues such as the quality of education or responsible sex.

If the child is in Will-Being, the parent tries to elicit the *ideals* of the group. He suggests ways in which these ideals can be put into action in ways acceptable to all. Challenging the young people, he meets them in their developmental moment. Trust begins to grow. Whenever he can, the parent looks for the good in each person and remarks upon it. If the conflict remains unresolved he can ask to bring in other parents, with the agreement that everyone play by the same rules. The parent does not threaten the child's support systems. Maintaining his courage and keeping his word, the parent gives respect and demands the same in return.

♦ Chores: Making It Work

227

Perhaps the most common conflict in a family's daily life revolves around chores. Some families pay their children to do chores, others punish them if they don't. Both payment and punishment are forms of coercion. The child is being trained instead of educated. She is being denied conscious access to her inner wisdom.

Resolving this conflict about housework begins with each family member, especially the parents, coming to a clear understanding of what they mean by the word "chore." For so many people a chore means an unpleasant activity that one is forced to do. It is akin to slavery and to be avoided wherever possible. Chores limit freedom. They are burdens; the opposite of "fun."

If the parent relates this way to chores, the children will also. Whether registering her feelings silently or aloud, a complaining parent adds to the conflict. Her best option is to restructure her own view of chores, admittedly a difficult task. Children know their parent's intention however, so the task is unavoidable. If the parent avoids restructuring her own negative relationship to chores, it smells strongly of hypocrisy to insist that the children do them.

The acknowledgment by all family members that the family is a single unit helps with this problem. Chores can then be defined as that which is necessary to keep the family healthy and together. Nature can be used as an example of how all parts of a whole are interrelated. Each child can relate to this understanding of chores as crucial to family togetherness in accordance with her developmental moment. Chores can then be seen as a service to the family, which values and supports each of its members equally.

When the child refuses to do her share, attempt to mutually arrive at a compromise. Be careful in choice of words, paraphrase, and try to suggest appropriate alternatives.

One such alternative might be to combine your chores with hers and then do them all together. Chores are especially onerous to a child if they isolate him from the rest of the family. Many times all family members cleaning the house together works much better than the command, "Go clean your room."

By spelling out the natural consequences of lack of cooperation, many chore-related conflicts can be resolved. The parent must be careful to avoid punishment. Make it clear that time consumed by arguments or by the parent doing the child's chore takes away from "fun" time. Telling a child she is to stay in her room until she completes a chore is a punishment.

Specifically state where fun time fits into the family schedule. Fun time usually does not begin until chores and important tasks are accomplished. Parents have the natural right to factor in time for themselves as an important task. Inform the child of the priorities. Be sure she understands so she can make a decision and directly experience its consequences. If you've applied these tools and the child still refuses to do a chore, don't belittle her. Do tell her how you feel about the situation. Though it may be hard to remember sometimes, whatever her decision, she is not "bad." Such shaming goes nowhere and only does damage

No matter what the conflict is, no matter how aggravated or perplexed we may feel, we must meet our children's developmental needs. In doing so we provide a context for solving conflicts, for honoring a commitment to health in the family

☘

During the last two decades, the trauma to children resulting from the breakup of families has shaken our families and our communities Many of the conflicts of today's parents and children are the products of the guilt and pain attendant to divorce. These circumstances and effects will be specifically addressed in the special section on Divorce found in the back of this book.

*S*ociety & Natural Learning Rhythms

We know that parents and teachers taking the time to read this book care deeply about children. For many of us, the motivation for working so hard to understand children is twofold: First, we have children in our lives whom we love dearly and for whom we want the very best. Second, we are concerned with the state of the world today—war, domestic violence, substance abuse, pollution, the wasting of our natural resources, unresponsive government—and we believe that the way we parent and educate children will be an important factor in improving the state of the environment and society.

This book has been dedicated to revitalizing the bonds with children in our lives—whether family members, students, or friends—and to restoring our connection to our natural learning rhythms. To complete our inquiry, we'll look at the way in which education determines our social reality.

Hurt Children

Children who have not had their developmental needs met often display antagonistic social behavior. We've already had some glimpses of this: Sean, abandoned by his biological father and then by a step-father, resorted to domestic violence. Helen, using sex as a way to numb herself to her family's hypocrisy, ended up with unwanted pregnancies. Jack, lacking inspiration in his life and feeling rejected by his mother, became a compulsive substance abuser. Had their predicaments gone

Often, in fact, the older a child gets the more extreme the behavior becomes, as the following case illustrates.

We first met Lucas eight years ago, when he was six years old. His parents had just agreed to a divorce. Both had serious problems with alcohol, and the father was abusive to the mother. At the time we first met them, the father had just moved out; Lucas was displaying his displeasure through aggressiveness toward the girls and bullying the weaker boys in his first-grade class, swearing almost continuously, and lying and being rude to the teacher. At home, the boy adopted a "man of the house" posture with a righteousness that would have seemed almost comical, were it not so sad. Lucas would question any male visitor about his intentions toward his mother. The child would insist on carrying packages that were too heavy for him and make his mother account for every minute that she was away from him.

Lucas's mother, Angela, sought our help, but his father, Roy, saw counseling as a waste of time and money. He continued to drink and treat women abusively. But according to court order, Roy had visitation in his own home about one-third of the time. As a result of this arrangement, any remedies the mother attempted the father undermined, either deliberately or as a result of his lifestyle.

Much of the violence Lucas expressed was a direct imitation of his father. Furthermore, Lucas expected females to passively accept rudeness and aggressiveness because that had been his mother's response when she was treated in a degrading way.

Once the divorce was final, however, Angela changed her ways. She began to date non-aggressive males who liked Lucas, and she began to model feminine strength. Lucas responded positively: After spending time in this new atmosphere, the dysfunction temporarily died away and his fun-loving, curious nature resurfaced. Once Lucas would return to his father's, however, all the trouble would begin anew.

So it went for three years. We had only intermittent contact with Lucas, but the strain of his dual existence showed in many places: On the positive side, he had female friends with whom he was gracious and kind, he excelled in sports, had respectful relationships with his coaches, and did whatever his mother asked. At the same time, Lucas had lost interest in nature; he preferred stories with superficial "good guys" who conquer nature; he preferred stories with superficial "good guys" who conquer only through the use of force, lied gratuitously, had continual fights, and did mediocre work in school.

At twelve, Lucas broke another boy's nose in a fight during a football game. At thirteen, he began to experiment with crack cocaine. He dated a girl three times, tried to have sex with her, then hit her when she refused. Increasingly disdainful toward his mother, he requested that he live exclusively with his father. Before they had a chance to talk about it he ran away from home, stole a car, and landed in juvenile hall.

These are desperate and difficult behaviors echoed by many young, disaffected teens in our society. Like them, Lucas has fine natural talents and intelligence that would flourish in a supportive environment. Like them, he is confused and hurt and searching for a world that makes sense.

Hurt Adults

The pernicious effects of developmental deprivation do not disappear at the end of childhood. Almost every approach to psychology recognizes the tremendous importance of an individual's childhood on his adult behavior. Whether that individual's problem is an inability to work, a bitter divorce, exaggerated behavior (such as extreme competitiveness to prove self-worth), or a loathing of people of another race or religion, the seeds of this conduct were usually sown in childhood.

233

In some cases, no human being actually inflicted the child's wound, yet the pain still runs deep and society still suffers. Sixty-five-year-old Ann, for instance, had a father who died in an auto accident when she was eleven. Although she was miles from the accident, Ann, like so many children, saw herself as personally responsible. Fifty years later, describing her memories in counseling, Ann echoed the same kind of feelings expressed by of most children of divorce: "I thought I must have done something wrong or Dad wouldn't have left me." After he died, Ann was left to grieve alone—unbearable for most people and crippling for an Emotional-Being child. Although she had three sons and a husband whom she loved, Ann suffered from seasonal anxiety attacks during those fifty years. During these attacks she couldn't provide the home life she knew her family needed, and this only increased her anxiety. In short, Ann lived about a third of her life incapacitated. Those of us fortunate enough to know her after her anxiety dis-

Unresolved childhood wounds will often express themselves even more blatantly, as in the case of our client Will. Two years ago, Will came to us frustrated, angry, and tense. He worked for a chemical company that illegally dumped toxic waste in a nearby river. He said he hated it. Worse yet, he spent sixty hours a week there, commuted two hours every day and pushed for every promotion that had even a remote possibility of coming his way. Will's wife, who called him a workaholic, was getting ready to take their two children and leave.

In looking at Will's life, I (Josette) shook my head, bewildered, and asked the obvious question: "Why not simply change jobs?"

"I can't," Will answered, wringing his hands. "I need the money."

"You say, 'I need the money.' Don't you mean your family needs the money?"

"Yeah, I guess so." Will seemed distracted. "Well, I mean Nancy says she doesn't care. But I do. We must get this money even if she can't understand it."

It took an hour, but Will eventually saw his attachment to the money and the long hours were due to his aversion to his father's lifestyle. His father had been, in Will's words, "lazy and a crummy provider." Will would not turn out that way. He would work long and hard to earn lots of money, even at the expense of his family and the environment.

Will's behavior came about for a good reason. As a child, he had been hurt and threatened by his father's actions. By compulsively overworking himself, Will was protecting himself from the pain of having to re-experience those difficult sensations and feelings—thus, unintentionally, preventing himself from moving past them. Therefore, becoming aware of his motivations did not completely open him to a new way of living. Will couldn't simply say, "Oh, I see the light and now I'll go home, take an environmentally responsible job, and save my marriage." He needed to penetrate and confront his feelings.

After six months of intensive counseling, Will accessed the feelings of fright, anger, and vulnerability as he had when he was a child. After this moving experience, he contacted his father and siblings and told them his honest perceptions of his childhood. Feeling ever more empowered, he turned to Nancy, who had supported him throughout counseling, and reaffirmed his commitment to her and their children. Last, he found a job that met his standards of social responsibility.

and reaffirmed his commitment to her and their children. Last, he found a job that met his standards of social responsibility.

Using "Common" Sense

Will's story ends positively, but it raises the disturbing possibility that many of us may actually be perpetuating interpersonal strife and environmental destruction as a result of early violation of our natural learning rhythms. Consider this: If security and flexibility were adequately supplied during Body-Being, would we really choose to spend so much money on weapons? Would we even be capable of blowing up our own body, or that of the planet we depend upon? And if we remembered Emotional-Being's wisdom of interconnectedness and fairness, could we desecrate natural habitats? Are such actions as spying and such attitudes as prejudice a response to the damage done to our individuality and freedom during Will-Being? How could genuine Reasoning-Being wisdom support highway gridlock, corruption in government, or the fouling of a country's water supply?

Specific questions such as these lead to clear conclusions: If body wisdom is not nourished during our earliest years, we lose our ability to evaluate our world by its sensations. We may, for instance, disregard the life-preserving message our body sends us when we become nauseated at a toxic dump, or the meaning of illnesses such as cancer that are linked to radioactivity. These messages, presented in the unambiguous language of body wisdom, say: "Horrible. Life does not live here."

Once we accept the simple relationship between developmental deprivation and suffering, examples of it can be found very easily in many areas of our society.

With poverty and prejudice eating away at the social structure, inner-city teens have few strong models during Emotional-Being and are offered little sensitive respect during Will-Being. They have few community ritual rites and no personal space that is truly theirs. Desperate, they turn to each other to mark territory, create an identity, and find some fairness and justice. Hungry for thrilling challenges in a desolate environment, a number choose to take substances that temporarily boost feelings of personal power. Having been stripped of security and warmth during Body-Being, they are often heedless to personal safety.

235

goods to Satan reveal these teens' desperate search for adventure, transcendence, and meaning.

What can concerned parents and teachers do about developmental deprivation and it effects? How can we help young people in a really fundamental way?

Creating Trust

The ability to trust is inherent in human beings, but its actual growth depends upon education. Trust *develops*.

The more developed the individual's ability to trust, the more she will trust herself. Paying attention to a child's natural learning rhythms builds trust; neglecting them diminishes it. Trust means the ability to rely on the integrity, strength, and surety of yourself and the people around you. And so we ask: How does trust develop? How can we use it to create a society in which each person has a chance to express her natural talents and realize her natural destiny?

The wisdom inherent in each of the life stages contributes to the development of trust in a unique and important way.

Body-Being: A Trust for a Trust

As we've learned, Body-Being brings to consciousness the knowledge of body-as-environment. A give and take, the rhythm of sensation, leads to perceiving justice as retributive.

Provided with a balanced diet and plenty of loving touch, Body-Being's call for "an eye for an eye" transforms into "trust for trust." The child learns to explore body-as-environment without fearing that the world is inherently hostile or that worry is a necessary defense while exploring.

Trust in Emotional-Being: A Sense of Justice

Healthy eleven- and twelve-year-old children are kind, just, and empathic. Were they able to comprehend a deeper meaning of the past and the future, they would make excellent judges. Unlike the healthy Body-Being child who experiences war and pollution as an unpleasant *bodily* sensations, the healthy Emotional-Being child *feels* these social and the future, they would make excellent judges. Unlike the healthy Body-Being child who experiences war and pollution as an unpleasant *bodily* sensations, the healthy Emotional-Being child *feels* these social atrocities in the form of emotional revulsion. We learned this lesson clearly one autumn from the children in our Nature Class.

It was a cool October day, and the class hiked into a forested region of the Sierra high country where fragrant ponderosa and sugar pines cover the granite hillsides. Around midday we happened upon a steep mountain face that had been clear-cut—every tree that grew there had been felled—by a local timber company.

Six of the eight children in the group started to cry. Everyone of them sat down, stunned. When we returned home, they decided to write letters of protest to the forest supervisor. These letters could not fail to touch the heart of a sensitive person: They spoke of the trees' *feelings* and the loss of habitat for the animals. They also spoke of the children's own feelings: "I am hurt that you've hurt all the creatures of the forest," wrote one ten-year-old boy. "I love them and they love me. How would you feel if I destroyed the home of your friend? Where will they live? Why do I feel so lonely? I am angry with you. Your ex-friend, Peter."

237

The child entering Emotional-Being experiences feelings of separation, loneliness, and vulnerability, for she has just come to understand her own mortality. Through this realization, the child feels connected with all life. If she is able to contact the intangible spirit that permeates life, she then trusts her feelings, for they have allowed her to cope not only with the most frightening challenge of her life, but to actually feel a moment of transcendence.

Children access their emotional wisdom with the proper diet of caring, adventure, honesty, and justice. They gain the knowledge and power of how to cope with resentment and frustration, as well as joy and caring. People in touch with emotional wisdom can handle their emotions. The fullness of emotional wisdom gives us power; this power leads to feelings of strength and surety, the basic components of trust.

Will-Being: Discovering Trust in Ideals

As we have shown, Will-Being is a time of rapid individualization. Treating this self-definition with sensitive respect allows the child to assert herself according to her ideals. Unsophisticated and often unattainable,

If her authentic developmental needs are violated, the child's assertions turn to rebellion. Ideals switch from "making it better" to "tearing it down." Mocked by parents and teachers as stupid or unrealistic, the violated Will-Being child mocks society by highlighting the cynicism, sarcasm, and hypocrisy in every aspect of life.

Children entering Will-Being with early developmental damage often project their ideals onto an institution. They may attach themselves to a country, a team, a career, or a religion, binding the potent Will-Being energy to the chosen institution. The bound child is charged with "creative" energy when the institution's actions meet her ideals. She resorts to "destructive" action when the institution fails to meet her ideals.

For the child in Will-Being, trust develops when her needs for personal space, challenges, opportunity for peer interaction, and the freedom to express her ideals inform the child that her family supports her movement toward individualization and freedom. Family support means respect for her attempts to take responsibility her own life, no matter how awkward these first attempts appear. She trusts those who encourage and support her. Only when she experiences trust can she interact harmoniously with her world.

Can you imagine a world in which healthy young teens were engaged in working on their ideals? Lively debate and many important actions would be carried out concerning important ethical questions such as abortion, war, and the national debt. After years of seeing teens powerfully engaged in their own ideals and natural rhythms, we are sometimes moved to ask: Would substance abuse, unwanted pregnancies, or random acts of violence among teens even exist in such a world?

Trust in Reasoning-Being: The Right to Adult Information

Reasoning-Being children have a particularly delicate task in establishing trust. Yet it is most important they do so, for they are about to reach maturity, have children of their own, and exert strong influence in society.

If trust can be actualized during Reasoning-Being, the child lives with a fundamental awareness of the integrity and wholeness of life. He can bring this awareness into his work and social life as he enters adult life. He and others like him will become the foundation for a sounder society.

If trust can be actualized during Reasoning-Being, the child lives with a fundamental awareness of the integrity and wholeness of life. He can bring this awareness into his work and social life as he enters adult life. He and others like him will become the foundation for a sounder society.

Reasoning-Being children ask the most difficult question a human can ask: "Who Am I?" Confused at the failure of his Will-Being assertions to answer all questions about life, and awed by his expanded knowledge of time, the Reasoning-Being child has a hard time trusting himself, not to mention others. The confusion is compounded by romantic desires. Who is this woman whom I fancy? And how does she fit into my life? Handled poorly, confusion manifests as cynicism. No one is to be trusted. Selfishness follows. I'll take care of myself and worry about the rest of the world later.

Cynicism and selfishness are not inherent despite their ubiquitous appearance in Western youth. Their source lies in the societal belief that children are ignorant and dependent upon "adult" information for success in life—information such as how to handle finance, how to become comfortable with themselves as sexual beings, or how to understand and impact power structures. Big dues are demanded in order to be allowed access to this adult knowledge, and the older the child, the bigger the dues. Being forced to pay dues for basic information inevitably leads to the defensive selfishness and cynicism. The child stops trusting.

When we offer free access to knowledge, on the other hand, we support the child's natural proclivities. She can absorb the information she needs to make sense of the world. She can interact with others equally, on the basis of mutual interests. In the midst of confusion and doubt, she is offered a hand. Her sense of trust coupled with reasoning wisdom allows Reasoning-Being's child to enter the adult world strong and intact.

A Partnership of Opposites

Cooperation and competition, two opposing aspects of natural human behavior, have both been fundamental to our survival as individuals and as a species: In a more primitive era, hunters competed with one another for who would capture the most during the hunt. This approach ensured that the hunting party would strive to use their utmost abilities. Later, however, the same hunters cooperated, sharing the bounty and thereby assuring that every member of the tribal group would survive. In today's

But to emphasize one at the expense of the other leads to crises. In today's world we have not only created systems that produce great wealth, but we have found ways to interact with the world to bring even more wealth. What we have not created are ways of distributing those resources to all human beings so that they might enjoy a prosperous life, and then contribute their skills to the resource base. We have become effective at destroying one another. What we have not created is a way to interact peacefully, so that the precious resources now used for destruction could be added, instead, to the "common wealth." We must relearn cooperative skills and teach them to our children if we are to survive.

Cooperation is a natural behavioral response when human beings feel trust. We *cooperate* when we have a solid grounding in the four stage-specific wisdoms: when we know we belong, and sense the dynamic interconnection between our body and others; when we know our own feelings and the feelings of others; when we find expression for our ideals; and when we are able to develop a cogent plan for our life that integrates our ideals and needs.

When humans beings cooperate, we discover that there are indeed enough resources to provide a secure, comfortable life for all the planet's inhabitants. We come to realize that the apparent scarcities threatening humanity actually reflect a lopsided accumulation and sharing of natural resources. And this imbalance is due, in large measure, to the way in which we are educated.

In a society dominated by fierce competition, human beings lose the ability to hear the wisdom of the body. We cannot reconcile our feelings of separation and loneliness. A hostile competitive reaction surfaces when only a tiny group of "winners" have access to individual expression; reasoning is drowned out by the obsession to compete, and we lose our ability to integrate a concept of life in its entirety.

Based on the fractured education it offers its citizens, a competitive society declares that certain people are more important than others. A pecking order is necessary to ensure that each person knows (and stays) in her proper place. Any human or natural resource—be it love, land, petroleum, or something else—is perceived as "scarce." And the act of competition becomes the proving ground where the individual's worthiness is measured.

petroleum, or something else—is perceived as "scarce." And the act of competition becomes the proving ground where the individual's worthiness is measured.

Excessive competition creates a protection/punishment dynamic in human behavior: To *protect* accumulated resources, we must *punish* those we perceive as competing for those resources. Such behavior is driven by a *logic of fear,* an unmistakable reflection of the kind of education that society has produced. Yet most ironic of all, blind competition is leading human beings to destroy the very basis of their accumulated wealth, the earth itself.

People caught in this competitive mode learn to absorb themselves in personal comfort and salvation, and to make war upon supposed competitors. We easily distinguish this pattern when we look at historical examples of competition. Time after time, for instance, Germany and France have fought over the hilly province of Alsace-Lorraine because of the coal deposits there. Not only has this binational conflict over energy resources resulted in tremendous loss of life and destruction of land, but it has indeed only led to larger battles—some even contend that the Alsace-Lorraine conflict contributed to the outbreak of World War II.

241

The policies of the Catholic Church hierarchy in the Middle Ages provide another example of the way in which people caught up in the protection/punishment dynamic behave. That religious body preached that Catholics alone would attain holy salvation after death. After declaring that membership in the Church was the only road to heaven, they positioned themselves at the tollbooth—the collection plate. By charging exorbitant prices for access, an institution of vulgar and opulent luxury was built on the backs of peons and the urban poor. This competitive ethic was no easy one to change. In the last two decades, radical reformists like those in Latin America's Liberation Theology movement have demanded that the Church actively support all of its members, working in a cooperative manner with those members, including the poor and the desparate. This rift, and the viewpoints it represents, has very nearly split the institution in two.

Evolution: Antagonistic or Synergistic?

When we cooperate, human evolution is viewed synergistically—the whole is greater than the sum of the parts. Nature's interconnected parts are seen as mutually supportive to one another, rather than mutually antago-

In general, cooperative social structures seldom have need for hierarchies. Each person comes to the group with her unique talent. By principle, cooperative institutions do not view human beings as a number; no one is considered for her effect on the balance sheet. And because each talent represents a vital contribution to society, chauvinism cannot take root.

With synergistic cooperation, each person's needs are met. In the case of children, their natural learning rhythms are honored. People trust themselves and each other. We've all seen people rally together during natural disasters—think of the hurricane that struck the south Atlantic coast, or the earthquake and fire that hit the San Francisco Bay Area. In these cases, people threw off their routine worries, volunteered their time and personal resources for the good of the community at large, and, in no small number of cases, spontaneously came to the aid of human beings they had never before laid eyes upon.

Somewhere in our minds, most of us know we have that capability in us, and we can use this same energy and spirit in more sustained efforts as well during crises. We've noticed this sustained, synergistic cooperation at different times during our Friday Nature Classes; we've also seen it in some intentionally formed communities, in some progressive businesses, and in several families.

The values of cooperation, care for children, and respect for the environment have merged in the Cohousing Movement, which is rapidly gaining popularity throughout the United States and Scandinavia.

In cohousing, a group of families and individuals purposely decide to cooperatively build an entire small community together. Using consensus, they create bylaws that determine how the title to the land will be held, which facilities will be shared and which will be owned privately, and how finances are to be managed. Often responsibility for cooking, shopping, or childcare may be shared, allowing more leisure time for each family and a greater variety of choice in fulfilling these commitments. Thus, for the same investment as the cost of a single family dwelling, a family can live on a large tract of land, choose who will be neighbors, and have a close relationship with the people that live nearby. In many ways, this kind of cooperative effort recaptures the best parts of small-town living, which has largely disappeared in our country.

Like the cohousing movement in the United States, the Mondragon cooperatives in the Basque region of Spain provide another example of group

Like the cohousing movement in the United States, the Mondragon cooperatives in the Basque region of Spain provide another example of group members working together for the benefit of all. Begun over forty years ago and now employing more than 21,000 people, this cooperative network includes a worker-controlled bank, department stores and machine shops, and worker-owned high-tech firms. By developing increasingly sophisticated forms of democratic self-government, Mondragon has been able to create systems in which workers enjoy unlimited health care and where hiring, firing, and distribution of common resources are decided collectively. There are cooperative schools for the young and old, daycare for small children, and vocational training that may include attendance at other educational institutions. Recognizing the natural human impulse toward individual expression and innovation, Mondragon's entrepreneur program offers members incentives to start new businesses that become part of the cooperative framework.

American farmers have been sucessfully distributing and marketing their produce for generations through cooperative organizations. On a large scale, the Grange movement, founded in 1867 and continuing today with chapters throughout the United States, has cooperatively established farmer-owned stores, developed expensive grain elevators, created its own insurance company, and appointed agents to deal directly with manufacturers of farm equipment for better prices. On a smaller scale, such cooperative networks as Eugene, Oregon's Organically Grown Cooperative provide markets for farmers who do not use pesticides or harmful chemical fertilizers. The Eugene cooperative also publicizes the sale of produce, helps locate loan sources for farmers, and organizes equipment sharing. Both the Grange movement and the organic farmers' movements are compelling examples of people working together for the advantage of everyone in the group.

❦

In a society that emphasizes competition above all else, its members must try to maximize their personal control of the resources, often at the expense of others. People simply become less concerned about the effects of their actions and more concerned about their own personal gain. In this way, if competition retains the upper hand, environmental degradation (making the mess, or cleaning it up) and war (waging it or

How else could we manage resources? Can you imagine space—the galaxies—from both a competitive and a cooperative perspective? Viewed competitively, space is a military resource, a base for defense against enemies. Earth's citizens live under a sort of sky-wide black umbrella, separated by walls of mutual aggression. And in practical terms, the militaristic exploitation of space consumes resources and human labor without replenishing them.

Now imagine space viewed with a more cooperative outlook: Peaceful exploration there reaps information about the universe we live in. The solar system reveals its secrets. Imagine the salubrious effect on the human spirit at having an entirely new frontier to explore. Think of how it might encourage the search for knowledge and meaning in life. Imagine the unity we would feel with our neighbors on Earth.

When cooperation becomes the prevailing ethic of a society, unbridled competition takes a back seat. The primary aim of the society becomes helping each person access his own intuition. For humans educated according to Natural Learning Rhythms, cooperation is a *natural* expression, not an unattainable ideal. Natural Learning Rhythms can be practiced now, by anyone reading this book. The time and effort spent on consistent adherence to nature's rhythms gives way to a general atmosphere of cooperation—an atmosphere in which we accept the responsibility and pleasure of educating our children. By accepting this extremely important responsibility, we participate in their evolution and our own future.

Natural Responses: A Plea for Support

Parenting and education are the most important jobs on the planet at this time. Why don't we support our citizens while they do this work? Teachers are poorly paid, parents are not paid at all. Competitive societal attitudes demand more time from every mother and father. Parents are out of the home and the children suffer. Multi-billion dollar defense systems are a common fact of life. Wall Street embezzlers rob billions each year. Thousands of teenagers, alienated, turn to drugs, irresponsible sex, and violence. Oil companies ravage the planet, then extort exorbitant sums of money for needed fuel. And still millions of young people cannot afford to attend college.

exorbitant sums of money for needed fuel. And still millions of young people cannot afford to attend college.

The present distribution of resources simply does not reflect the real priorities of our times. It is impossible for both parents to work full-time and attend to the natural learning rhythms of their children. As a society we need educated grown-ups consciously parenting their children far more than we need a new type of plastic cup, another shopping mall, or another electronic labor-saver. The time and resources exist now for humans to support one another in their efforts to access self-knowledge. We *must* reprioritize.

Funding the dissemination of information about child development is a step in the right direction. Restructuring the educational system is another. Supporting students is a third. Supporting parents genuinely engaged in parenting is a fourth. Seeking knowledge of one's self and about natural law is a fifth. Supporting personal and societal efforts at peace and cooperation is a sixth. None of us can do all six steps. All of us can do something. All efforts help. Do what you can.

Recognizing education as the number one priority, practice Natural Learning Rhythms with every child you meet. Allow that child to become conscious of stage-specific wisdom. Support the children as they make contact. Support the grown-ups helping the children to contact their own body, emotional, will, and reasoning wisdom.

245

On Divorce

Harmony in the home lays the basis for peace in more complex social structures, up to and including the state. But today, divorce is a reality, and it rarely comes about peacefully. In the United States, nearly fifty percent of all marriages end in divorce. Close to two-thirds of the country's children have experienced the bitter pain of the broken family.

While the unique characteristics of each divorce must be considered, our experiences in counseling many parents and children of broken families suggests general principles to help mitigate the trauma of divorce. As an offering toward future peace on a global scale, we begin with the basics, offering a set of Natural Learning Rhythms responses to the difficulties attendant to divorce.

Keeping the Burden off the Children

First and foremost, divorcing parents must communicate with their child *within* the limits of the child's developmental capabilities.

Ross, a thirty-eight-year-old father, made the mistake of assuming that his son Jonah, age ten, would understand issues such as the sexual incompatibility between the parents and the mother's desire for an "open marriage." Jonah, in the midst of the Emotional-Being stage, simply felt his father's painful feelings of failing to be a good husband, but he could not comprehend Ross's explanations. Two years later, in counseling, Jonah admitted that had felt uncomfortable listening to his father explain his position. He still resented that his father talked about abstract issues as a way to cover his pain. Ross believed that he had been talking about the reasons *for* his pain. He was hurt that his honesty hadn't resulted in closeness with his son. At this crucial moment they lost contact.

After months of counseling, Ross realized that he had been unconsciously looking for support from his son. Jonah felt this and, quietly suffering, he recoiled. Ross imposed on his son and increased everyone's suffering. Children are not counselors. They need respect for their own pain, not additional responsibilities to support a parent in a dispute they don't fully understand. Ross and Jonah are still trying to pick up the pieces of their relationship.

The Myth of Easy Adjustment

Not long ago, a middle-aged couple, Joyce and Richard, came for pre-divorce counseling. As so many others parents who have decided to separate, Joyce insisted, "The children are the least of our problems. They'll adjust." She simply could not put down her own pain and feel the very obvious desperation of the children. Psychologists call this type of behavior *denial*.

Richard, on the other hand, began to place the needs of the children as his priority. Using the appropriate vocabulary in the appropriate environment, he continually reassured the children that he was there for them. He explicitly told them that the divorce was not their fault. Conscious of keeping his word, Richard made sure they knew where they would be and who would be with them. They decorated their new home together. When he had to break a dark mood in the children, he used creative confrontation. He did not speak disparagingly of their mother behind her back

Two months after the separation, Joyce took in a new boyfriend. One day, the children came home and learned their house had a new occupant. They had known the man, but did not know that he was to be their "new dad." Joyce loved her children, she kept them well fed, read to them before bed, and even built them a corral in the front yard. Still, she frequently brought the children to daycare even though she did not have to work, and she often neglected them emotionally. When speaking on the phone with their father, she would yell and curse when angry.

Six months later, the boyfriend—to whom the children had finally become close—moved out. More pain. Their father kept quiet but continued to provide the Body-Being and Emotional-Being food his children needed.

Not surprisingly, the children came to prefer living with their father. More pain. Since the divorce the children had been living half-time with each parent. As it became clear that Richard's household more closely approximated the natural needs of the children, he asked for primary custody.

Joyce was shocked. She believed she was a good mother and therefore resisted. Legally, they'd agreed to joint custody, so there was nothing Richard could do.

A child's family should include those people who honor his natural learning rhythms. In this case, however, and in many others, the children's natural learning rhythms were not the main issue considered.

Why Children Feel Guilt

Every child experiences guilt when the home breaks up. Safe space disappears in front of the child's eyes. How did it happen? What was her part in it? She does not understand, and she cannot understand: Primary support systems are not supposed to crumble. They make up the firm ground in which she anchors her life. Did she do something wrong?

The experience of guilt turns into severe trauma when the child becomes the focus of the parents' disagreement. If the parents have not honestly evaluated their motivations for the split-up, their displaced anger focuses on the issues surrounding the child. Or, if they have examined themselves, they don't communicate their understanding to the child in a way he can understand.

Absolving the child from guilt is a critical but, unfortunately, often-neglected, responsibility of the parents. In the previous case, the father, Richard, did this by refraining from arguing in front of the children and by refusing to "bad mouth" the mother when she wasn't present. Staying calm and consistent within *Natural Learning Rhythm*'s guidelines, he let them know by word and deed that the divorce was not their fault. In the midst of a difficult situation, he kept himself from leaning on the children for advice. Through creative conflict he breathed life back into the experience of interconnectedness.

Keeping the Children Together: Inclusion

Several times parents have approached us with a plan to separate siblings as part of the visitation settlement. They contended that the siblings had been fighting continuously and that the logistics would work more easily if there were separation. But in each of these cases, investigation revealed a dynamic that occurs often when conflict threatens a family: The children were playing out the roles of their parents, each child taking one side. Perhaps, unconsciously, they were trying to reach a solution for the family. Perhaps, without knowing it, they were mimicking the parents' antagonistic behavior as a way of crying out for help. But certainly, they were keeping in contact—perhaps their only way to maintain contact at the time.

Empower the children of divorce through inclusion. Siblings should not be separated. In family crises, siblings make compensation bonds. They find strengths in one another to offset the powerlessness brought on by the pain and guilt of divorce, and they often "test" each other. These bonds may arise in their oppositional as well as peaceful interactions, and they are extremely important to their emotional survival. The plans to separate the children invariably reflect power struggles between the parents and have nothing to do with the welfare of the children. Keep the children together.

Introducing New Partners

In the preceding case, Richard, the father, practiced inclusion when he had the children help decorate the new house. The mother violated their sense of home and belongingness by inviting a man to live there without their prior understanding or agreement.

Joyce's mistake is not at all uncommon. Many parents enter into intimate contact with partners oblivious to its effect on their children. But the child's perspective must be considered if damage to her is to be avoided. Even if the child cannot "understand" it, she keenly feels the power of romantic and sexual bonds between adults. From the child's perspective, that is *her* mother (or father) going to bed with *that* guy (or woman). All support systems, already shaky, receive another violent blow. The child worries, "How will I know that Mom (or Dad) will be there to take care of me?"

Introduce a new partner to the children slowly and gently. Let them all become friends at the children's pace. Remind the children of the importance of their feelings. Keep them informed of the status of your own feelings, but do not pressure them into feeling the same way as you. Let the possibility of a long-term partnership arise naturally, within the context of the entire family. Always allow children full access to you, the parent. If the new romance means that you're not available to the children there is little likelihood that family unity will develop.

In Joyce's case, her children grew to like their mother's new boyfriend. Six months later he was gone. The children learned that commitment has no predictable duration. The pain of rejection by a grown-up man shattered them once again. It became increasingly harder for them to trust the elders in their lives, especially, in this case, older males. For even though their father was doing his best to care for the children, their home of origin had broken down, partially destroying his credibility as a trusted male.

Sean, whose case history we introduced in the Emotional-Being chapter, experienced the devastating effects of the new dad switching allegiance to his newly born biological child. Both Sean's story and the story of Richard and Joyce's family offer an important message for new partners: Don't enter into a child's life without genuine intent to connect and to keep your word. Know the limits of your commitment and communicate them directly and honestly to the children. Coming and going as a friend of the child's parent represents one level of commitment; being a lover is different; being a potential mate is different again.

Stating the nature of your relationship clearly supports the need for security in Body-Being children, and the need for honesty and fairness of the child in Emotional-Being.

Blending Families

If each partner has children, bring both families together, and let all members meet in a casual way. If the relationship grows closer, try group discussions for a frank expression of feelings and needs of family members. Make sure each child knows the particulars of where and when they will be with the various members of the biological family and those of the new family. Honoring each person's needs, don't side-step; answer all complaints and questions thoroughly.

Patience and a comprehensive understanding of Natural Learning Rhythms can provide the atmosphere for blended families to grow together harmoniously. If the grown-ups' relationship is authentic they can make the effort

251

to support all the children. Denial of the needs of any of the children disrupts family balance. When the children accept the new arrangement, the blended family bonds. These connections build a healthy and trusting atmosphere. After so much hurt, we can risk opening our hearts again.

Natural Learning Rhythms: Solutions for the Children of Divorce

The pain of divorce manifests in many different ways. When the birth parents can't agree on a school, or can't develop an accurate vocabulary for communicating about the child, or parent in contradictory ways, guilt and confusion beset the child.

Awareness of Natural Learning Rhythms as a system brings forth responses to each of these situations. It provides the parents with a common vocabulary that is at once precise and usable. It allows for a consistent approach to parenting that allows for everyone's uniqueness, leaving ample opportunity for the expression of individual parenting style. Natural Learning Rhythms offers ways to speak with children so they won't feel fear, blame, or guilt. In our own practice of Natural Learning Rhythms, we've seen its remarkable potential for healing.

Beyond general responses, each divorce must be considered individually in order to construct a worthwhile response. Have there been other marriages? Are there children from these marriages? What is the financial situation? What are the preferences for schooling? How far away do the separated parents live from one another? Are there any medical problems? What is the legal agreement? Is one home more clearly suited to the needs of the children than another? What is the relationship to aunts and uncles and grandparents?

In blended families there are additional considerations. What is the child's relationship with the absent biological parent? Does the new dad or mom get along with the absent one? Does each parent have adequate time to provide the emotional support the child needs to adapt to the new family?

After considering every detail and recalling the principles and practices of Natural Learning Rhythms, it is possible to devise a strategy that meets everyone's wisdom needs. Like the turtle, move slowly, examining the ground carefully before taking each step. It's a challenge, for it takes a delicate touch to successfully survive divorce and to recombine families.

The Evolution of Peace

As a species, we human beings sometimes stubbornly retain old habits that no longer serve us. By continuing to fearfully protect our resources, sometimes harming others to do so, we demean the grace, power, intelligence, and beauty inherent in each individual. As soon as we find a way to let go of the psychologically and physically wasteful attachment to protection and punishment, we will make the conscious evolutionary leap to a far more peaceful, environmentally secure society.

Education is the springboard for our next collective developmental leap. The substance and character of that evolutionary process lies within each individual. Not in a book, not at the university, not in government, and not in any preordained plan. Religious and psychological practices serve only to open the door to our innate wisdom; they cannot provide the answers.

Why are human beings here? Where did we come from? Where are we going? We carry the information to answer these questions, and to live peacefully and with abundant resources. When we accept our responsibility as the bearers of the evolutionary message, we will do all we can to allow each person access to it. We will educate each child so that he becomes conscious of his own unique, innate wisdom.

Let us begin the great experiment of educating with the intent of bringing about the peaceful human evolution. Let us cease to educate primarily for cultural convention or the goal of fiscal gain. Let us hone our skills in understanding our own psychology and spiritual self, so that we can directly experience the full breadth of our birthright. Let us reprioritize in accordance to the genuine needs of the planet.

Peace truly *does* begin in the home and in the classroom. It is here that children spend the greatest part of their life. As parents and teachers, we are far and away their most important influences: Let's rise to the occasion and the honor.

The question parents ask us most often?

"How can I teach my children what I've never experienced myself?"

Work hard. Don't be afraid to ask questions or tell a child, "I don't know." Every family has the capability to help their children find peace through inherent human wisdom. Yes, many of us were not brought up in peace-inducing environments, and perhaps we have forgotten or never learned how to create this for our children. But judicious application of Natural Learning Rhythms will help parents over the gaps in their own education. Understanding our natural learning rhythms will let us reclaim the responsibility for our community, our culture, our planet, and, most importantly, our young.

PHASES

	Body-Being	Emotional-Being	Will-Being	Reasoning-Being
RECEPTIVITY	I am Receptive from the moment of conception through some time in my second year. Body wisdom takes over and accounts for my survival needs while I drink in my world. Every sound, and word, impinges on my senses. Subconsciously, I begin to sort both the individual sounds and movements, and the sensation ambiance in which these events occur.	I become aware of my own personal death at approximately eight years of age. I feel soft, tender, vulnerable, quivering with feeling. My egocentricity, based on my competent use of my body-as-environment is wiped out. I am inundated with the feelings of the world, from those around me, and from myself.	I close off to the world as I try to establish my individual identity. I'm fully receptive, as paradoxical as it may seem, to the possibilities of my own freedom and self. This receptivity begins around the age of thirteen. It doesn't include you. Why should I?	I'm born in confusion and doubt at around the age of sixteen. I'm just becoming aware of the vastness of time/space and I need some time to absorb it. I'm receptive to any and all data that helps define my relationship to myself, my past and future, my environment, the planet, and the universe.
TRIAL & ERROR	I push, pull, test, and select the limits of my natural, social, and communicative environments. I can successfully move my body over varied terrain, speak in short paragraphs, get the food to my mouth and the poop in the toilet and touch others in a safe way.	I look to grown-up models for ways to deal with my expanded feelings. I try out new modes of friendships with various peers. Prejudice does not enter my selection process. I test all and everything for the possibility of allowing me transcendent feelings.	In the bright fire of Will for all to see, I try on all the possible "I's" I can. From green hair to ballet dancer, from loner to groupie, from freedom lover to disciplinarian, I assert my ever-changing I. As peers are important for support, I try on some of the same personas that they do.	I study, or at least dabble, in as much as I can. I learn a lot. I specialize. I attempt to consider what it means to ask "Who Am I?" I try to come to terms with my past, play with projecting the future, and experiment with intimacy.
COMPETENCY	I fill up the whole world. I'm omnipotent and immortal. I'm a conqueror. I can marry a grown-up and defeat any enemy. I can move my body over long distances and almost any terrain. I am aware of the effects of my contact on others. I like to explore genitals. I am often good with infants.	I can be fair, honest, and just. I can account for everyone's feelings, including my own, and fix the world according to what feels fair. I'm in time with the beat of the heart of the world.	I have an "I" and it is a darn good one. I am strong and able and know the right way for myself and often for everyone. I'm still not very interested in your perspective unless it somehow affects my freedom. I can do what I want to do.	I use my data to find out who I really am. My specialization has led me back to a systemic overview of life. I have the power and competency to organize myself and my environment. I accept my humility in the face of the vastness of the universe, including the possibility that reasoning may not be the final step to discovering my true nature.

HESITANCIES

Hesitancies—

○ are often accompanied by *regressive* behavior

○ are often accompanied by nightmares, poor health, or refusing *favorite* events

○ are not to be mistaken for malfunctioning—handle with caring contact

○ allow a pause, which prepares for new physiological and psychological growth

○ signal parent that change is about to occur

○ manifest, in part, the *natural rhythm* of growth

Approximate Age	Characteristics
2½	Obtuse, difficult, demanding, testing, manipulative, autocratic, fussy. Child regressively wants to be treated like an infant.
6	Very active, fearful, tantrums, violent. Unable to accept criticism. Easily upset by altered routines or broken promises. Often prefers playing with younger children at their games. Father especially important.
10½	Recurrence of old fears, fussy, dislikes uncertainty and criticism. Bossy or timid, lonely, despairing, possessive, concerned with death.
15	Confused, cynical, fixated on emotional highpoints of previous ages, fears strangers, fears opposite sex, dominant or wimpy, blindly follows peer group, rejects parents.

L I F E   S T A G E S

Attributes	Being	Transmitting Mode	Age	Key Attitude / Key Foods	Characteristics
Womb					

Womb – Environment provides the foundation for future growth

Birth – Unbridled love

Attributes	Being	Transmitting Mode	Age	Key Attitude / Key Foods	Characteristics
Receptivity Life-affirming or *"I'm Alive"*	**Body-Being**	Sensation	0-7	*Key Attitude* Loving touch *Key Foods* Security, warmth, nourishment, flexibility.	The child learns a working knowledge of personal and planetary bodies. Secures the body on the planet. Provides for future growth. Absorbs by sensation-impressions and observation-imitation. What you see is what there is. **The Child Is** – I am the center of the world, the world is an extension of my body. I am alive.
Vulnerability *"I and Others"*	**Emotional-Being**	Feeling	8-12	*Key Attitude* Right modeling *Key Foods* Fairness, justice, caring, concern, adaptability, adventuresomeness, honesty	The child learns a deciphering of personal and social feelings. Needs the example of someone and is very susceptible to inspiration. Provides a foundation for future growth. Absorbs by feeling Impressions and observation. **The Child Is** – aware of personal death for the first time in her life. I care about the feelings of others and what they feel about me.
Assertion *"I Alone"*	**Will-Being**	Probing	12-15	*Key Attitude* Sensitive respect *Key Foods* Challenges, adventure, active activities, peer-sensitive, beginning of responsibility, protector of personal space, opportunity to express and work with ideals.	The child solidifies previous experience and defines a "self" to deal with puberty changes. Will provides a definite basis for Reasoning-Being comparisons by attempting to define an "I." The child appears to be very confident in her convictions. The child operates on ideals. **The Child Is** – absorbed with her own individuality. But Will ends in confusion as the assertions prove inadequate.
Questioning *"Who Am I"*	**Reasoning-Being**	Thinking	16-21	*Key Attitude* Mature recognition *Key Foods* Comparison, exploration, experimentation, recapitulation, suggestion, investigation, discernment.	The child evaluates past and future. She is able to tap Body-Being wisdom, Emotional-Being wisdom and Will-wisdom. She is also able to now research alternatives for herself. **The Child** – recognizes that there is such a thing as Intuition.
Recognition *"I Am"*	**Intuition**	Synchronization	21 & Up	*Key Attitude* Openness.	Access to ever-more refined "Love." Access to non-thought intelligence. Realization of personal history. Always more indefinable, simultaneous, and spontaneously non-habitual. **The Individual Is** – open and non-prejudicial.

R I T U A L S

Birth	Celebration of the Naming	Keynote The Earth	The Birth
First Year	Celebration of the First Coordination	Keynote Mother	Ritual bath, perhaps in a river or ocean, child's movement noted by elders without too much intensity.
Third Year	Celebration of the First Individuality	Keynote Father or Mother	Presentation of quality creation tool and teacher who will guide that craft. In the home, a very boisterous celebration.
Fifth Year	Celebration of Introduction to Nature	Keynote Parent or elder sibling	Quiet, fire circle. Mythical stories or ritual dance to awaken sense of natural cycles. Child participates.
Eighth Year	Celebration of Consecration of Earth Birth of Second Identity	Keynote Child with choice of elder	New name, partly referring to nature, chosen by child in accord with parents. Wilderness experience culminating in drama-dance-celebration of emergence of humans in nature. Celebration of humanity and the earth.
Tenth Year	Celebration of Sociability	Keynote Siblings, Cousins, Friends	Mountain climbing, daylong campout with spiritual guide. Mountain-top talk about death and God and the approach of adolescent changes.
Thirteenth Year	Celebration of Third Individuality	Keynote Spiritual Guide	Rite of Passage Part One–*Inner Keynote Fasting:* vision quest, psychedelic ritual with spirit guide for three full days in natural setting. Part Two–*Community:* child names self, performs dance-song-story-prayer. *Thanking Ceremony:* to those who have helped in her life to bring her thus far.
Fifteenth Year	Celebration of Access to Study	Keynote Special Interest Teacher	Quiet presentation of teacher and tools.
Seventeenth Year	Celebration of Sexuality	Keynote Teacher of Sexuality	Acknowledgment by parents of entry into her own sexuality.
Nineteenth Year	Celebration of Gratefulness	Keynote Voluntary Gratitude to Parents & Teachers	*Recapitulation Ceremony* in which parents review the child's life with her.

Selected Bibliography

The books described below represent a cross-section of writings related to the subject of education; they do not exhaust these subjects by any means. Themes range from pure psychology to home schooling, from cooperative games to science fiction. We hope that you will be able to find information on the aspect of education that suits you best and to use it to access related material. We offer the annotations as a way to make that task easier.

Adler, Alfred. *The Education of Children*. Henry Regency Co., Chicago. 1930.
> Pioneering psychological work on the way children form perceptions and how those perceptions can last a lifetime, though now a bit outdated. Emphasis on "individual psychology" and the strong influence parents have on determining the personality of the child. Both Dreikus and Glenn found this man inspirational.

Armstrong, Thomas. *The Radiant Child* The Theosophical Publishing House, Wheaton, IL. 1985.
> A theosophical look at transpersonal child development. Armstrong argues that children have natural access to spiritual realms; harmful education destroys that link.

Ashton-Warner, Sylvia. *Teacher*. Simon and Schuster, New York. 1963.
> An excellent exposition of Ashton-Warner's discovery of "organic" reading and the way to teach it, with an interesting account of her experience teaching children from the Maori tribe in Australia.

Bateson, Gregory. *Mind and Nature*. Dutton, New York. 1979.
> Bateson's search for "the pattern that connects" and its application to how humans learn. He applies ecological observations and principles to education. Precise, elegant, wonderful. An extension of general semantics into environment-as-human.

Bennett, J.G. *The Spiritual Hunger of the Modern Child*. Claremont Press, Charles Town, WV. 1984
> A collection of essays by educational practitioners from various spiritual disciplines, this book highlights the multi-level ever-present bond between education and spiritual awakening.

Berends, Polly Berrigen. *Whole Child, Whole Parent*. Harper and Row, New York. 1987.
> A tender practical treatment of the parent-child relationship. Even handed, easy to read, written with a great deal of caring. Recommended.

Brown, Tom. *The Tracker* and *The Search*. Prentice Hall, New Jersey. 1978 and 1980.
> As a young boy Brown was taught to track. These books have stimulated thousands of youngsters to pay better attention to nature. He now gives workshops in tracking and wilderness survival.

Chinmoy, Sri. *A Child's Heart & A Child's Dreams*. Aum Publications, Jamaica, New York. 1986.
> A guru's traditional response to education: lots of discipline, formal schooling in state sanctioned institutions and meditation by the parents. No recognition of child development, or help for parents, except to remind them to meditate and pray. Sri Chinmoy believes children should be taught to meditate, and that life was better in the olden days.

Citizens Policy Center. *Our Future At Stake*. New Society Publishers, Philadelphia, PA. 1985.
A classic and a must. Read it twice for its teachings, and use it often for your effortless learning enjoyment.

Activist teenagers share their ideas and experiences in working for peace. Good book to stimulate ideals in teenagers.

Cornell, Joseph Bharatt. *Sharing Nature with Children*. Ananda Publications, Nevada City CA. 1979.
A classic and a must. Read it twice for its teachings, and use it often for your effortless learning enjoyment.

Deacove, Jim. *Games Manual of Non-Competitive Games* and *Sports Manual of Non-Competitve Games*. Family Pastimes, RR4, Perth, Ontario, Canada, K7H3O6.
Low key publications of innovative cooperative activities. Send for their catalog of inexpensive game kits.

Dreikus, Rudolf. *Children the Challenge*. Hawthrone Books, New York. 1964.
A caring, skill filled book designed to bring the family closer together. It has been in print over twenty years. Emphasizes democracy in the home and the classroom.

Erickson, Erik. *Childhood and Society*. W.W. Norton, New York. 1963.
The great psychologist presents the stages of life. Clearly written, this book is a resource for many. Along with collegue Eric Fromm, Erikson opened the door to a humanitarian way of looking at ourselves.

Faber, Adele, and Mazlish, Elaine. *How to Talk So Kids Will Listen and Listen So Kids Will Talk* and *Siblings Without Rivalry*. Avon, New York.
A respectful "how-to" compendium for communicating with children. Sensitive to the integrity of the child. Worth considering, though insight and theory on the fundamental nature of the child is limited.

Flugelman, Andrew, ed. *The New Games Book* and *The Second New Games Book*. Doubleday, NY. 1979.
Lots of game ideas, some of them competitive, some worth little, but generally vibrant and relevant.

Gardner, Howard. *Frames of Mind*. Basic Books, New York, 1983.
The complete account of the Gardner's Theory of Multiple Intelligences, unashamedly academic in language and style.

Gessel, Arnold. *The First Five Years of Life* and *The Child From Five To Ten*. Harper and Row, NY.
Gessel was the most famous of the many developmental psychologists working in United States in and around World War II. While at Yale he observed thousands of children of all ages and wrote several books reporting his findings. Although culturally biased and clinically based, these books still make interesting reading in their description of childhood stages.

Gibbs, J., and A. Allen. *Tribes*. Centre Source, Berkeley CA. 1978.
Excellent compendium of self-esteem building activities. Primarily designed for teachers, this is a treasure trove for all. Used intelligently, it provides a way to explore your child's values in ways consistent with developmental needs. If public school is your educational choice, insist your teacher read a copy.

Glenn, Stephen and Nelsen, Jane. *Raising Self-Reliant Children in a Self-Indulgent World*. Prima Publishing, Rocklin, CA. 1988.
Recognizes that the way children perceive the world is the fundemental issue in education. Good, practical insights into how to influence perception to allow for capable children. Weak understanding of development; no distinction made between behavior and *stage specific wisdom*.

Grinspoon, Lester, and Bakalar, James. *Psychedelic Drugs Reconsidered*. Basic Books, New York, 1979; *Marihuana Reconsidered*. Harvard University Press, Cambridge, MA. 1977.
Excellent, unbiased appreciation of the science and sociology of these substances. Other books in the same series cover additional drugs.

Grof, Stanislaus. *Realms of the Human Unconscious*. Dutton, New York. 1976.
A transpersonal look at the birth experience from one of the leading researchers in the use of psychedelics in psychotherapy. Grof and his wife Cristina are the founders of Holotropic Breath Therapy. This therapy confirms his research on LSD. Grof's work cannot be ignored by any serious investigator of human psychology.

Gurdjieff, G. I. *Meetings with Remarkable Men*. Dutton, New York. 1968.
The fascinating psycho-history of a very aware human being. Laced throughout with a deep and meaningful understanding of children. Emphasis on creating the conditions necessary for nurturing children's strength, courage and willingness to take responsibility as mature, meaningful people.

Harrison, Marta. *For the Fun of It; Selected Cooperative Games*. New Society Publishers, Philadelphia PA. 1976.
A few good games by an American Friend (Quaker). Other more complete cooperative games manuals have been published but this is a good place to start.

Harwood, A. C. *The Way of the Child*. Rudolf Steiner Press, Spring Valley, New York. 1979.
A year-by-year description of child development and educational process from the perspective of Steiner and Waldorf education. Clearly written; a good introduction to Waldorf education.

Hegener, Mark and Helen. *Alternatives in Education*. Home Education Press, Tonasket WA. 1988.
An excellent compilation of articles on all alternative schooling possibilities in the U.S. today. The Hegeners are the editors of *Home Education Magazine*. They also have a brief, excellent publication on getting started in home schooling.

Holt, John. *Teach Your Own.* Delacorte, Seymour Lawrence, New York. 1981.
Holt is the most well-known advocate of family centered education, and this is his most direct dissertation of home study. He writes clearly, and from the vantage points of parent, teacher and member of society. Lots of good legal advice. His *How Children Learn* and *How Children Fail* are classics; *What Do I Do Monday* is full of creative ways to teach math and science.

Houston, Jean. *The Possible Human.* J.P. Tarcher, Los Angeles. 1982.
A series of innovative exercises designed to awaken all aspects of ourselves. Useful for parents self-exploration which can also be adapted for children. Houston is an avid educator and explorer of the self. Previous works include *Mind Games,* and *Life Force: The Psycho-Historical Recovery of Self.*

Huston, James. *The White Dawn.* Harcourt, Brace and Janovich, New York. 1971; *The White Archer.* Harcourt, Brace and World, New York. 1967.
Two of James Houston's many marvelous accounts of native life in the arctic circle. Exciting and meaningful tales.

Huxley, Aldous. *Island.* Harper and Row, New York. 1962.
Huxley's last novel is set in a modern world Utopia, and contains excellent chapters on education, parenting and rites of passage. The wisdom in this book continues to grow on us. Huxley's collection of essays, *Brave New World Revisited,* describes many of the psychological impediments to healthy education inherent in our culture.

Huxley, Laura, and Ferrucci, Pierro. *The Child of Your Dreams.* CompCare, Minneapolis. 1987.
A simple and moving description of the need and method for conscious conception. Ms. Huxley has initiated many innovative programs which honor children, including "Prelude to conception", a high school program in which teens "parent" toddlers on a regular basis to get hands-on information about what it's like to be a parent. She's also authored useful works in self-help psychology, including *You Are Not the Target* and *Between Heaven and Hell.*

Ilg, Frances, and Ames, Louise Bates. *Child Behavior.* Harper and Row, New York. 1955.
Standard Gesell Institute fare: the stages are identical with the behavior of the child. Specific recommendations for coping with the various behaviors, such as whining or sexual desire.

Illich, Ivan. *Deschooling Society.* Harper and Row, New York, 1983; *Toward A History Of Needs.* Pantheon, New York. 1977.
Ivan Ilich's seminal work on the social base that produces the ills of public schools. Intellectually profound. If a wider population truly understood Illich's message, the public schools would be empty.

Janov, Arthur. *The Feeling Child.* Simon and Schuster, New York. 1975; *Imprints.* Putnam, New York, 1984.
Through his extensive Primal Therapy work, Janov has gained a compassionate, intimate understanding of the problems we face as children and continue to perpetuate in parenting our own children. Excellent physiological justifications for his theses.

Judson, Stephanie, ed. *A Manual on Nonviolence and Children.* New Society Publishers, Philadelphia, PA. 1975.
A compendium of Judson's experiences helping children come to nonviolent resolutions to conflicts in their lives. (This publisher, incidentally, steadily produces award winning books on the subject. Get their catalog at 4722 Baltimore Avenue, Philadelphia PA 19143. After having read many of their publications, we've come to bestow upon them the title of "foremost children's peace publisher.")

Jung C.G. The Development of Personality. Princeton University Press, Princeton, NJ. 1975.
Jung's seminal work, which includes his early recognition of the deeper aspects of the psyche. Earth-shattering 70 years ago. Speaks to the whole child, concentrates on the psychological. Interesting, though not mandatory.

Kagan, Jerome. The Nature of the Child. Basic Books, New York. 1984.
Harvard's expert on child development puts forth the current academic gospel. The work offers many important insights, though it lacks an understanding of stage-specific wisdom. Many theoretical deductions and assumptions. Includes a short, interesting refutation of Piaget. Kagan admits he has little practical applications to offer families.

Korzybski, Alfred. *Science and Sanity* and *Manhood of Humanity.* The International Non-Aristotelian Library Publishing Company, Lakeville CT.
Classic writings by the father of General Semantics. Difficult to read but worth it. Korzybski concludes that, we are, to a large extent, what we think we are. Our thinking is conditioned by our language/body/environment: our general semantic. Recognize that semantic, he says, change it, and change yourself. Applies to every field, especially education.

Krishnamurti. *Education and the Philosophy of Life.* Harper and Row, New York. 1953.
Perhaps the best book we have ever read on education. It places educational responsibility where it belongs, on us—our attitude and awareness, our values and our ability to work on ourselves to dissolve our conditioned blindness. Equally stimulating are the dialogues recorded in *Beginnings of Learning.* These dialogues are superb models of the techniques of Inquiry.

Kubler-Ross, E. *On Children and Death and Dying*. Macmillan Publishing Company, New York. 1983.
> A heart-opening text, with lessons absolutely necessary for real acceptance of the child as wise in her current moment. Also vital for recognizing the way in which children of different ages acknowledge death.

Laing, R.D. *The Politics of the Family*. Pantheon, New York. 1969.
> An insightful look at how family structures evolve and the way in which each family member internalizes those structures. Laing challenges many of our beliefs as to the nature of family. Any family wishing its members to be "free" needs to understand the meaning in this book. All Laing's books are valuable reading. They are based on years of non-traditional psychiatric work which is helping to shape a new definition of the human mind.

Lao Tsu. *Tao Te Ching*. Translated by Gia-Fu Feng and Jane English. Random House, New York. 1972.
> The ancient verses of the Chinese master communicate how to live life in harmony with nature. We also recommend the Archie Bahm translation of *Tao Te Ching* from Ungar Publishing of New York. He translates the title as "Nature and Intelligence." A new version by Stephen Mitchell and published by Harper and Row is most easily readable, without losing the meaning.

LeGuin, Ursula K. *Always Coming Home*. Harper and Row, New York. 1985.
> Science fiction writer LeGuin's masterful treatment of the world of the Valley of the Na has many hints for appropriate integration of children and society.

Lessing, Doris. *The Making of the Representative from Planet 8*. Random House, New York. 1984.
> Another science fiction book?! Indeed. Lessing's little known novel is an insightful psychological portrait of the sacrifices necessary for becoming a true educator and a true human being. Not easy to read, it requires much time for contemplation.

Liedloff, Jean. *The Continuum Concept*. Warner Books, New York. 1977.
> When Lieldoff went to live with South American Indians, with no theory to prove, she came back with a remarkable understanding of the natural energy fields inherent in the relationships between elders and children.

Lifton, Betty Jean. *The King of Children*. Schocken Books, New York. 1988.
> Moving biography of Janusz Korczak, a Polish-Jewish educator who lived during the first half of this century. Korczak ran large scale orphanages with many innovative programs, including the first children's newspaper and children run courts. He was killed, with his children, by the Nazis.

Luvmour, Josette, and Luvmour, Sambhava. *Towards Peace*. CEG Books, North San Juan, CA. 1989.
> A manual of 170 cooperative games and activities aimed at improving communication skills, building self esteem and resolving conflict. Cross-referenced for easy access while playing.

Mahler, M.S. "Developmental Aspects in the Assessment of Narcissistic and So-called Borderline Personalities." in P. Hartocollis, Ed., *Borderline Personality Disorders*. International Universities Press, New York. 1977.
> In this and a series of other papers, Mahler establishes the developmental phenomena of *rapprochement*, very similar to our concept of the *hesitancy*. As far as we are aware, this is the only reference in which this phenomena, cited in *Natural Learning Rhythms* fieldwork, appears.

Maurer, Daphne and Charles. *The World of the Newborn*. Basic Books, New York. 1988.
> A strictly scientific account that challenges many popular notions about how babies perceive the world. Interestingly, it refutes the idea that the birth experience is negative and traumatic for the baby.

Miller, Ron. *What Are Schools For?* and *New Directions in Education*. Holistic Education Press, Brandon, Vermont, 1991.
> Miller is quickly establishing himself as a premier historian of holistic education. In these books he explores the history of holistic education in the United States and its many functioning contemporary examples.

Montagu, Ashley. *Touching*. Columbia University Press, New York. 1971.
> Montagu's work in human development is unparalleled in scope and accuracy. In this book he reminds us of the skin's sacredness and its importance to all arenas of health.

Montessori, Maria. *The Absorbent Mind*. Dell Publishing, New York. 1967.
> The great pioneer of aligning education with allowing the natural, intelligent wisdom of each child to unfold with as little interference as possible, Montessori addresses child development, requirements of a teacher, the importance of contact with children of different ages and her own very interesting experience as an educator. Other books, such as *The Secret of Childhood*, and *The Discovery of the Child*, cover much the same ground.

Neill, A.S. *Summerhill*. Hart Publishing, New York. 1960.
> Freudian psychologist A. S. Neill, one of Reich's foremost students, is a compassionate educator who ran a private school in England for some of the most difficult, unwanted children of that society. With neither rules nor regulations imposed from "above", the success of the school shocked traditionalists and stretched the minds of all educators. A fascinating account, with an introduction by Erich Fromm.

Orlick, Terry. *The Cooperative Sports and Games Book* and *The Second Cooperative Sports and Games Book*. Pantheon, New York. 1978 and 1982.
Good stuff! The second one is better than the first. Both have games from other cultures. Both make a lot of sense. The best place to start for an appreciation of cooperative games.

Ornstein, Robert, and Sobel, David. *The Healing Brain*. Simon and Schuster, New York. 1987. Ornstein, Robert, and Thompson, Richard. *The Amazing Brain*. Houghton Mifflin, New York. 1984.
Lucid, simple descriptions of the human brain. These books serve inquiries in education and psychology

Pagnoni, Mario. *The Complete Home Educator*. Larson, New York. 1984.
Nice ideas about computers and home schooling. Because he home-taught for just one year, Pagnoni is less in touch with the deeper natural significance of home schooling. Interesting, though culturally limited

Pearce, Joseph Chilton. *Magical Child* and *Magical Child Matures*. Dutton, New York. 1976 and 1984.
Excellent attempt at correlating brain research and education, though much of the information is stretched to support the author's spiritual experiences, theories and aspirations. Very stimulating and challenging. A groundbreaking and fundamentally important work by a man commited to children Very attentive to parenting in a non-sentimental way.

Piaget, Jean. *The Grasp of Consciousness*. Harvard University Press, Cambridge, MA. 1976.
The Swiss biologist who, in many books, charts the development of cognition. The books are not easy to read. There are some good introductions and expositions by other authors. The books by Pearce and Pulaski are a good place to start.

Prutzman, Stern, Burger and Bodenhamer. *The Friendly Classroom for a Small Planet*. New Society Publishers, Philadelphia, PA. 1988.
Specific manual with many excellent ideas on creating cooperation in the classroom. Straightforward and easy to read and use.

Pulaski, Mary. *Understanding Piaget*. Harper and Row, New York. 1971.
Easy to understand introduction to Piaget's theory.

Rasberry and Greenway. *Rasberry*. Freestone Publishing Co., Albion, CA. 1971.
A manual on how to start your own school written from the perspective of the free school movement of the sixties. Lots of innovative ideas.

Reich, Wilhelm. *The Mass Psychology of Facism*. Simon and Schuster, New York. 1970.
A classic work on Nazi madness by the incisive German psychologist. He saw it happen and dissects it brilliantly. Clear description of the dangers of symbols, behavior modification, and living to please others, including parents. It can be read as companion to Aldous Huxley's collection of essays, *Brave New World Revisited*, to appreciate the importance of allowing centered, self-referring children.

Rohnke, Karl. *Silver Bullets: A Guide to Initiative Problems, Adventure Games, Stunts and Trust Activities*. Project Adventure, Hamilton, MA. 1984.
Directed primarily at teens, there are many cooperative activities in this book. Excellent as a companion for Ropes Course work. Lots of good ideas, especially for physical education teachers looking to change the curriculum in their gyms.

Shah, Idries. *The Pleasantries of the Incredible Mulla Nasruddin*. Dutton, New York. 1971.
A marvelous collection of teaching stories in two companion volumes. Shah has other teaching story collections but none so suitable for children.

Schoel, Prouty and Radcliffe. *Islands of Healing*. Project Adventure Co. NY. 1988.
Specific, detailed application of cooperative and initiative activities with teenagers with emphasis on their theraputic value. A stimulating approach to the problems facing teens. Recommended

Sobel, Jeffrey. *Everybody Wins*. Walker Publications, New York. 1984.
Good compendium of cooperative games, especially for the very young.

Spock, Marjorie. *Teaching As A Lively Art*. The Anthrosophic Press, Spring Valley, NY. 1978.
Classic Waldorf education as applied to the eight-to thirteen-year-old child. Guidelines for home and school, along with supporting philosophy.

Steiner, Rudolf. *Understanding Young Children*. International Association of Waldorf Kindergartens. Stuttgart, Germany. 1975.
These ten lectures summarize Steiner's appreciation of the young child. He's written many other books on biodyanamic gardening, architecture, education, occultism and *anthroposophy*, the spiritual path he founded. His autobiography tells of the way he gained insight into such varied disciplines. Other books (such as Harwood's) give a more complete account of Waldorf education.

Stern, Daniel. *The Interpersonal World of the Infant*. Basic Books, New York, 1985.
Stern, a pediatrician, combines psychoanaysis with development in an attempt to portray how the child develops a sense of self. Excellent detailed work on the life of an infant, but excessively academic and hard to read.

Wallace, Nancy. *Better Than School*. Larson Publications, New York. 1983.
A first hand account by a frequent contributor to *Mothering* magazine, this book touches on Suzuki musical instruction, and the trials and joys of home schooling.

263

Walters, J. Donald (aka Kriyananda). *Education for Life*. Ananda Publications, Nevada City, CA. 1986.
The founder of Ananda Cooperative Village and disciple of Yogananda states his belief about child development and education practices. Hindu scheme of development; some innovative educational practices.

Weingartner and Postman. *Teaching as a Subversive Activity*. Delacorte Press, New York. 1969.
Written in the heyday of the alternative schooling movement, this is worth skimming for its effective responses to public school. It is worth attentive study in the section in which it elucidates the relationship between language and learning. Excellent suggestions for enlivening high school classrooms. Wise in its correlation between psychology, general semantics and education. Postman in particular continues to publish excellent books in the field.

Weinstien, M., and Goodman, J. *PlayFair*. Impact Publishing, San Luis Obispo, CA. 1980.
Exuberant account of many unique cooperative games and the way to introduce and play them.

Wichert, Susan. *Keeping the Peace*. New Society Publishers, Philadelphia, PA. 1989.
Theory and practice for creating cooperation and resolving conflict with preschoolers. Useful for anyone working with children.

Wickes, Frances. *The Inner World of Childhood*. New American Library, New York. 1968.
Wickes, a contemporary of Jung, co-developed many of the understandings that are attributed only to him. She then applied these understandings to children. This inspiring record of hundreds of case histories brings home one ruthless truth: the psychic health of the parent is the most important determinant of the wellbeing of the child. Highly recommended.

Wilber, Ken. *The Atman Project*. Theosophical Publishing House, Wheaton, IL. 1980.
Human development as seen as *atman*, or the God within, becoming, according to Hindu scripture. Excellent summaries of the various approaches to human development succinctly stated. Read this and save a lot of other reading. Great background for *Natural Learning Rhythms*. Purely psychological and philosophical, with no educational deductions. Exciting and informative.

Bio Notes

Josette and Geoffrey Sambhava Luvmour are co-founders of the Center for Educational Guidance and the Pathfinder project in North San Juan, California. Family counselors for more than a decade, they offer workshops in Natural Learning Rhythms throughout the United States.

Geoffrey S. Luvmour holds masters degrees in psychology and early childhood education. He has been a preschool founder and teacher, and has taught fourth grade in the Philadelphia public schools. From 1972-73, he was a research fellow at the Van Kleinsmid Center at the University of Southen California.

Josette Luvmour is a counselor and educator. She trained in Gestalt and other forms of psychotherapy at the Esalen Institute. In addition to her work with children and families, she leads workshops in family reunification and intimacy for couples.

The Luvmours have co-authored *Everyone Wins*, a book on cooperative games and activities (New Society Publishers, 1990). They are parents of a daughter, Amber, and live and work in the foothills of California's Sierra Nevada mountains.

$\mathcal{I}$ndex

A

Academic subjects. *See* Curriculum

Acting, as educational tool
  during Body-Being stage, 169
  during Emotional-Being stage, 179

Adaptability
  expressions of, xx
  as nutrient of Emotional-Being stage, 48-49

Adjustment, myth of for children in divorce situations, 248

Adults, effects of childhood hurts, 233-34

Adventure
  as nutrient of Emotional-Being stage, 48-49
  through travel study programs, 194

Affront, personal, child's conflictive behavior seen as, 217-18

Age, chronological
  association with others during Will-Being stage, 66, 68
  and life stages and wisdoms, 8
  and reactions during hesitancies, 14

Alsace-Lorraine, conflicts over as example of resource competition, 241

Alternatives, in resolving conflicts, 220

Anger, situational, leading to confrontation, 217-18

Animals, caring for during Emotional-Being stage, 179

Anthropology, xi
  as part of background for Natural Learning Rhythms system, 9, 11

Anthroposophy, 6

Anti-drug campaigns, effect on Will-Being children, 82

Anxiety, in adulthood, 233

Apprenticeships, during the Will-Being stage, 183, 185-87

Arguments, intensification by further arguments, 220-21

Armstrong, Thomas, *Radiant Child*, 6, 10

Assertion
  adult reaction to during Will-Being stage, 71-73
  during Reasoning-Being stage, 88

Atman Project, The (Wilber), 7, 10

Attachment/separation paradox, during Body-Being stage, 34-35

Attention, undivided
  Chinese character for, 108, 109
  during communications, 106-8
  during creative confrontation, 148

Attunement, to system(s) during Reasoning-Being stage, 90-91

Authority
  decentralization during Will-Being education, 184
  willingness to admit mistakes, 148

Autonomy
  balance with humility, 152, 154, *chart* 151
  at different ages, 12-13

B

"Badness", as unpleasantness during Body-Being stage, 20

Bakalar, James, 188

Behavior, children's, xii, xix, xxi
  effect on of threats and violence, xv, 145, 212, 213, 219
  during hesitancies, 13-14, 27-29, 155
  imitative mode during Body-Being stage, 19
  problem manifestations of, 152-53

use of rewards and punishment, xiv, xxi, 9, 183, 187
Behaviorism, and Natural Learning Rhythms, 11
Being. *See also* Body-Being; Emotional-Being;
    Reasoning- Being; Will-Being
    definitions of, 7, 11
Belongingness, balanced with strength, 152, 154, 160,
    chart 151
Belousov-Zhavotinski reaction, as chemical chaos
    theory, 188
Birth, sensory input during, 20-21
Body, physical and psyche traits at different ages, 12
Body-Being stage, 7-8, *chart* 255
    case studies of, 17-35
    communication as recognition of a reality, 112
    curriculum for, 53-54, 172-73, 197, *chart* 198-99
    educating the child during, 168-73
    egotism, 17, 20, 28-29, 30
    experimenting with new behavior during, 14
    flexibility during, 21, 23-24
    height differential during adult-child
        communication, 113
    hesitancy periods, 27-29
    importance of body language, 24-27, 31-32, 117
    interaction with nature, 29-31
    problem behavior traits, 152, 154, 156, *chart* 151
    ritual rites of passage, 140-42
    transition to Emotional-Being stage, 37-39
    as a trust in trust period, 236
Body language
    during Body-Being stage, 24-27, 31-32, 117
    observance during communications, 115
Body wisdom, 8, 10
    denial in many education systems, 166
Bonding, parent/child
    created in meeting child's natural needs, xx
    weakening during Will-Being stage, 79
Boredom, reactions to by suburban teenagers, 235-36
Boundaries, for young explorers, 115-16
Boy into Man (Weiner), 139-40
Brain, human, during Body-Being stage, 20
Breast feeding, weaning as separation, 35
Bribery, use in discipline, xxi, 10
Butterfly (*Lepidoptera*), as example of life stages, 3-4,
    5-6, 67

C

Careers, case studies on means of attaining, 90-91,
    94-95, 96-97
Caring, for others
    during Body-Being stage, 18-19
    during Emotional-Being stage, 39-40
    during Will-Being stage, 74-75
Carrots and sticks, as educational method, 183-85
Caterpillars, as example of life stage, 3-4, 5-6
CDs (compact discs), use as teaching tools, 191-92
Celebration, as part of rites of passsage, 125, 132
Challenge(s)
    in cooperative games, 176
    lack for inner-city teenagers, 235
    Ropes Courses as, 190
    during Will-Being stage, 71, 73-74, 183, 190-92
    nature as, 75-78
Change
    awareness of during Emotional-Being stage, 55-56
    and conflict during hesitancies, 13-14
Chanting, ritual, during rites of passage, 136, 137
Chaos Theory, investigation of, 188
Character traits, 12-13
    of the changing human psyche, 150, 152, *chart* 151
Cherry Festival story, as illustation of conflict
    resolution, 208-17, 218, 219, 221, 222
Child abuse
    Alice Miller on, 5
    case studies of, 231-33
    effects of in adulthood, 233-34
    seeking therapy for, 153
Choice, during Will-Being stage, 71
Chores, family, as source of conflict, 227-29
Circles
    use as teaching formations, 177-78
    use in resolving confrontations, 210
Civil Rights movement, as example of caring during
    Will- Being stage, 74-75
Cliques, minimization of, 176, 192
Cocoons, role in life cycle of *Lepidoptera*, 3-4
Co-exploration, with Reasoning-Being children
    as communication tool, 119-20
    as necessary to development, 91-92, 93, 98
    on the university level, 193
Cohousing, growth of, 242
College
    case study on concerns about, 94-95
    life at and the Reasoning-Being student, 193-94
Coming-of-age Ritual. *See* Rites of passage
Commitment, during Reasoning-Being stage, 92-93
Communication, xii, 146, 148
    as interaction between persons, 105-20
    teaching of during Emotional-Being stage, 174

Community
  and Emotional-Being stage, 12, 39, 44-45
Community education, examples in rural California, 178-80, 185
Compassion, use by mentor during conflict resolution, 222
Competency
  during childhood phases, *chart* 255
  as life stage, 14-15, 28-29
Competition
  fostered in public school systems, 183
  paired with cooperation, 239-41
Computer programs, as teaching tool, 191
Concerns, personal, as distractions during communication, 107-8
Conditioning, as limiting Body-Being exploration, 23
Confidentiality, during resolving conflicts, 210, 212
Conflict
  attitudes of parental figures during, 145-46, 208
  and change during hesitancies, 13-14
  between children, 208-17, 218, 219, 221, 222
  confidentiality during, 210, 212
  lack of favoritism during, 210, 223, 225
  resolution of, xii, xvii, 201-29
  use of stage-specific vocabulary, 219-20
Conformity, as form of rebellion during Will-Being stage, 70-71
Confrontation, creative, during periods of crisis, 147-48, 207-8
Confusion
  becoming cynicism, 239
  beginnings of during Will-Being stage, 86
Connections, striving for during Emotional-Being stage, 39-40
Consciousness, human
  age-old quest for key to, xi-xiv
  aspects of explored in each life stage, 5
  during emergences from hesitancies, 14
  and human development, 3, 10-11
Cooperation, paired with competition, 239-41
Cooperative games, during Emotional-Being stage, 174-77, 180
Cooperative life
  Grange movement marketing as, 243
  Liberation theology demands for, 241
"Co-op Juggle", as example of cooperative game, 176
Costumes, use in rites of passage, 140
Counseling. *See* Therapy
Cultural exchange programs, 195
Curiosity

during Body-Being stage, 22-23, 115-16
  during Will-Being stage, 190-92
Curriculum, xii-xiv. *See also* Education
  chart for development stages, 197-200
  teaching mathmatics, xv, 169, 172
  teaching reading to young children, 53-54, 172-73
Cynicism, confusion manisfested as, 239

D

Dance, the, xviii-xix
  with children during Body-Being stage, 32-33, 97
  honesty of during Emotional-Being stage, 56-57
  during Reasoning-Being stage, 99-100, 193
  with Will-Being stage children, 78
Dancing
  as emphasizing rhythm, 179
  as part of ritual rites of passage, 129, 131
Data retrieval, value of in Western society, 167
Death
  awareness of during Emotional-Being stage, 39-42, 56, 57, 87, 237
  discussions on, 160, 161
  as part of a rites of passage myth, 129
  to the reasoning mind, 99
Decision-making, xvi, 184
Defensiveness, child's, effect of natural environment on, 15
Development, children's. *See* Consciousness, human; Life stages
Disabilities, physical, teenagers' feelings about, 189-90
Discipline, xi-xii
  use of rewards and punishments, xiv, xxi, 9, 183, 187
Discrimination
  balanced with perspective, 152, 154, 158, *chart* 151
Disputes, childhood
  benefits of resolving, 58
  Cherry Festival example, 208-17, 218, 219, 221, 222
Distance, physical, between communicating people, 107
Divorce
  effects on children, xii, 156, 229, 232, 247-52
  rate increases, xvi, 247
  and ritual rites of passage, 127
Doubt
  beginnings of during Will-Being stage, 86
  in Reasoning-Being stage, 86-87, 88, 91
Drama
  acting as an educational tool, 169, 179

influence of during Emotional-Being stage, 53-54, 179

Drugs. *See* Substance abuse

Dual existence, of children in divorced famillies, 232-33

Dumbing Us Down: The Hidden Curriculum of Compulsory Schooling (Gatto), xv

Dysfunctional behavior
remedies for, 143-63
and ritual rites of passage, 127-28

e

Ecology. *See also* Nature
interconnectiveness, 152, 154, 156, *chart* 151
Lepidoptera life stages as example, 3-4, 5-6, 67
teaching to Emotional-Being children, 182

Education. *See also* Curriculum; Parenting; Schools
carrot and stick method, 183-85
CDs and computers as tools, 191-92
community programs, 178-80
early childhood, 9
fostering access to stage-specific wisdom, 6
methods for the Body-Being stage, 168-73
for the stages of childhood, 165-200
teacher as inquirer, 188-90

Egoism
during Body-Being stage, 17, 20, 28-29, 30, 170-71
death as destroyer of, 39

Elder(s)
healing attitudes, 145
role in co-exploration during Reasoning-Being stage, 91-92
as role models during Emotional-Being stage, 4, 45-46, 46-48, 49-52, 57-58

Emotional-Being stage, 7-8, 12, 30, 113, *chart* 255
case studies, 37-59
communication during, 117, 119, *chart* 118
cooperative games during, 174-77
curriculum for, 197, 200, *chart* 198-99
education during, 173-82
hesitancy periods, 52-53
influence of adult models during, 44, 45-46, 46-48, 49-52, 57-58
interaction with nature, 54-56, 177-78
as period of trust in justice, 236-37
problem behavior traits during, 152-53, 154, 156, 158, *chart* 151
realization of death and mortality, 39-42, 56, 57
rites of passage to Will-Being stage, 128-33

trial and error during, 53-54

Emotional wisdom, 8, 10
denial in many education systems, 166

Emotions. *See* Feeling

Empowerment, xvi
of self during Body-Being stage, 23-24

Empty, being, during communications, 108-13

Environment(s)
child's ability to integrate with, 5-6
creating for Body-Being children, 171-73
human ability to harmonize with, 4
for successful communications, 106, 108

Eugene, Ore., cooperative movement, 243

Eurythmy, as Waldorf education technique, 180

Everyone Wins (Luvmour), 177

Evolution
as antagonistic or synergestic, 241-44
human, 4-5
Lepidoptera's as example, 3-4
of peaceful humans through education, 253-54
stage-specific wisdom choices, 5

Exaggeration, during family conflicts, 206

Exploration. *See also* Challenge(s); Co-exploration
during Body-Being stage, 22-23, 115-16

Eye contact, during communications, 107

f

Failure, threat of, during Will-Being stage
in education systems, 183
reaction to, 70

Fairness, sense of. *See* Justice

Family, xi-xvi, 5. *See also* Parent(s); Parenting
blending of his and her children, 251-52
and divorce, 247-52
role of humor during difficulties, 149-50, 205

Far East, case studies of effects on Reasoning-Being travelers, 195

Fasting, as part of ritual rites of passage, 134

Fault, children's view of selves in divorce situations, 248, 249

Favoritism, in conflict resolutions, 210, 223, 225

Fear
in behavior modification programs, xxi
in competition modes, 241

Fearlessness
balanced with incisiveness, 152, 160-61, *chart* 151

Feeling(s)
during Body-Being stage, 20
earlier unfulfillments and Reasoning-Being stage, 89

during Emotional-Being stage, 37

representation during Emotional-Being stage, 44-45, 53

results of not honoring, 5

Films, use as teaching tools, 191-92

Flexibility

during Body-Being stage, 21, 23-24, 116

of mentor during conflict resolution, 221

Frames of Mind: The Theory of Multiple Intelligences (Gardner), xvii, 166-67

Freedom, personal, for Will-Being children, 119

Free School movement, on flexibility during Body-Being stage, 24

Friday Nature Class, cooperativeness during, 175-76, 242

Frustration, leading to confrontation, 217, 221

Fun time, and family chores, 227-28

G

Games, cooperative, during Emotional-Being stage, 174-77, 180

GAP, the, as suspension period in rites of passage, 123, 124, 128-30, 141

Gardner, Howard, xvii, 166-67, 180, 197

Gatto, John, xv

Genital exploration, during Body-Being stage, 29

Gifts, during rites of passage, 125, 140

Goals, during Will-Being education stage, 184-85

Goodall, Jane, 10

Good Mother, The (film), 191

Gossip, leading to confrontation, 215-16

Grange movement, as example of cooperative marketing, 243

Grinspoon, Lester, 188

Growth pattern

confusion between first signs and permanence, 202

role of hesitancies, 27

Guidance

during Body-Being stage education, 170-71

during Emotional-Being stage education, 173-74

Guilt, children's feelings of in divorce situations, 248, 249

Gymnastics, as emphasizing rhythm, 179

H

Harmony, and divorce, 247

Healing Brain, The (Ornstein), 145

Healing process

among participants in resolved confrontations, 218-19

parent(s)' role in, 145-46

patient's role in, 143-44

Height differential, equalization of during communication, 113

Hesitancies, 13-14, *chart* 256

during Body-Being stage, 27-29

during Emotional-Being stage, 52-53

mistaking for malfunctions, 155

at onset of Reasoning-Being stage, 87-88

and ritual rites of passage, 127

Hierarchies

lack of in cooperative institutions, 242

undermining during cooperative games, 176

High school, graduation and future, 94

Hiking (walking), as part of ritual rites of passage, 124, 130

History

methods of teaching, 187-88, 191

personal background as healing tool, 154, 160

Holistic education, values of, 168

Home, leaving during Reasoning-Being stage, 89

Home schooling, 9, 178-80

Honesty

balanced with humor, 152, *chart* 151

in conflict resolutions, 222-23

importance of during Emotional-Being stage, 46-48, 58

striving for in educational systems, 181

Horme (Montessori term), as stage-specific wisdom, 6, 9

Horses, caring for during Emotional-Being stage, 179

Houston, James, 182

"Hug A Tree", as sensation game, 29

Human beings (*Homo Sapiens*), natural life stages, 4-5

Humility

of adults in conflicts with children, 202-3

balance with autonomy, 152, 154, *chart* 151

of parents during crisis periods, 148-49

of teacher during inquiry process, 185

Humor

balanced with honesty, 152, *chart* 151

role during family difficulties, 149-50, 205

I

"I", ever-changing role of, 75

I-and-Other relationships, during Emotional-Being stage, 45, 56, 157

271

Ideals
  as curriculum goals, 187
  during Will-Being stage, 74-75
Identity, personal
  revaluation in Reasoning-Being stage, 87
  search for in Will-Being stage, 62, 140
Imitation
  as behavior mode during Body-Being stage, 19, 24
  as learning method during Body-Being stage, 170
Impartiality. *See also* Cherry Festival story
  of role model during Emotional-Being stage, 57-58
Imperfection, impatience with during Will-Being stage, 74
Impersonal approach, to confrontation resolution, 218
Incisiveness
  balanced with fearlessness, 152, 160-61, *chart* 151
Inclusion
  of family members during problem periods, 146-47
  feeling of in conflict resolutions, 206, 222
  keeping children together after divorces, 250
Individualism, during Will-Being stage, 12, 70, 71
Information
  adult data availability to Reasoning-Beings, 238-39
  compared to communication, 105
  integration of that received during communication, 114
  received during hesitancies, 13
Innate wisdom, during hesitancies, 13-14
Inquirer, teacher as, 188-90
Inquiry
  as tool during Reasoning-Being stage, 93-96
  as Will-Being teaching technique, 184-85
Insecurity, during Will-Being stage, 61, 62
Intelligence
  listening with during communications, 113-14
  multiple types for Gardner, xvii, 166-67, 180, 197
  for Pearce, 6
Interests, specialized, pursuit during Reasoning-Being stage, 196-97
Integration, as intermediate communication step, 114-16
Interruptions, during communications, 107
Intuition
  as the direct expression of inner wisdom, 97
  during the Reasoning-Being stage, 197
Isolation, during boys'ritual rites of passage, 136, 137-38
Issue, specific, responding to during communication, 117

J
Job security, need for during Reasoning-Being stage, 90
Jungian psychology, xix, 168
Justice, sense of
  during Emotional-Being stage, 48, 58, 161
  examples of systems used in schools, 181-82
  lacking for inner-city teenagers, 235
  as retributive during Body-Being stage, 20, 48, 171

K
Kagan, Jerome, xvi-xvii
"Kid-ness", desire to leave behind during rites of passage, 133-34
King, Martin Luther, Jr., 195-96
King of Children, The (Lifton), 181
Knowledge
  of child during communication, 115
  search for, xv-xvii
Korchak orphange (Poland), as example of justice system, 181-82
Kübler-Ross, Elisabeth, 40-41

L
Labeling
  cost to the child, 203-5
  discouragement of in confrontaion resolutions, 212, 224
Language, learning of, during Body-Being stage, 6, 19
Lepidoptera (Butterfly), as example of life stages, 3-4, 5-6, 67
Leslie, Robert Franklin, 182
Liberation Theolgy, demands for cooperative life, 241
Life (Developmental) stages, xvi-xvii, xxii, *chart* 257. *See also* Body-Being; Emotional-Being; Reasoning-Being; Stage-specific wisdom; Will-Being
  hesitancies during. *See* Hesitancies
  of human beings, 4-5
  of the *Lepidoptera*, 3-4, 5-6, 67
  myths on, xiv-xv, xix-xxi
  three phases of, 14-15
  unfolding of governed by stage-specific wisdom, 5-7
Limits, imposition of. *See also* Trial and error
  on Body-Being children, 14, 23, 115-16
  during Will-Being stage, 70, 186
Listening, importance in communication, 117
Losers
  in cooperative games, 175

in educational systems, 183

Love, falling in, during Reasoning-Being stage, 92-93

Lulls. *See* Hesitancies

Luvmour, Josette and Sambhava, *Everyone Wins*, 177

M

Magical Child (Pearce), 9

Magical Child Matures (Pearce), 9

Malfunctions, children's, case histories and remedies, 143-63

Manifestations

    behavior symptoms as, 144, 152-53

    natural rhythms of children, 3

Masks, use in ritual rites of passage, 130

Mathmatics, xv

    teaching to Body-Being children, 169, 172

Maturity

    fostering of during Reasoning-Being stage, 93

    during Will-Being stage, 61

Me-against-Them

    during Emotional-Being stage, 45

    during family conflicts, 206

Meaning

    creation of during Reasoning-Being stage, 83

    desire for in Reasoning-Being stage, 91

    found by child through stage-specific wisdom, 6

Miller, Alice, 5

Mirroring, by children, xix, 19, 24, 170

Mistakes, ability of authority figures to admit, 148

Modeling Remedy, for Perspective/Discrimination malfunctioning, 158

Mondragon cooperatives (Spain), growth of, 242-43

Montessori, Maria, xxii, 6, 9, 11

Montessori Method, use during Body-Being stage, 171

Mortality. *See* Death

Motivations, and behavior, 155-56

Music

    appreciation during Body-Being stage, 172

    singing during Emotional-Being stage, 179

Myth(s)

    of adjustment for children in divorce situations, 248

    on boys and girls playing together, 177

    on children and development, xix-xxi

    creation of for ritual rites of passage, 129-30

    on developmental stages, xiv-xv, xix-xxi

    as explaining the unknown to a child, 46

    and Natural Learning Rhythms, 11

    use in Waldorf educational techniques, 180

N

Name, new, taking of during rites of passsage rituals, 125, 131-32

Name-calling, discouragement of in resolving confrontaions, 211, 223

National Home Schoolers' Association, 185

Natural Learning Rhythms. *See* Rhythms, natural, children's

Nature

    case study of parents learning from young adults, 100-101

    as challenge during Will-Being stage, 75-78

    child's reaction to, 15-16

    interaction with during Emotional-Being stage, 54-56, 177-78

    lessons of during Body-Being stage, 29-31

    redefining during Reasoning-Being stage, 97-99

Nature of the Child, The (Kagan), xvi-xvii

New Self, acknowledgement of during rites of passage, 123, 125, 130

Non-biological children, parenting of, xx-xxi, 251-52

Non-favoritism, use in resolving confrontations, 221, 210, 223

Nonviolence, as curriculum ideal, 187

North San Juan Community Education program (Calif.), 178

O

Old self, role in ritual rites of passage, 123, 128

On Children and Death (Kübler-Ross), 40

Organically Grown Cooperative (Eugene, Ore.), 243

Ornstein, Robert, *Healing Brain, The*, 145

Outer space, as cooperative venture, 244

Outward Bound program, Rope Course of, 190

P

Paraphrasing, as communication technique, 111-13, 221

Parent(s). *See also* Divorce; Family

    case study of learning from young adults, 100-102

    healing attitude of, 146

    rejection of during Will-Being stage, 79

    separateness feelings during Body-Being stage, 34-35

    views on children's peers, 226-27

Parenting, xi-xviii, xxii, 6

    humility during crisis stages, 148-49

    of non-biological children, xx-xxi, 251-52

Partners, new, introducing to children, 250-51

Patience, of mentor during conflict resolution, 222

Peace
Emotional-Being stage desire for, 58-59
evolution of through education, 253-54

Pearce, Joseph Chilton, xxii, 6, 9, 11

Pecking order, in competition modes, 240

Peers
manipulation by malfunctioning person, 159, 160
role in Will-Being stage, 68, 70, 74-75, 84, 146, 192
seen as "bad" by parents, 226-27

"Person becoming", child seen as, 10

Perspective
balanced with discrimination, 152, 154, 158, *chart* 151

Pets, caring for during Emotional-Being stage, 179

Phase changeovers, timing rites of passage during, 126-27

Philosophy, study of during Will-Being stage, 188

Playgrounds, school, territoriality on, 173-74

Postman, Neil, 184

Prejudice, listening without during communications, 108-13

Professors, college, as sometime hindrances, 193

Project Adventure, Rope Course of, 190

Promiscuity, sexual, as emotional answer during Reasoning- Being stage, 89-90

Protection/punishment, in competition modes, 241

Psychology, 9, 11
inquiry method of teaching, 188-90
Jungian, xix, 168
teaching to Waldorf-method educators, 180

Puberty changes, at onset of Will-Being, 61, 62

Punishment, as discipline method, xiv, xxi, 9, 183, 187

Purpose
fulfillment of by children, 5
fulfillment of by *Lepidoptera*, 5

Put-downs, discouragemnt of in conflict resolutions, 223

Q

Question, ability to, beginnings of during Will-Being stage, 86

R

Radiant Child (Armstrong), 6, 10

Ramayana, The, as teaching tool, 168-70, 173

Reading, teaching to young children, 53-54, 172-73

Reality
change in perception during rites of passage, 133
checks on during Will-Being education stage, 184

Reasoning, based on sensory experience during Body-Being stage, 20

Reasoning-Being stage, 7-8, 15, *chart* 255
case histories, 83-102
curriculum for, 200, *chart* 198-99
doubt factor during, 86-87, 88, 91
education during, 192-97
family communications during, 119-20
hesitancies at onset, 87-88
problem behavior traits during, 154, *chart* 151
rational justice capabilities of, 48
redefining nature during, 97-99
trust actualized during through adult information, 238-39

Reasoning wisdom, 8, 10

Rebellion
due to labeling expectations, 203
during Reasoning-Being stage, 88
during Will-Being stage, 70-71, 73

Recapitulation Ceremony, between parents and Reasoning-Being children, 157

Receptivity
during childhood phases, *chart* 255
as life stage, 14-15
during Reasoning-Being stage, 90-91

Recognition, mature, accorded to Reasoning-Being children, 91, 119-20

Rejection, of parents during Will-Being stage, 79

Religion
beliefs conflicting with ritual rites of passage, 127
child development influenced by practices, 10
as means for child to pursue transcendence, 46
salvation beliefs of Catholicism, 241
spiritual concerns during Emotional-Being stage, 57

Remedies, for malfunctioning behaviors (manifestations), 143-63

Resentment
benefits of resolving, 58
leading to violence, 174

Resources, material, distribution of, 240-41, 245

Respect, sensitive, during Will-Being stage, 69-70

Responses
means of communicating, 115, 116-20

Responsibility
awareness of during Will-Being stage, 86
overemphasis in adulthood due to childhood hurts, 234

and Will-Being curriculum, 184, 186
Rewards, as discipline method, xiv, xxi, 9, 183, 187
Rhythms, natural, children's, 3, 6, 8-12. *See also* Life stages
  effect of, 15-16
  of stage-specific wisdom, 5-6
  use in educating during Emotional-Being stage, 178-79
Rhythms, natural, of *Lepidoptera*, 3-4, 5-6, 67
Ridicule, reaction to during Will-Being stage, 70
Rights of others, reactions to during Will-Being stage, 74-75
Rites of passage
  devising developmentally appropriate rituals, 11
  ritual steps and examples of, 121-42, *chart* 258
  timing of, 201-2
  during Will-Being stage, 62, 126, 133-38, 138-39, 191
Role models
  adults as during Emotional-Being stage, 44, 45-46, 46-48, 49-52, 57-58
  in the inner city, 235
  parents' failure as, 161
  parents' need for, xii
Ropes Course, as challenge for young people, 190
Roshi, Suzuki, 184, 186

S

Safety, loving touch felt as, 21
School(s). *See also* Education
  home and community programs, 178-80
  territoriality on playgrounds, 173-74
  the Unicorn experiment, 180-81
  the Waldorf technique, 180-81
Science, value placed on, 167
Security
  during Body-Being stage, 21-23, 145
  lack of during periods of crisis, 147
Self-inquiry, as teaching method, 189
Selfishness, arising out of cynicism, 239
Self-protection
  behavior geared toward, xv
  during Emotional-Being stage, 44-45, 174
Sensitivity, during Body-Being stage, 30
Sensory input
  during birthing process, 20-21
  during Body-Being stage, 17, 19-20, 22, 29-30, 141
  and education, 170, 171
Separateness, feeling of
  by parent during Body-Being stage, 34-35

during periods of crisis, 147
  weakening of parental bond during Will-Being stage, 79
Sexuality
  characteristics at onset of Will-Being stage, 61, 62
  explaining during boy's rites of passage, 136
  exploring during Will-Being stage, 78-79
  genital exploration during Emotional-Being stage, 29
  during Reasoning-Being stage, 89-90
Silence, as part of ritual rites of passage, 134
Singing
  chanting during ritual rites of passage, 136, 137
  for Emotional-Being children, 179
Skepticism, healthy, during Reasoning-Being stage, 91-92
Sound, power of during Body-Being stage, 19
Space, personal
  communications about with Will-Being children, 119
  search for during Will-Being stage, 62-63, 67, 69, 76, 146
Specializations, evolving of during Reasoning-Being stage, 93
Spirituality, 11
  concerns during Emotional-Being stage, 57
Spiritual traditions, conflicting with ritual rites of passage, 127
Stage-specific wisdom, 4, 5-8, 61, 70, 221
  and character traits, 12, 152
  during "dysfunctional" behavior, 144
  effect of natural environment on, 15-16
  as factor in communication, 113, 115, 117
  for Montesorri, 5
  obscuring through bad education, 165-66
  optimum conditions in each type, 10-11
  for Pearce, 6
  role during hesitancies, 13
  for Steiner, 5, 9, 11
  word choice during conflict resolutions, 219-20
Stand By Me (film), 191
Steiner, Rudolf, xxii, 168
  methods used by Waldorf teachers, 180
  on stage-specific wisdom, 6, 9, 11
Stories. *See also* Myth(s)
  reading and telling techniques, 173
Strength, balanced with belongingness, 152, 154, 160, *chart* 151
Stress, periods of, and ritual rites of passage, 127
Study programs, independent, value of, 179-80
Substance abuse, during Will-Being stage, 80-82, 188

Sufi traditions, stories illustrating conflict resolutions, 203-4, 205

Suggestions, use in resolving conflicts, 220

Sulking, applying conflict-resolution tools, 226

Summerhill (Neill), 181

Summerhill school (England), as example of a justice system, 181-82

Support, mutual, in cooperative games, 175

Sweat lodges, as part of ritual rites of passage, 134-35

Synergy
in communications, 105-6
natural evolution as, 241-44

Systems
seeking access to in Reasoning-Being stage, 88, 90
understanding of during Reasoning-Being stage, 83

T

Taboos, regarding acknowledgments of death, 44

Tantrums, applying conflict-resolution tools during, 226

Tao Te Ching, on conflict resolutions, 224

Taste, as sensory experience during Body-Being stage, 22

Teaching as a Subversive Activity (Postman & Weingartner), 184

Teenagers. *See also* Will-Being stage
"bad" peers predicament, 226-27
family communications with, 119
feelings toward physical disabilities, 189-90
lack of role models in the inner city, 235
reaction to cooperative games, 176
search for identity, 140
suburban youth reaction to boredom, 235-36

Tendencies, natural, of human beings, 166-68

Tension, easing during cooperative games, 174-75

Territoriality, on school playgrounds, 173-74

Thanksgiving ceremonies, as part of ritual rites of passsage, 125, 132

Themes
during Body-Being stage education, 170-71
use in the Unicorn experiment, 181

Therapy
versus behavior remedies, 153-54
for unresolved conflicts, 204
use of cooperative games, 174-75

Threats
discouragement of in resolving confrontaions, 212, 213, 219
effect on children, xv, 145

Time
commitment by parents during Body-Being stage, 33-34
perception of in Reasoning-Being stage, 87
as unstructured in children's stories, 173

Touch
as love during Body-Being stage, 35, 141, 170
as primary sensation during birth process, 20-21, 33
use during tantrum resolutions, 226

Transcendent possibilities, search for during Emotional-Being stage, 45-46

Transitions
during Emotional-Being stage, 37-39
between life stages, 8
during Reasoning-Being stage, 88-90

Transpersonal psychology, 9, 11

Trauma(s)
brought on by childhood labeling, 204-5
guilt becoming in divorce situations, 249

Travel study, for the Reasoning-Being person, 194-96

Trial and error, *chart* 255
during the Emotional-Being stage, 53-54
as life stage, 14-15, 28-29
during Reasoning-Being stage, 92-93, 196
use in family problems, 154
during Will-Being stage, 75

Tribes (Gibbs & Allen), 180

Trust
development of, 236
erosion of during Emotional-Being stage, 45
in information received during Body-Being stage, 21
as part of real communication, 105, 110

U

Understanding
role in communications, 106, 115
of systems during Reasoning-Being stage, 83

Unicorn (educational experiment), 180-81

Uniqueness, recognition of other person's during communication, 113

Universe
outer space as cooperative venture, 244
realization of during Emotional-Being stage, 39

University life, and the Reasoning-Being student, 193-94

V

Violence, xv, xxi

in children's stories, 173

as outgrowth of resentment, 174

Violin, study of, as example of attunement to a system, 90-91

Vocabulary

communication with Emotional-Being children, 117-19

during creative confrontation, 148

use of stage-specific in resolving conflicts, 219-20

Vulnerability, during Emotional-Being stage, 44-45, 220

w

Waldorf education, 6, 9, 180-81

Warmth, during Body-Being stage, 21, 24

Weaning, as separation process, 35

"Web, The", as example of cooperative game, 175-76

Weiner, Bernard, *Boy into Man*, 139-40

Weingartner, Charles, 184

Weistar, Debbie, 177

"Who Am I", as Reasoning-Being quest, 239

Wholeness

concept of during Reasoning-Being stage, 83

as exemplified by the natural world, 15

"Why?", during the Reasoning-Being stage, 192

Wickes, Frances, xix

Wilber, Ken, 6, 10

Will-Being stage, 7-8, 12, *chart* 255

case studies, 61-82

curriculum for, 200, *chart* 198-99

education during, 183-92

family communications during, 119

as gestation period for Reasoning-Being stage, 84, 86

importance of chronological age during, 66

inclusion in problem and decision periods, 146-47

nature as challenge, 75-78

onset of sexuality, 61, 62, 78-79

as period of trust in ideals, 237-38

problem behavior traits during, 153, 154, *chart* 151

reaction to earlier labeling, 203

rites of passage during, 62, 126, 133-38, 138-39

role of peers, 68, 70, 74-75, 84, 226-27

search for personal space, 62-63, 67, 69, 76

Will wisdom

denial in many education systems, 166

Winners

competitiveness in educational systems, 183

in cooperative games, 175, 177

Wisdom, inner. *See also* Stage-specific wisdom

during hesitancies, 13-14

intuition as expression of, 97

listening to during communication, 110-11

role of ritual rites of passage, 122

Woman, role in boys' rites of passage, 137, 140

Word choice, use of stage-specific in resolving conflicts, 219-20

World, the

as extension of body during Body-Being stage, 17-20

global peace and Emotional-Being, 58-59

longing for perfection in during Will-Being stage, 74

Wounds, family, and ritual rites of passage, 127